MAP OF THE MEDITERRANEAN REGION

20°
30°

BLACK SEA

TRIESTE
VENICE
FIUME
POLA
REPUBLIC

ADRIATIC SEA

FLORENCE
GDOM OF RURIA

SPALATO

PAPAL STATES

RAGUSA
CATTARO

ROME

KINGDOM OF NAPLES

DURAZZO

CONSTANTINOPLE
BOSPORUS

GALLIPOLI

SEA OF MARMARA

NAPLES
TARANTO

PALERMO

DARDANELLES

IMBROS IS.

LEMNOS IS.

C. ST. MARIA
CORFU

TENEDOS IS.

40°

C. COLONNA

AEGEAN

GREECE

CHIOS IS.

SMYRNA

ETIMO IS.
PALERMO
REGGIO
MESSINA
STR. OF MESSINA

MOREA

ANDROS IS.

SEA

SICILY

C. BON
PANTELLARIA IS.

SYRACUSE

C. PASSARO

MILO

RHODES

GOZO IS.

MALTA

R A N E A N

CRETE

GABES
JERBA

SEA

PT. TAJORA

C. RAZAT

C. RAZATIN

TRIPOLI

C. MESURATA

DERNE

BOMBA

C. TRABUCA

BENGHAZI

TABARSA

ROSETTA

GULF OF SIDRA

ALEXANDRIA

RIPOLI

CAIRO

30°

20°
30°

THE 200 YEAR LEGACY OF STEPHEN DECATUR

Painting of the USS *United States* versus HMS *Macedonian* on October 25, 1812, by Arthur N. Disney, Sr. Photograph courtesy of the Naval Historical Center.

THE 200 YEAR LEGACY
OF
STEPHEN DECATUR
1798–1998

BY
BEN BIRINDELLI

HALLMARK

Print of "The attack made on Tripoli on the 3rd August, 1804, by the American Squadron under Commodore Edward Preble to whom this plate is respectfully dedicated by his Obedient Servant John B. Guerrazzi." Colored print in the Naval Historical Society of New York, 1935. Photograph courtesy of the Naval Historical Center.

Hallmark Publishing Company
B. L. Walton, Jr., Owner and Publisher
Elizabeth B. Bobbitt, Editor and Designer
Hallmark Publishing Company, Inc.
Post Office Box 901
Gloucester Point, Virginia 23062

Library of Congress Cataloging-in-Publication Data
Birindelli, Ben
        p.   cm.
  Includes bibliographical references and index.
  ISBN 0-9653759-4-3 (alk. paper)
  1. Decatur, Stephen, 1779-1820. 2. Admirals--United States--
Biography. 3. United States. Navy--Biography. 4. United States--
History, Naval--To 1900. 5. Decatur, Stephen, 1779-1820--Pictorial
works. 6. Decatur, Stephen, 1779-1820--Influence. I. Title.
E353.1.D29B5   1998
973.4'7'092--dc
[b]   98-7647
                                                         CIP

Printed in the United States of America

DEDICATION

This book is dedicated to those sailors who sailed with Stephen Decatur from the time of his warrant as a midshipman on April 30, 1798, through his demise in 1820 and to all of those sailors who have sailed and will sail in subsequent ships of his name. It is especially dedicated to those sailors who are about to embark in the latest *USS Decatur* (DDG-73) to be commissioned some 200 years later on or about August 29, 1998. May they "always be in the right," as they sail "in search of peace."

This book is also dedicated to the loving memory of the author's sister,
Charlotte Anne Laughon.

October 2, 1948–August 22, 1997

TABLE OF CONTENTS

Launching of *Decatur* (DDG-73), November 10, 1996.
Photograph by and courtesy of Bath Iron Works Corporation,
A General Dynamics Company.

FOREWORD

For those of us who grew up in "my generation," Stephen Decatur was one of the great names in our history. We read about his daring recapture and destruction of the grounded frigate *Philadelphia* under the guns of the "Bashaw" of Tripoli, and of his defeat of the proud British frigate *Macedonian* during the War of 1812, feats of valor and leadership that went far toward setting a solid foundation for the powerful and victorious American navy of our own time. Ben Birindelli's work fleshes out these general impressions, and, skillfully drawing in the words of the persons involved, draws a picture of Decatur the sailor and Decatur the man. We finish with a broader appreciation of his versatility. We all know, for instance, of Stephen Decatur the naval officer and national hero; but how many of us know of Stephen Decatur, the accomplished diplomat?

Over the years, Decatur has been fittingly commemorated by the nation he served with such devotion. For his victory over HMS *Macedonian*, Congress voted him a gold medal. As we might expect, five Navy ships have borne his name, from a wooden sloop-of-war completed in 1840 to a new *Arleigh Burke*-class missile destroyer. But we now find that, even before his untimely death, three privateers took his name to sea during the War of 1812.

Beyond this, though, we are reminded that cities, towns, and counties in no fewer than fourteen states are named Decatur. Schools—including high schools in Berlin, Maryland, Decatur's birth place, and at the Naval Air Station at Sigonella, Sicily, appropriately located near the coast of "High Barbaree" where he won his first honors—and libraries bear his name. A highway in Maryland and a hospital in Illinois keep his memory before us. Decatur House, his home on Lafayette Square just across the street from the White House, is preserved as a historic landmark. This work ends, fittingly enough, by listing the places that go to make up "Decatur Country" and remind us, once more, of the impression that Stephen Decatur has left on America's national memory.

Speaking at Amherst College less than a month before his death, President John Kennedy told us that "a nation reveals itself not only by the men it produces, but also by the men it honors, the men it remembers." In this work Ben Birindelli helps us to honor and remember one of the truly great men of our history. It should do much to ensure that Stephen Decatur's proud legacy of duty to country, well and truly done, will continue to be a living presence in the years to come.

JOHN C. REILLY JR.
Ships History Branch
Naval Historical Center

Portrait of Stephen Decatur by Chappel. Engraved by G. R. Hall, published by Johnson, Fry & Co. Photograph courtesy of the Naval Historical Center.

Painting of the USS *Decatur* (DDG-31) by Jack Vogelman,
October 1967. Courtesy of the Naval Historical Center.

PREFACE

The genesis of this book was to provide a monograph of Commodore Stephen Decatur, Jr.'s, life and the histories of the subsequent ships bearing his name. It was intended to dedicate his 200 year legacy, starting with his warrant as a midshipman signed by President Adams on April 30, 1798, and culminating with the commissioning of the latest of these ships, the USS *Decatur* (DDG-73), on or about August 29, 1998. However, as the historical research progressed, it became evident that the subject deserved better treatment than a mere monograph. As more and more anecdotes and pictures were identified, the project began to steer more towards a pictorial history book.

Since there has been no history of Decatur in many decades, the book began to take on an aura of a project intended for more than just a few past and current Decatur sailors. It became evident that there were many Decatur schools, libraries, towns, counties, and organizations that might be anxious for some update to their Decatur legacy. Therefore, the final chapter, Decatur Country, has been added to allow their involvement, as well as the Navy's. All of these entities may enjoy and benefit to some degree from the pages that follow.

EM1 Ferrell ready to shift the load. Photograph by B. D. Sullivan. Courtesy of the USS *Decatur* (DDG-31), The First Year, 1968 Cruise Book, Taylor Publishing Company and the Naval Historical Center.

Above: ETC McKeithman, SK1 Joyce, and ET1 Paris aboard *Decatur* (DDG-73). Photograph by and courtesy of the author.

Kids at Glenlake Park, Decatur, Georgia, August 1997. Courtesy of the Decatur Recreation & Community Services department.

ACKNOWLEDGMENTS

The author would like to acknowledge the efforts of several individuals associated with the Naval Historical Center who provided assistance and support in the research and development of this book. I am grateful to Messrs. John C. Reilly, Jr., and Ray Mann of the Ships' History Branch, Messrs. Bernard F. Cavalcante, and Mike Walker and Ms. Kathy LLoyd of the Operational Archives Branch, Messrs. Chuck Haberlein and Ed Finney of the Photographic Section of the Curator Branch, Ms. Jean Hort, Director of the Navy Department Library, and Ms. Christine Hughes and Mr. Chuck Brodine of the Early History Branch. I would also like to thank Captains Woody Tiernan, Mike Sessions, Tom Hilt, and Mike Roberts of the Naval History VTU 0615 for their constant encouragement and support in the undertaking of this project.

Special thanks are also due to a considerable list of people who helped in the lengthy search for Chief Smith's roots. These included Ms. Ann "Tex" Moyer, National Medal of Honor Museum; Ms. Becky Livingston, National Archives; Messrs. Al Taylor, Fred Watson, and Jim Adamson, Veterans Administration; Mr. Bill Mason and LCDR Ken Kronk, Office of Naval Information; and Capt. Norris Jones, Commanding Officer, U.S. Naval Reserve Public Affairs Office Unit, Chicago, Illinois.

The author is also indebted to Hallmark Publishing Company, Inc., especially Mr. Bernie Walton, Publisher, for giving me the opportunity that I was searching for. I am grateful to the editor, Ms. Betsy Bobbitt, for her perservering support and patience with my inexperience with photographs. Many thanks to my colleague, Mr. Bob Moore, for his invaluable assistance in obtaining all sorts of connections and data from the Internet and to Mr. Pat Wells for his discerning help in overcoming various word processing idiosyncrasies. My thanks also to Ms. Netra Jacob for her editing and word processing assistance in bringing this project to fruition.

My thanks also extend to the staff of the Decatur House, whose hospitality and assistance contributed greatly to the initial steps of this project, as well as providing much of the information for Decatur's final years. I am especially indebted to Mr. Paul Reber, director and Mr. Chris Slusher, curator.

My thanks also extend to my good friend and superb artist, Ms. Marty Vinograd. Without her unflagging faith in and generousity towards the U.S. Navy the magnificent artwork to be exhibited in the USS Decatur's Wardroom and copied in this book could never have been made available. Indeed the whole project would not have gone forward without her devotion to its cause.

I am further indebted to my ex-shipmate and then First Lieutenant Mr. Jeff Wilson, who not only resurrected the story of the mooring buoy anchor chain fouling complete with sketches, but also first introduced me to the wonderful world of SCUBA diving in St. Thomas harbor. I also greatly appreciated the photographs provided by my one time assistant supply officer and shipmate, Mr. Bruce Babbitt.

Additional thanks are well deserved by Mr. Mike Wolfe of NSWC, Port Hueneme Division, for all of his input on the Ex-*Decatur* Self Defense Test Ship, and to Sandy Williams, Navy Office of the Judge Advocate General, for her input in response to my requests. Also, my sincere thanks to Mr. Larry Lee, an ardent *Decatur* enthusiast, who provided many pictures and much additional information, especially on the DD-936 on which his uncle served.

I am also grateful to the officers and crew of the new *Decatur* (DDG-73) and Bath Iron Works for their hospitality in inviting me to cruise with them and allowing me to observe some of the training and take pictures for the book. Similarly, I am appreciative of the support provided to me from Lt. Comdr. Ted Hleba and Ms. Barbara Jakowski, Aegis Program Executive Office, which is responsible for these marvelous new ships. Also many thanks to Messrs. Bob "Bear" Hastings and Tim Henkle of LOGICON for providing the Bath Iron Works DDG-73 and Navy pictures and other DDG-73 information.

My most sincere appreciation is extended to the many people, who in response to cold calls from me, went out of their way personally to provide me with pictures and information for Decatur Country. They included Ms. Pam Swanner and Ms. Squee Bailey of Decatur, Alabama; Ms. Linda Martin of Decatur, Arkansas; Ms. Lyn Menne, Ms. Linda Harris and Ms. Susan Illis of Decatur, Georgia; Ms. Vanessa Arthur and Ms. Frances Willis of Bainbridge, Decatur County, Georgia; Ms. Mary Talbott of Decatur, Illinois; Ms. Linda Morris and Mr. Gordon Gregg of Decatur, Indiana; Ms. Sondra Phipps of Decatur City, Decatur County, Iowa; Ms. Marsha Seck of Decatur County, Kansas; Master Chief Dave Reynolds of Decatur High School, Berlin, Maryland; Ms. Toni Benson of Decatur, Michigan; Messrs. Melvin Tingle and Bubby Johnston of Decatur, Mississippi; Ms. Peggy Davis and Ms. Pam Nelsen of Decatur, Nebraska; Ms. Lvera Seipelt of Georgetown, Ohio, and Ms. Eva Mae davis of Winchester, Ohio; Ms. Susan Williams of Decatur, Texas; and Mr. Edwin Townsend of Decatur County, Tennessee; and Ms. Lavon Johns and Ms. Gloria Schouggins, Decatur, Meigs County, Tennessee; and Ms. Frances Pollard, Richmond, Virginia.

I would also like to thank my own Falls Church folks for their invaluable assistance with this project. They include Ms. Deane Dierksen and Ms. Brenda Crowley, Mary Riley Styles Public Library; Mr. John Ballou, George Mason High School Art Teacher and Photographer; and Mr. Tony Socarras and Cuong Tang, Dominion Camera.

Last but not least, I would like to thank my wife Nancy for her forbearance throughout the development of this book. It was her long enduring patience that made it all possible. It was also her insistance that I chair the Falls Church Tricentennial Committee that indirectly led to this book's publication.

As the author, I take total responsibility for any mistakes or ommisions either in the information or pictorial representations within this book. My most sincere apologies to any person or place that I may have missed or misrepresented. It was not within the scope or timeframe allowed to have possibly covered everything as I would have desired.

Portrait of Stephen Decatur, Sr., (Decatur's father). Print by Stapco. Courtesy of Decatur House, photograph by John Ballou.

Portrait of Ann Pine Decatur (Decatur's mother). Print by Stapco. Courtesy of Decatur House, photograph by John Ballou.

Oval shaped Silver Medal-lion engraved with Masonic Insignia and a ship "The Royal Louis" honoring Stephen Decatur, Sr.'s command on the obverse. Courtesy of Decatur House, photograph by John Ballou.

Decatur Family Coat of Arms on the reverse side of the Silver Medallion honoring Stephen Decatur, Sr's. command of the *Royal Louis*. Courtesy of Decatur House, photograph by John Ballou.

CHAPTER 1

STEPHEN DECATUR, JR., THE EARLY YEARS

Stephen Decatur, Jr., was born on January 5, 1779, in Sinepuxent, Worcester County, Maryland, in a small two-room log house during the Revolutionary War. Although Sinepuxent no longer exists, today nearby Berlin, Maryland, claims to be his place of birth. (Knight, "Stephen Decatur," pp. 3 and 14). His mother, Ann Pine Decatur, had taken refuge there upon fleeing Philadelphia in 1777, when General Howe's British Army occupied the city. From there she could keep in touch with her husband, Capt. Stephen Decatur, via either the Atlantic Coast or the Chesapeake Bay, as he carried out his privateering against the British merchantmen. A few months after Stephen's birth, Mrs. Decatur returned to their home in Philadelphia, since the British had been forced to evacuate the city during the previous summer. There she also had the additional support of her mother-in-law, Priscilla Decatur, as she awaited the return of Captain Decatur. Priscilla had married a young man in the French Navy, Lt. Etienne Decatur, who was not in good health, and she had been widowed shortly after Stephen Senior was born. So young Stephen's grandfather and father preceded him in a naval tradition.

After several successful smaller commands, in 1781 Captain Decatur took command of the *Royal Louis*, a 22-gun Pennsylvania privateer. He soon fell in with the British sloop of war *Active* and in a brief engagement captured this regular ship of the Royal Navy and brought her home as a prize. (Anthony, *Decatur*, p. 10)

Following the Revolutionary War Stephen's father returned to the merchant service as a ship's master for Gurney and Smith of Philadelphia in both the European and East Indian trade. In 1786, at the age of eight, Stephen was allowed to accompany his father on one of his voyages to Europe to help him recover his health after a severe bout with whooping cough. Although this voyage probably launched the call of the sea in young Stephen's mind, upon returning home he was subject to the dictates of his mother and there were no more voyages with his father. Young Stephen enrolled in the Episcopal Academy under the direction of Reverend Doctor Abercrombie for his elementary education. Two of his schoolmates were Charles Stewart and Richard Somers, who would also later join him in the naval service. (Lewis, *The Romantic Decatur*, p. 6) When Stephen completed his preparatory studies at the Academy, he entered the University of Pennsylvania. Although his mother had hoped that one day Stephen might enter the Episcopal clergy, his heart was not in such a classical course of study. After one year his parents allowed him to leave the University before finishing and take a clerical position with his father's business associates at Gurney and Smith.

Meanwhile, at the close of the Revolutionary War the United States had only three ships in her infant navy, since all the others had been captured or destroyed.

When the last of these, the *Alliance,* was sold in Philadelphia on June 3, 1785, the United States was without a naval combatant ship for a period of approximately ten years. Recognition of this fact soon came from the pirates of the Barbary Coast of North Africa, as they learned that the American merchantmen were from a young and weak country and began intercepting them. The worst of these Barbary States was Algiers. Beginning in 1785 her corsairs repeatedly captured American merchantmen and enslaved their crews. After a Congressional appropriation in 1792 failed to buy peace with Algiers, a bill was finally passed on March 27, 1794, to provide for four ships of forty-four guns and two ships of thirty-six guns. Congress appropriated $688,888.82 to fund the ships, but a provision was added that if peace were made with Algiers, work on the ships was to stop.

When negotiations were renewed with Algiers, the Dey held out for $525,500 in ransom, a frigate of thirty-six guns, and an annual tribute of approximately $25,000 in naval stores. The treaty was ratified by the Senate on March 2, 1796. Fortunately Congress realized the extent to which funds had already been expended on the earlier authorized ships and allowed for the completion of two of the forty-four gun and one of the thirty-six gun frigates. The three ships to be completed were the *United States,* the *Constitution,* and the *Constellation.* Coincidentally, Gurney and Smith of Philadelphia were not only owners of merchantmen, but also shipbuilders, who had been awarded the contract to build the *United States.* Young Stephen Decatur, recently in their employment, was assigned to duties assisting with her construction. Thus he indirectly came under the influence of her supervisor, Joshua Humphreys, the designer of all the frigates, and Capt. John Barry of Revolutionary War fame, who was to be her first commanding officer. The forty-four gun *United States* was the first of the new frigates to be launched on July 10, 1797. Young Stephen Decatur was traditionally thought to be on her deck as she slid down the ways. The smaller thirty-six gun *Constellation* was launched at Baltimore in September 1797 followed by the forty-four gun *Constitution,* which was launched at Boston on October 21, 1797. (Lewis, pp. 10–13)

Following the French Revolution and the beginning of a general war in Europe in 1793, the French government sent its minister Edmond Charles Genet to the United States. Citizen Genet overstepped his bounds by issuing privateering commissions and fitting out a cruiser in Philadelphia in spite of the protests of Secretary of State Thomas Jefferson. During this period of high enthusiasm for France, a crowd of French sympathizers were gathered near the Buck's Head Tavern wearing their liberty caps, when young Stephen Decatur and some friends happened by wearing their blue cockades marking them as sympathizers with the party supporting Washington's neutrality policy. When the young men refused to trade their American cockades for liberty caps, one of the leaders attempted to take Decatur's cockade by force. Stephen immediately answered with his fists, ignoring the fact that they were far outnumbered. Fortunately, some of his father's apprentices made a timely appearance and entered the fray in typical sailor fashion. They soon extricated a considerably bruised young Decatur, but with his blue cockade still in his possession. In the beginning of this European war, American neutrality rights were violated by both France and England until John Jay negotiated a treaty in London on November 19, 1794, and war with England was averted. When the Jay Treaty

was officially proclaimed in February 1796, the French, believing they had been discriminated against, published a series of decrees that caused great losses to American shipping. After three envoys sent by President Adams were rebuked, Congress abrogated the French Treaties of 1778 on July 7, 1798, and two days later authorized the seizure of French ships.

During this period of awakening to French injustice to American shipping Capt. John Barry, a close friend of the Decaturs and aware of young Stephen's love of ships and the sea, obtained an appointment as a midshipman for him. Stephen Decatur, Jr., was warranted as a midshipman in the U.S. Navy by President John Adams on April 30, 1798. (Lewis, p. 19) At the age of nineteen Stephen accepted his warrant with his mother's consent and began his naval service on the frigate *United States* under Capt. John Barry. While the *United States* was completing fitting out for sea, Midshipman Decatur managed to take a few lessons in navigation from a Mr. Talbot Hamilton, a former British naval officer, who kept a nautical academy near Philadelphia.

Meanwhile, Stephen Decatur, Sr., was appointed a post captain on May 11, 1798, and given command of the *Delaware*. Captain Decatur made the first capture of the Quasi-War with France on July 7, 1798, taking the French schooner *Croyable* of twelve guns and fifty-three men off the entrance to Delaware Bay. Captain Decatur captured three more prizes with the *Delaware* before he was given command of the new frigate *Philadelphia* in the later months of the war. In the *Philadelphia*, which had been given to the government by the citizens of Philadelphia, Captain Decatur captured five more French privateers. The Quasi-War with France led to the recommencement of construction on the *President*, *Congress*, and *Chesapeake* on July 16, 1798. These were the other three frigates on which work had been stopped when peace with Algiers was imminent.

When Captain Barry had the *United States* ready for sea and war near the middle of June 1798, he set sail from Philadelphia down the Delaware River. On board were some four hundred men, officers, and midshipmen, including two of Stephen Decatur's former schoolmates, Lt. Charles Stewart and Midshipman Richard Somers. The duties of the midshipmen included ensuring that all orders of the officers of the deck were carried out, going aloft to direct the crew in handling the sails, assisting the division officers in gun drills or in battle, inspecting the crew's clothing, and supervising the issuing of provisions, water, and spirits. A midshipman was in charge of each boat crew and every midshipman had to keep a journal for the periodic inspection of the commanding officer. The midshipmen in general served as buffers between the captain and his lieutenants on one hand and the sailors on the other. They were quartered in the gun room on the berth deck just forward of the wardroom, where they ate together and slung their hammocks. The midshipmen also spent their idle hours there, singing and joking, hazing the younger ones, and sometimes quarreling and fighting. They sent their challenges and fought their duels heeding the code of honor equally the same as the older officers.

One noteworthy incident during this time of growing friendship between Decatur and Somers would undoubtedly leave a memory with Decatur that probably had significant influence in his final year. In response to some remark by Somers about his carelessness in dress, Decatur in jest called Somers a fool. However, their messmates took it seriously and a couple of days later when Somers called for a toast, they refused to drink with him until he challenged Decatur's familiarity. Decatur was not present at the time and was unaware of Somer's embarrassment until Somers brought the matter to his attention and requested him to be his second, as he met each of the messmates an hour apart. Somers was determined to prove his courage and would not listen to Decatur's offer to have a dinner party and assure each of their messmates that he had meant no offense to Somers.

Somers met the first officer and was wounded in his right arm. The second officer wounded Somers in the thigh. When the third officer appeared, Decatur offered to take Somers' place. However, after recovering from a faint from blood loss, Somers insisted in firing from where he sat. Decatur had to prop up Somer's right elbow, but at the word Somers fired and wounded his opponent. The rest of the challenged messmates were convinced and acknowledged Somer's courage. (Anthony, pp. 103-104)

Captain Barry received his orders for a cruise to the West Indies from Secretary of the Navy Stoddert just two days after Congress passed the Act of July 9, 1798, authorizing the capture of French ships wherever found. Barry's squadron was to include the *Delaware* under Capt. Stephen Decatur, Sr., the *Herald* under Capt. James Sever, and the revenue cutter *Pickering* under Capt. Jonathan Chapman. Upon reaching Boston, Barry found that the *Herald* and *Pickering* were not ready for sea, so the *United States* and the *Delaware* sailed without them on July 26, 1798. Before ending the cruise after only six weeks due to the impending hurricane season, the squadron captured the schooner *Le Jaloux* of fourteen guns and seventy men and the sloop *Sans Pareil* of ten guns and sixty-seven men. Nine days after the *United States* embarked on her second cruise in late September, she ran into a gale that caused so much damage that she was forced to return to port for repairs.

In December Captain Barry set out for the Caribbean in command of one of four squadrons, which included the frigates *United States* and *Constitution*, the *George Washington*, *Merrimack*, and *Portsmouth* of twenty-four guns, the *Herald* of eighteen guns, and four revenue cutters. In February 1799 off the coast of Martinique, the *United States* overhauled the French privateer *Amour de la Patrie* and put a twenty-pound shot through her. When Midshipman Decatur approached the sinking ship in the first boat, he managed to get the panicking crew to steer towards the *United States*, enabling all of the crew of some sixty men to be saved as their ship sank. The *United States* next took the *Tartuffe* with sixty men and eight guns. Captain Barry then entered Basse Terre Roads, Guadeloupe, under a flag of truce, to attempt to exchange his prisoners, but was fired on. After bombarding the fort, the *United States* continued on her cruise and in late February captured a British prize from the French privateer *Democrate*, but the *Democrate* escaped. The *United States* then returned to Philadelphia on May 9, 1799, since her crew's one year enlistment was up.

Decatur Monument in Decatur Park, Berlin, Maryland. Photograph by and courtesy of Bob Moore.

On May 21, 1799, Stephen Decatur, Jr., received his promotion to lieutenant. (Lewis, p. 29) Not long after that Lieutenant Decatur had his first personal involvement in a duel. While assigned to recruiting duty in Philadelphia, a group of seamen, that he had enlisted, entered into service on an India ship instead. When Decatur demanded that the first officer of the merchantman return the deserters, he was insulted by the officer. Decatur demanded an apology which was refused, but his challenge was accepted. They met on the banks of the Delaware River near New Castle several days later as circumstances permitted. Decatur escaped without injury, but wounded his opponent in the hip as he declared that he would prior to the encounter. (Sabine, *Notes on Duels and Dueling*, pp. 139–140)

The *United States* next sailed down the Atlantic Coast and received a new bowsprit in Norfolk before proceeding to Newport, where she arrived on September 12, 1799. Captain Barry was then ordered to transport the newly appointed envoys Ellsworth and Davie to France and sailed for Lisbon on December 3, 1799. The *United States* departed Lisbon for L'Orient to disembark the envoys, but they had their fill of sailing and requested a landing at the nearest port of Corunna, Spain. Captain Barry then returned home to the Delaware, arriving off Chester on April 3, 1800. After determining that the *United States* needed her decayed outer planking replaced, she was taken upriver to Marcus Hook for extensive repairs. Lieutenant Decatur obtained a temporary transfer to the brig *Norfolk* commanded by Thomas Calvert in order to stay at sea. The *Norfolk* sailed for Cartagena in the West Indies in May and on the way encountered two French privateers. One escaped on a light wind using her sweeps and the other escaped after a thirty-minute engagement in which Captain Calvert was severely wounded. The *Norfolk* arrived at Cape Francois on July 30, 1800, and was ordered to return to Cartagena from where she was to convoy merchantmen to America. Decatur soon after returned to the *United States*, which by December was ready for sea. On December 6, 1800, Captain Barry was ordered to take command of the squadron off Guadeloupe. The *United States* had barely arrived at St. Kitts, when Captain Barry learned that a convention had been signed between the United States and France on September 30, 1800, putting an end to the Quasi-War with France. (Lewis, pp. 29–31)

Painting of the grounded American frigate *Philadelphia* by Charles Denoon. "A perspective view of the tops of the U.S. Frigate Philadelphia in which is represented her relative position to the Tripolitan Gun-boats when, during their furious attack upon her, she was unable to get a single gun to bear upon them." Photograph courtesy of the Naval Historical Center.

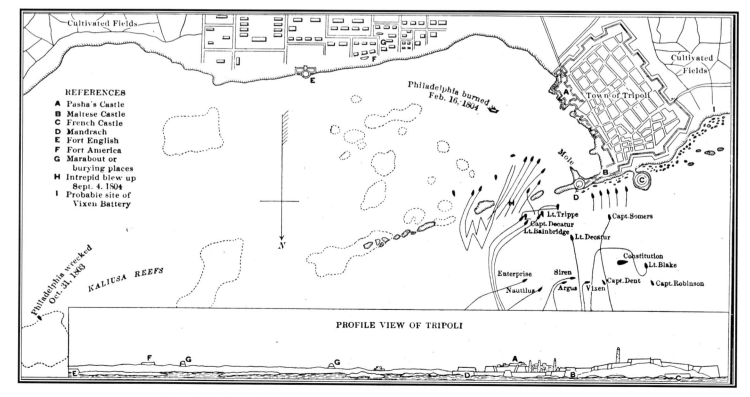

Map of Tripoli, 1804, from Allen's "Our Navy and the Barbary Corsairs." Photograph courtesy of the Naval Historical Center.

CHAPTER 2

LIEUTENANT TO CAPTAIN DECATUR IN THE TRIPOLITAN WAR

In 1796 the treaty with Algiers was looked at with envy by the other Barbary States. However, in 1800 President Adams complained that the American tribute was three times what Sweden and Denmark had to pay. When Captain Bainbridge carried out the annual payment in the *George Washington*, the Dey of Algiers reminded him, "you pay me tribute, by which you become my slaves." (Anthony, p. 68)

When President Jefferson assumed office in 1801, he was soon confronted with a demand from the Bashaw of Tunis for 10,000 stands of arms. Jefferson's response was to prepare a squadron of three frigates and a schooner under the command of Commodore Dale to sail for the Mediterranean. Commodore Dale sailed in the frigate *President* along with the frigates *Philadelphia* and *Essex* and the schooner *Experiment*. Captain Bainbridge commanded the *Essex* and Lt. Stephen Decatur was assigned as his first lieutenant. (Anthony, pp. 69–70)

In an age of strict discipline, use of the cat-o'-nine-tails, solitary confinement, and irons were quite common, but Decatur would have none of it. From this first assignment as first lieutenant through his first commands in *Argus* and *Enterprise*, and continuing thereafter, he led by example. It stood him well, as evidenced by the response from his crews.

In April 1801 the American consul Eaton at Tunis sent word to the United States that affairs at Tripoli were approaching potential violence and that our merchantmen should be prepared. Commodore Dale was sailing into rumors of war in the Mediterranean, but his orders limited his action to show his frigates from Gibralter to Smyrna with no authority to make captures. After arriving in Gibraltar on July 1, 1801, Commodore Dale left the frigate *Philadelphia* to cruise the straits and watch the two Tripolitan corsairs they encountered there. When the *Grand Turk* out of Salem came up to the squadron, the *Essex* was assigned to convoy her to Tunis. The *President* now joined by the *United States* cruised the Barbary Coast off Algiers and Tunis before taking up station off Tripoli. (Anthony, pp. 72–73)

While continuing her independent duty, the *Essex* arrived in Barcelona with a convoy of merchantmen to await some stragglers. Captain Bainbridge was returning from shore one evening, when a Spanish xebec guard ship fired several shots over his boat demanding him to come close to be recognized. Bainbridge refused and continued on to the *Essex* without further interference. When a boat carrying a group of American officers was treated similarly the next night, Decatur, as ranking officer, tried to establish some understanding and was rebuked and abused. The next morning Decatur went aboard the xebec and asked for the commanding officer. When told that he was ashore, Decatur pronounced him "a cowardly scoundrel" and returned to the *Essex*. Word of the incident spread rapidly and the captain-general of the province of Catalonia asked Captain Bainbridge to keep his

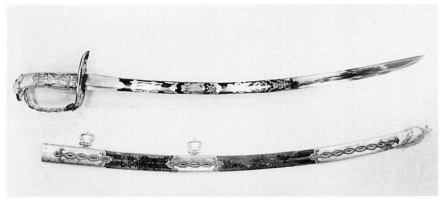

officers on board. Bainbridge refused, because there was work to be done ashore in obtaining necessary supplies. Furthermore, if the captain of the xebec did not know how to deal with gentlemen, his actions would be his responsibility. Although the captain of the xebec was forced into an apology and never sent a challenge aboard the *Essex*, Bainbridge escalated the affair to the American minister at Madrid, who put the matter before the Spanish minister of state. The Bourbon monarch satisfied Captain Bainbridge, ordering all commanders to "treat all officers of the United States with courtesy and respect, and more particularly those attached to the United States frigate *Essex*." The small but proud United States Navy was commanding courtesy. (Anthony, pp. 75–76)

Dress Sword owned by Commodore Stephen Decatur, presented to him by the U.S. Congress for burning the frigate *Philadelphia* under an Act approved November 27, 1804. Courtesy of Mr. Stephen Decatur, 1938. Photograph courtesy of the Naval Historical Center.

The *Essex*, badly in need of repair, was relieved by Commodore Richard V. Morris in the *Chesapeake* and set sail for home, arriving in New York on July 22, 1802. Decatur then became the first lieutenant of the thirty-six gun frigate *New York* under the command of Capt. James Barron. The *New York* soon joined the next squadron heading for the Mediterranean, consisting of the *Constellation*, the *New York*, the *Adams*, the *John Adams*, and the schooner *Enterprise*. They would report to Commodore Morris ready for action, since Congress had authorized war on Tripoli if peace could not be arranged. The *New York* first stopped at Algiers to deliver $30,000 to Consul O'Brien to offer to the Bey in lieu of the annual dues of naval stores that he demanded. The *New York* then crossed over to Malta, which had been designated as the rendezvous for Commodore Morris' fleet. There was a considerable delay at Malta, while Commodore Morris waited for his slowly assembling fleet.

Unfortunately, the delay allowed tension to build between the Americans and their British hosts. One night in the theater some British officers found themselves sitting near two young officers from the *New York*. The British talked about the American war with Tripoli and how the Americans would never stand the smell of powder. The two Americans left for the lobby to decide what to do. The British soon followed. As they passed in the lobby, the more vocal British officer jostled the American Midshipman Joseph Bainbridge. Twice again the British officer jostled Bainbridge and on the third offense Bainbridge knocked him down. The next morning a challenge came on board the *New York* from the British officer, who was the secretary of the governor of Malta, Sir Alexander Ball, and the most dangerous duelist on the island. News of the affair spread rapidly, as Bainbridge looked around for another midshipman to be his second. When Decatur heard about it, he sent

Semi-porcelain Pitcher depicting Commodore Edward Preble's Squadron at the Battle of Tripoli. Courtesy of Decatur House. Photograph by John Ballou.

for the boy, realizing that he was the brother of his old commander. Decatur asked Bainbridge if he knew that his challenger was a professed duelist and meant to kill him. He knew. Decatur then asked if Mr. Bainbridge would accept Lieutenant Decatur's services as his second. Bainbridge gratefully accepted.

Soon after Decatur met with the secretary's second and accepted the challenge. Decatur then chose pistols at four paces. The other second claimed that it looked like murder. Decatur countered that it looked like death, but not murder. Decatur then pointed out that the secretary was a duelist and that his friend Bainbridge was totally inexperienced. He offered to exchange places with Bainbridge, if the secretary's second insisted on ten paces. However, the second refused, saying that they had no quarrel with Decatur. Decatur then insisted on his terms.

When they met, the two fighters walked off the four paces and extended their pistols, covering each other. After delaying the count until the hand of the duelist began to tremble, Decatur called out the order to fire. The duelist, who was trained to kill at ten paces, missed and Bainbridge's shot went through his opponent's hat. As the pistols were reloaded the British officer could have apologized, but he was now even more anxious to kill Bainbridge. Decatur told Bainbridge to lower his aim, if he wanted to live. On the second firing the duelist fell mortally wounded just below the eyes. Bainbridge had defended the honor of the American Navy. However, the governor, Sir Alexander Ball, demanded that Decatur and Bainbridge be turned over to the authorities for trial in the civil courts. After careful deliberation Commodore Morris relieved the two from duty and took them to Gibralter in the flagship. When he transferred his flag to the *New York*, Decatur and Bainbridge remained on the *Chesapeake* headed for home on April 7, 1803. (Anthony, pp. 77–83)

Four months after returning home Decatur was placed in command of the *Argus*. Apparently the Navy Department approved of its fighting officers and their Maltese encounter. The *Argus* was one of four light vessels built to successfully blockade Tripoli. Since their draft was much less than the frigates, they could cruise closer to the shore with less fear of grounding. The *Argus* was one of two brigs and was square-rigged for speed. She carried sixteen twenty-four-pound carronades and two long twelve-pounders.

Decatur soon received his orders, which were to take the *Argus* to Gibraltar as soon as she was ready for sea. He was to deliver her to Isaac Hull, who was his senior. Then he was to take command of the *Enterprise*, which was schooner-rigged and mounted twelve guns. Decatur would be under the command of Commodore Edward Preble, who was to take the next relief squadron to the Mediterranean. Preble's squadron included his flagship, the frigate *Constitution*, the frigate *Philadelphia*, the brigs *Argus* and *Siren,* and three schooners, the *Vixen* and the *Nautilus*, as well as the *Enterprise* which was already on station in the Mediterranean. The squadron sailed independently as each was ready for sea and rendezvoused at Gibraltar. Preble arrived in Gibraltar on September 12, 1803, along with the *Philadelphia* and

Commodore Preble Congressional Medal. An engraving of the obverse and reverse sides of the medal presented to Commodore Edward Preble by Congress. Photograph courtesy of the Naval Historical Center.

Nautilus. The *Vixen* followed two days later. At the same time Commodore Rodgers arrived in the *New York* along with the *John Adams.* Commodore Morris arrived in the *Adams* on September 22 and the *Siren* came in on October 1. While both squadrons were together, Preble convinced Rodgers to accompany him in a show of force to Morocco before returning home. This would neutralize a potential threat to his flank and supply line to Gibraltar, when dealing with the more truculent Tripoli. Meanwhile, Preble sent the *Philadelphia* and *Vixen* to begin the blockade of Tripoli.

After requesting a meeting with the Emperor Muley Soliman, Preble appeared off Tangier with his squadron and Rodgers' two ships. Their show of force and impressive twenty-one gun salute impressed the emperor that such friends were invincible. They were soon able to convince the emperor and his prime minister that free trade with all nations would be much more profitable than piracy. Preble then returned to Gibraltar and Rodgers and his squadron departed for home.

Decatur in the *Argus* finally joined Preble in Gibraltar on November 1, 1803. Decatur then turned over command of the *Argus* to Hull and Preble, ordering Hull to cruise along the African coast keeping an eye out for trouble. Decatur took command of the *Enterprise* and was ordered to convoy the supply ship *Traveler* to Syracuse to establish a base. After that he was to proceed to Tripoli to join the blockade. As a twelve-gun schooner, the *Enterprise* with a shoal draft was even handier than a brig. She was powerful enough to successfully attack gunboats, but speedy enough to escape more powerful ships. On board the *Enterprise* with Decatur was a crew ranging at different times from eighty to ninety-four men. His lieutenants were Joseph Bainbridge, James Lawrence, and Jonathan Thorn. They were joined by the surgeon and two midshipmen to complete the officers on board.

On the way to Syracuse the *Enterprise* and *Traveler* were overtaken by the *Constitution* off Cape Passero. The three ships then rounded north and arrived in Syracuse on November 28. Here Preble conveyed the bad news. He had communicated with the British frigate *Amazon* on November 24 and learned that the *Philadelphia* had been captured off Tripoli. He had lost one-third of his force. Preble immediately sailed for Malta, where letters awaited him from the now captured Bainbridge. (Anthony, pp. 105-16)

In the first letter from Tripoli dated November 1, 1803, Capt. William Bainbridge informed his superior, Capt. Edward Preble, of the loss of the *Philadelphia.* The letter conveyed the distressing information of how the *Philadelphia* under Bainbridge's command had been wrecked on the rocks about four and a half miles from Tripoli. For particulars of the unfortunate event Bainbridge referred to the enclosed copy of his letter to the Secretary of the Navy, which he wanted accepted by Commodore Preble as the full infor-

Engraving of "Prebles Boys," depicting Stephen Decatur in the center, William Bainbridge in the upper left, David Porter in the upper right, James Lawrence in the lower left, and Thomas MacDonough in the lower right. Courtesy of Decatur House. Photograph by John Ballou.

Sir, Misfortune necessitates me to make a communication, the most distressing of my life, & it is with the deepest regret that I inform you of the loss of the United States Frigate Philadelphia under my command by being wrecked on Rocks between 4 & 5 Miles to the Eastward of the Town of Tripoli; The circumstances relating to this unfortunate event are: At 9 A M about 5 Leagues to the Eastward of Tripoli, saw a Ship in shore of us, standing before the Wind to the Westward, we immediately gave chase, she hoisted Tripolitan Colours & continued her course verry near the shore; about 11 Oclock had approached the shore to 7 fathoms Water, commenced firing at her, which we continued by running before the Wind untill half past Eleven, being then in 7 fathoms water and finding our fire ineffectual to prevent her getting into Tripoli gave up the pursuit & was beating, off the land when we ran on the Rocks in 12 feet water forward & 17 feet aft. Immediately lowered down a Boat from the Stern, sounded and found the greatest depth of water a stern, laid all sails aback, loosed top Gallt Sails and set a heavy press of Canvass on the Ship, blowing fresh to get her off, cast Three Anchors away from the Bows, started the Water in the hold, hove overboard the Guns except some abaft, to defend the ship against Gun Boats, which were then firing on us, found all this ineffectual, then made the last resort of lightning her forward by Cutting away the Fore Mast. which carried the Main Top Gallt mast with it, but labour & enterprise was in Vain; for our fate was direfully fixed. I am fully sensible of the loss that has occurrd to our Country & the dificulty which it may further involve her in with this

regency, and feel beyond description for the Brave unfortunate Officers & Men under my command, who done every thing in their power worthy of the character & stations they filled, & I trust on investigation of my own conduct that I will appear to my Government and my Country, consistant to the station in which I had the honour of being placed.

Striking on the Rocks was an accident not possible for me to guard against, by any intimation of Charts, as no such shoals was laid down in any on Board, and every careful precaution (by three leads kept heaving) was made use of in approaching the shore, to effect the capture of a Tripolitan Cruizer, & after the Ship struck the Rocks, all possible measures were taken to get her off, and the firmest determination made not to give her up as long as a possible hope remained; although annoyed by the Gun Boats, which took their position in such a manner as we could not bring our Guns to bear on them not after cutting away part of the Stern to effect it, when my Officers & self had not a hope left, of its being possible to get her off the Rocks; & having withstood the fire of the Gun Boats for four hours & a reinforcement coming out from Tripoli, without the least chance of injureing them in resistance, to save the lives of Brave men, left no alternative but the distressing one of hauling our coulors down & submitting to the enemy whom chance had befriended—In such a Dilemma the Flag of the United States was struck however painfull it will be to our fellow Citizens to hear the news, they may be assured that we feel in a National loss equally with them, Zeal of serving our Country in doing our duty, has placed us in that situation, which can better be conceived than described & from which we rely on our Countrys Extricating us. The Gun Boats in attacking fired principally at our Masts, had they directed their shot at the Hull, no doubt but they would have killed many.

The Ship was taken possession of a little after sun set & in the evening myself and all Officers with part of the Crew were brought on shore carried before the Bashaw who asked several questions from the Palace the Officers were conducted to the House which Mr. Cathcart lived in, where we lodged last night & this day the Minister has become guarantee to the Bashaw for us Officers and we have given our parole of honour—Enclosed you will receive a list of the Officers and a few of the People to attend on them, who are quartered in the American Consular House and we are to be provided for by such ways & means as I can best adopt, which will be on as equinonomical a plan as possible, the remainder of the Crew will be supported by this Regency.

We have all lost every thing but what we had on our Backs & even part of that was taken off, the loss of the Officers is considerable as they were well provided for a long station—Mr. Nisson the danish Consul has been extremely attentive, & kindly offers every service of assistance—I trust Sir, you will readily conceive the anxiety of mind I must suffer, after the enclosed Certificate from the Officers on my conduct, should you be pleased to express the Opinion of Government, you will much oblidge me

P. S. Notwithstanding our Parole we are not at liberty of leaving the house, or going on the Top of it, they have prevented our View of the Sea which they allowed at first. (Knox, Naval

mation for himself. Bainbridge went on to note his distressed state of mind for not having kept the schooner *Vixen* with him. He noted that the accident might have been prevented or at least they could have extricated themselves from their precarious position. However, he had deemed it more prudent to send the *Vixen* off to afford more protection to our commerce than in keeping her with him.

Bainbridge then asked that Preble consider his decision as judicious under the circumstances and done with the best of intentions, although it proved to be most unfortunate. He continued with the reflection that his services under Preble had seemed so promising, but were now so cruelly terminated. Bainbridge stated the dire circumstances they were in with no additional clothing or money and that they had to rely on Preble's ability to aid and assist them, as much as was in his power. He further noted that Mr. Nisson, the Danish consul, had rendered them every assistance in his power and was very instrumental in alleviating their distress. In closing, Bainbridge said that Mr. Nisson thought that a Credit on Tunis would be the most proper place to meet their needs. (Knox, Naval Documents, vol. 3, p. 191)

On the first of November 1803 Captain Bainbridge also wrote a letter to the Secretary of the Navy, which he had referred to in his letter to Preble. The letter read as shown at right.

On November 10, 1803, Lt. Stephen Decatur, Jr., wrote to the secretary of the Navy from the United States Schooner *Enterprise* in Gibraltar Bay that he had arrived in Gibraltar on the first of the month after a passage of thirty-four days, twenty-five of which they had been up against easterly winds. He noted that the *Argus* sailed well and possessed a number of excellent qualities. Decatur then reported that on November 9 he had delivered the *Argus* to Lieutenant Isaac Hull and relieved him in command of the *Enterprise*. In closing, he noted that per the secretary's instructions he was enclosing Commodore Preble's receipt for the thirty thousand dollars that he had brought out. (Knox, Naval Documents, vol. 3, p. 212) An extract from the diary of Captain Edward Preble of November 24, 1803, read below.

At 9 A. M. spoke His B. M. ship Amazon on a cruize the Capn. of which gave me the melancholy and distressing Intelligence of the loss of the U. S. Ship Philadelphia. He said she ran on shore near Tripoly in chase of an Algerine schooner, that the Officers and Crew were made prisoners and the ship got off by the Tripolines and Towed into Tripoly. The loss of that ship and capture of the Crew with all its consequences are of the most serious and alarming nature to the United States; and it should not involve us in a war with Tunis and Algiers in consequence of the weakness of our squadron, yet still it will protract the war with Tripoly.

Extract from Captain Preble's diary of November 24, 1803.

On December 1, 1803, Commodore Preble of the frigate *Constitution* in Syracuse Harbor wrote to Lt. Stephen Decatur, Jr., commanding the schooner *Enterprise* that the articles he had requested to be supplied the *Enterprise* were ready to be delivered to the proper officers as soon as they applied to receive them. Preble then requested that Decatur have the *Enterprise* ready for sea as early as possible for a cruise. (Knox, Naval Documents, vol. 3, p. 244)

While at Syracuse on December 14, 1803, Commodore Preble transferred Midshipman Thomas Macdonough from the *Constitution* to the *Enterprise*. As ranking midshipman, Macdonough and Lieutenant Decatur quickly saw eye to eye and became good friends. Macdonough had been ordered out of the *Philadelphia* as prize master of the captured Moorish ship *Meshoba* and then became a passenger on the *Constitution*. As it later turned out, it was a very fortunate set of circumstances. (Anthony, pp. 116–117)

On December 17 Preble in *Constitution* sailed with the *Enterprise* in company to reconnoiter the harbor and defenses of Tripoli. Sailing Master Nathaniel Haraden, U.S. Navy, on board the frigate *Constitution,* noted the following event in his log for December 23, 1803. As they were cruising the coast near Tripoli, running to the southward after daylight at half past 8:00 A.M. on Friday, December 23, *Constitution* answered the *Enterprise* signal for seeing land to the southwest and a strange sail in the same quarter and gave chase. While in the act of setting studding sails, the wind veered to the southwest and brought the chase dead to windward. However, the chase continued steering towards *Constitution* until 10:00 A.M. at which time she was brought to by the *Enterprise* about two miles away from the *Constitution. Enterprise* was signaled to bring the chase to the Commodore. She was the ketch rigged *Mastico* with Tripolitan colors. The *Constitution* was showing British colors as she sent a boat for the captain. When *Constitution* hauled down the British and hoisted the American colors, the people on board the *Mastico* appeared to be in great confusion. Commodore Preble gave orders for taking charge of the

Mastico at noon. Tripoli was at this time nearly nine miles to the west-southwest from *Enterprise*. Commodore Preble noted in his Memorandum Book for December 23, 1803, that they captured the Turkish ketch called *Mastico* with about seventy Tripolines on board. (Knox, Naval Documents, vol. 3, pp. 288–289)

After reconnoitering Tripoli the *Constitution* and *Enterprise* along with their prize ketch *Mastico* returned to Syracuse. The fortifications at Tripoli were formidable. Preble noted batteries judiciously constructed and mounting one hundred fifteen heavy cannon backed by twenty-five thousand Arabs and Turks. He viewed a harbor protected by nineteen gunboats, two galleys, two eight-gun schooners, and a ten-gun brig. (Anthony, pp. 117–118)

Decatur also noted the defenses of Tripoli, as well as the *Philadelphia*, absent her foremast, stripped of her sails, and chained under the fort. He went to the Commodore with a plan. Decatur proposed to take the *Enterprise* into the Tripolitan harbor and burn the *Philadelphia*. Coincidentally, the same recommendation had been made by Captain Bainbridge in letters in sympathetic ink, which were sent through the Danish Consul to Commodore Preble. (Anthony, pp. 118–119)

After considerable deliberation Commodore Preble made his decision. On January 31, 1804, Preble aboard the U.S. frigate *Constitution* in Syracuse Harbor, wrote to Decatur, as shown at right above.

An extract from the diary of Capt. Edward Preble, Commodore of U.S. Squadron in the Mediterranean, February 3, 1804, is shown at right below.

On February 19, 1804, Commodore Preble wrote to the Secretary of the Navy from Syracuse that it was his honor to inform the secretary that the brig *Siren* under the command of Lt. Commandant Stewart and the ketch *Intrepid* under the command of Lieutenant Decatur arrived the previous evening from a cruise. He noted that they left this port on February 3 with orders to proceed to Tripoli and burn the late U.S. frigate *Philadelphia* at

SIR You are hereby ordered to take command of the Prize Ketch which I have named Intrepid and prepare her with all possible dispatch for a cruize of Thirty days with full allowance of Water, Provision &ca. for Seventy five men. I shall send you five Midshipmen from the Constitution and you will take Seventy men including Officers from the Enterprize if that number can be found ready to volunteer their Services for boarding and burning the Philadelphia in the Harbor of Tripoly, If not, report to me and I will furnish you with men to compleat your compliment. It is expected you will be ready to sail tomorrow evening or some hours sooner if the Signal is made for that purpose.

It is my Orders that you proceed to Tripoly in company with the Syren Lt. Stewart, Enter that Harbor in the night Board the Frigate Philadelphia, burn her and make your retreat good with the Intrepid if possible, unless you can make her the means of destroying the Enemy's vessels in the Harbor by converting her into a fire ship for that purpose and retreating in your Boats and those of the Syren. You must take fixed ammunition and apparatus for the Frigates 18 Pounders and if you can, without risking too much you may endeavor to make them the Instruments of distruction to the shipping and Bashaw's Castle. You will provide all the necessary Combustibules for burning and destroying ships. The destruction of the Philadelphia is an object of great importance; And I rely with confidence on your Intrepidity & Enterprize to effect it. Lt. Stewart will support you with the boats of the Syren and cover your retreat with that vessel be sure and set fire in the Gun room births, Cockpit Store rooms forward and Births on the Birth deck.

After the Ship is well on fire, point two of the 18 Pdrs. shotted down the Main Hatch and blow her bottom out—Return to this Place as soon as Possible, and report to me your proceedings. On boarding the Frigate it is probable you will meet with Resistance, it may be well in order to prevent alarm to carry all by the Sword, May God prosper and Succeed you in this enterprize.

Commodore Preble to Decatur, January 31, 1804, excerpt. (Knox, Naval Documents, vol. 3, pp. 376–377)

(Syracuse) Taking on board water and provisions; Setting up rigging &ca. At 5 P.M. Sailed the Syren Lt. Stewart and the Prize Intrepid with Lt. Decatur with 64 Volunteers from the Enterprize and Six Midshipmen and two Pilots from this Ship bound for the Coast of Tripoly to endeavor to burn the Frigate late the Philadelphia —From information which I have received from Tripoly that ship is now in the Harbor with all her Guns mounted: but that she has no ammunition on board and only a Guard of about 30 Men.

An extract from the diary of Capt. Edward Preble, Commodore of U.S. Squadron in the Mediterranean, February 3, 1804. (Knox, Naval Documents, vol. 3, p. 388)

SIR, I have the honor to inform you, that in pursuance of your orders of the 1st Inst. to proceed with this Ketch off the Harbour of Tripoly there to endeavor to effect the destruction of the United States late Frigate Philadelphia. I arrived there in company with the U S Brig Syren Lt. Commt. Stewart on the 7th, but owing to the Badness of the weather was unable to effect any thing untill last evening when we had a light breeze from N.E. At 7 O'clock I entered the harbour with the Intrepid the Syren having gained her station without the Harbour, in a situation to support us in our retreat at 1/2 past 9 laid her a long side the Philadelphia, boarded, and after a short contest carried her. I immediately fired her in the Store Rooms, Gun Room Cockpit & Birth Deck and remained on board until the flames had issued from the Spar Deck hatch ways & Ports, and before I got from alongside the fire had communicated to the rigging and tops. Previous to our boarding, they got their Tompions out, and hailed several times, but not a Gun fired—

The noise occasioned by boarding and contending for possession (altho' no fire arms were used) gave a general alarm on shore, and on board their cruisers which lay about a cable and a half's length from us, and many boats filled with men lay round, but from whom we recd. no annoyance. They commenced a fire on us from all their Batteries on shore, but with no other effect than one shot passing thro' our Top Gallt. Sail.

The Frigate was moored within half Gun shot of the Bashaw's Castle, and of their principal Battery; two of their Cruisers lay within two cables length on the starboard quarter and their Gun Boats within half Gun shot on the starboard bow she had all her Guns mounted and loaded which as they became hot went off as she lay with her Broadside to the town, I have no doubt but some damage has been done by them. Before I got out of the harbour, her cables had burnt off, and she drifted in under the Castle where she was consumed. I can form no judgement as to the number of Men that were on board of her; there were about 20 killed—A large boat full got off, and many leapt into the Sea. We have made one prisoner, and I fear from the number of bad wounds he has recd. will not recover, altho' every assistance & comfort has been given him—

I boarded with sixty men & Officers, leaving a guard on board the Ketch for her defence; and it is with the greatest pleasure I inform you, I had not a man killed in this affair, and but one slightly wounded—Every support that could be given I recd. from my Officers, and as each of their conduct was highly meritorious, I beg leave to enclose you a list of their names.—permit me also, Sir, to speak of the brave fellows I have the honor to command, whose coolness and intrepidity was such, as I trust will ever characterise the American Tars.

It would be injustice in me, were I to pass over the important services rendered by Mr. Salvador the Pilot, on whose good conduct the success of the Enterprize in the greatest degree depended. he gave me entire satisfaction.

I have the honor to be, Sir,
With great respect
Your Mo. ob Servt.
(Signed) Stephan Decatur
Commodore Edwd. Preble
Commanding the U S Squadron
in the Mediterranean

anchor in that harbor. Preble continued that it was impossible to bring out the Philadelphia under the circumstances and that, therefore, her destruction was necessary in order to favor his intended operations against that city.

Preble enclosed copies of his orders of January 31, 1804, and noted that they were executed in the most gallant and officer-like manner by Lieutenant Commandant Decatur, assisted by the brave officers and crew of the ketch Intrepid under his command. He went on to say that their performance of the dangerous service assigned could not be sufficiently estimated. It was beyond all praise. If Decatur had delayed one-half hour for the boats of the Syren to join him, he would have failed, since a gale started immediately after the Philadelphia was fired. Preble noted that the Syren had been forced to anchor out some distance because of the light breeze. However, Lieutenant Stewart had taken the best position to cover the retreat of the Intrepid and that his conduct was judicious and highly meritorious. Preble also observed that only a few of the officers of the squadron could participate, but that they had all volunteered their services. He was confident that whenever another opportunity was offered for them to distinguish themselves, that they would do honor to the service. Preble concluded by enclosing Lieutenant Commandant Stewart and Decatur's official communication with the names of the officers on board the ketch Intrepid. (Knox, Naval Documents, vol. 3, p. 413)

Lt. Stephen Decatur, Jr., had written to Capt. Edward Preble, from on board the ketch Intrepid at sea February 17, 1804, the letter at left.

Also enclosed was the letter to Capt. Edward Preble from Lt. Charles Stewart, aboard the Brig Syren in Syracuse Harbor of February 19, 1804, which passed on his observations during the expedition in company with Lieutenant Commandant Decatur in the ketch Intrepid to effect the destruction of the frigate Philadelphia in the harbor of Tripoli. He noted the happy termination of the enterprise and heartily con-

Lt. Stephen Decatur, Jr., to Capt. Edward Preble February 17, 1804, (Knox, Naval Documents, vol. 3, pp. 414–415)

gratulated Captain Preble. Stewart did lament the fact that he was unable to form a junction with the *Intrepid* by his boats of the *Syren* under the command of Lieutenant Caldwell. He had no doubt that they would have been able to carry and destroy one or both of the cruisers laying near the frigate. Stewart noted that the boats were dispatched in time to meet the *Intrepid*, but circumstances made it advisable for Lieutenant Commandant Decatur to enter the harbor much earlier than intended such that the junction of the boats was defeated until after the *Philadelphia* was on fire and the ketch was retreating out of the harbor. (Knox, Naval Documents, vol. 3, p. 415)

Captain Preble then wrote to the secretary of the Navy from the *Constitution* in Syracuse Harbor February 19, 1804, the letter shown at right above:

An extract from the diary of Capt. Edward Preble, Commodore of the U.S. Squadron in the Mediterranean, February 19, 1804 read as shown at right.

Thus, using the recently captured ketch renamed *Intrepid*, Decatur and his daring crew had successfully penetrated the harbor of Tripoli on the night of February 16, 1804. By letting his Maltese pilot Salvador Catalano answer the hail of the ship-keepers, Decatur and his men were able to swiftly board the captured American frigate *Philadelphia* and sweep the Tripolitan crew overboard in twenty minutes, sustaining only one wounded casualty. Decatur and his party had then set fire to the *Philadelphia* and escaped while under fire from answering shore batteries with the burning *Philadelphia* lighting the way. Upon hearing of the action Admiral Lord Nelson termed this "the most bold and daring act of the age." (Anthony, Decatur, P. 138)

The secretary of the Navy responded to Captain Preble's report with

Top: Captain Preble to the Secretary of the Navy, February 19, 1804, excerpt. (Knox, Naval Documents, vol. 3, p. 441)

SIR Lieutenant Decatur is an Officer of too much Value to be neglected. The important service he has rendered in destroying an Enemy's frigate of 40 Guns, and the gallant manner in which he performed it, in a small vessel of only 60 Tons and 4 Guns, under the Enemy's Batteries, surrounded by their corsairs and armed Boats, the crews of which, stood appalled at his intrepidity and daring, would in any Navy in Europe insure him instantaneous promotion to the rank of post Captain. I wish as a stimulus, it could be done in this instance; it would eventually be of real service to our Navy. I beg most earnestly to recommend him to the President, that he may be rewarded according to his merit.

By the Store Ship, I shall have the honor to write you again in a few days. With the highest respect

(Syracuse)

Wind NNE to ENE—Moderate and cloudy. At 10 A.M. the Syren & Ketch Intrepid appeared in the Offing; they sailed the 3d. Inst. for the Coast of Tripoly with orders to Burn the frigate Philadelphia. At 1/2 past 10 Lt. Stewart and Lt. Decatur came on board and informed me that my Orders were executed; On the night of the 16th. Lt. Decatur entered the harbor of Tripoly with the Ketch and in the most gallant manner laid her alongside the Frigate, boarded and carried her against all opposition, killed about 20 or 30 Tripolines and drove the rest overboard, excepting one boats crew which escaped on shore and made one prisoner. He then set fire to her and left her. She was soon in a complete Blaze from her birth deck to her tops and was totally consumed. In effecting the destruction of the frigate we had none killed and only one man wounded with a Sabre, on the head, Altho she had all her Guns mounted and loaded and a great number of men to defend her, and two Tripoline Corsairs full of men lay within half musket shot.

The names of the Officers on board the Ketch Intrepid who effected this Important business are,

Lt. Commt.	*Stephen Decatur Junr.*
Lieutts.	*James Lawrence*
	Joseph Bainbridge &
	Jonathan Thorn
Surgeon	*Lewis Hermen*
Midshipmen	*Ralp(h) Izard —Belonging to the [Constitution]*
	John Rowe - - - - - "
	Thomas McDonough - - - - - [Enterprize]
	Charles Morris - - - - - - - - [Constitution]
	Alexander Laws - - - - - - - - "
	John Davis & - - - - - - - - - "
	Thomas Oakley Anderson - - [Siren]
Pilot	*Salvadore Catalano*

An extract from the diary of Capt. Edward Preble, February 19, 1804 (Knox, Naval Documents, vol. 3, p. 443)

Navy Depmt.
22 May 1804.—
Commodore Edd. Preble.
Mediterranean.

Your several Dispatches have been received.
Your whole conduct has afforded us the highest satisfac-
tion. Justly are you entitled to our warmest Thanks. We
congratulate you on the glorious Enterprize achieved by
Capt. Decatur. As a testimonial of our high sense of the
brilliancy of this Enterprize, we send The Hero a
Captain's Commission. Knowing that you will feel great
pleasure in presenting it to him I herewith send it to you
for that purpose.

Rt. Smith.

Response of the Secretary of the Navy, May
22, 1804. (Knox, Naval Documents, vol. 3,
p. 427)

Navy Dept.
22d. May, 1804—
Stephen Decatur jr. esqr.
Captain in the Navy of the United States.
Care of Commre. Edd. Preble.
Mediterranean.

By Dispatches from Commodore Preble it has been
announced to us that the destruction of the late frigate
Philadelphia has been effected while lying in the Harbour of
Tripoli under circumstances of extraordinary peril to the parties
that achieved it. I find, Sir, that you had the Command of this
Expedition. The achievement of this brilliant Enterprize reflects
the highest honor on all the Officers and men concerned. You
have acquitted yourself in a manner which justifies the high
Confidence we have reposed in your valour and your Skill. The
President has desired me to convey to you his Thanks for your
gallant Conduct on this occasion, and he likewise requests that
you will in his name thank each Individual of your gallant
Band for their honorable and valorous Support rendered the
more honorable from its having been volunteered.

As a Testimonial of the President's high opinion of your
gallant Conduct in this Instance, he sends to you the enclosed
Commission.

Rt. Smith

The Secretary of the Navy to Captain
Decatur, May 22, 1804. (Knox, Naval
Documents, vol. 3, pp. 427–428)

the letter shown at left.

In a separate letter the secretary of the Navy wrote to Capt. Stephen Decatur, whose promotion had been dated from February 16, 1804, as shown at left below.

The "Statement of the Circumstances" attending the destruction of the frigate *Philadelphia* with the names of the officers and the number of men employed on the occasion was laid before the president by the secretary of the Navy on November 13, 1804. The secretary noted that Commodore Preble lying with his squadron at Syracuse on January 31, 1804, ordered Lt. Charles Stewart in command of the brig *Siren* of sixteen guns and Lt. Stephen Decatur in command of the ketch *Intrepid* of four guns and seventy-five men to proceed to Tripoli and destroy the frigate *Philadelphia* of forty-four guns. He stated that Decatur had orders to enter the harbor at night, board, and set fire to the *Philadelphia* and that Stewart was ordered to take the best possible position outside of the harbor to cover the retreat.

The secretary continued that under these orders they were to proceed immediately, but that very heavy gales prevailing there in winter kept the enterprise from being undertaken until February 16. Lieutenant Stewart took the best possible position to effect his instructions and at seven o'clock that night Lieutenant Decatur entered the harbor of Tripoli, boarded and took possession of the *Philadelphia*. At the time the frigate was boarded she had all her guns mounted and charged and was lying within half a gun shot of the Bashaw's Castle and his principal Battery, as well as two cruisers within two cable's length on the starboard quarter and several gunboats within half a gun shot on the starboard bow. About twenty men of the *Philadelphia* were killed and a large boat full got off, as many men leapt into the water. One prisoner was taken. Lieutenant Decatur set fire to the storerooms, gun room, cockpit, berth deck and he and his officers and men remained on board until the flames were issuing from the ports of the gun deck and the hatchways of the spar deck. They continued in the ketch alongside until the fire had reached the frigate's rigging and tops, while all the batteries on shore were opened up on the assailants. Decatur did not lose a man and had only one wounded. The list of officers and men employed in the destruction of the *Philadelphia* are listed in Appendix A.

The secretary concluded with the statement that Lieutenant Decatur had stated that all his officers and men behaved with the greatest coolness and intrepidity, and Commodore Preble had informed him that Lieutenant

Stewart's conduct was judicious and meritorious. (Knox, Naval Documents, pp. 422–424)

On November 27, 1804, Congress passed the resolution shown at left in honor of the gallant conduct of Capt. Stephen Decatur, the officers and crew of the United States ketch *Intrepid*, in attacking and destroying the Tripolitan frigate of forty-four guns in the harbor of Tripoli.

After passing the remainder of the winter at Syracuse, Commodore Preble began a real blockade of Tripoli on March 27, 1804. He personally reconnoitered the harbor defenses and realized he needed additional help. Preble appealed to the King of the two Sicilies and his majesty loaned him six gunboats and two bombards. These vessels were not good sailers, being flat bottomed and built for harbor defense. The gunboats mounted one twenty-four-pounder each and the bombards a thirteen-inch brass sea mortar each. Preble recruited twelve Neapolitan sailors for each boat and then convoyed them to Syracuse. Off Tripoli he made one more attempt to arrange for the release of the prisoners which was to no avail. Preble then sailed to Tunis to keep the Bey friendly to the Americans and returned to Syracuse on July 14, 1804. He then sailed for Tripoli via Malta, where he was delayed by summer gales too unfriendly for his gunboats until July 21.

Resolved, &c., That the President of the United States be requested to present, in the name of Congress, to Captain Stephen Decatur, a sword, and to each of the officers and crew of the United States ketch Intrepid, two months' pay, as a testimony of the high sense entertained by Congress of the gallantry, good conduct and services of Captain Decatur, the officers and crew, of the said ketch, in attacking, in the harbor of Tripoli, and destroying, a Tripolitan frigate of forty-four guns.
Approved, November 27, 1804.

Congressional resolution, November 27, 1804. (Knox, Naval Documents, vol. 3, p. 428)

Preble finally appeared off Tripoli on July 25 with his squadron ready for battle. The squadron included the frigate *Constitution*, schooners *Intrepid*, *Nautilus*, and *Enterprise*, brigs *Siren*, *Argus*, and *Scourge*, six gunboats, and two bombards. The *Scourge* had been the Tripolitan privateer *Transfer*, captured by Lieutenant Stewart in the *Siren*. Delayed again by a gale, the squadron was finally positioned for the attack on August 3, 1804.

Decatur commanded a gunboat division during the subsequent attacks on Tripoli. In the first attack on August 3, 1804, Decatur swept down on the Tripolitan gunboats. All were firing as they closed, but soon Decatur boarded his first gunboat opponent with Midshipman Macdonough and twenty-three of his crew. They cleared the deck with cutlass, axe, and pike within ten minutes, although outnumbered almost two to one. Decatur put Lieutenant Thorn in charge of the prize and took her in tow.

Stephen's brother James Decatur also plunged into the fray with such a rapid and accurate fire that when he came alongside his opponent to board, the Tripolitan captain surrendered. However, as James started to board to take possession of his prize, the Tripolitan captain suddenly shot him through the head and he fell backward into his gunboat. Midshipman Brown managed to get their gunboat clear and started carrying his mortally wounded officer back for aid. As he passed close to Stephen Decatur's gunboat, he reported the treachery.

Decatur's men heard the report and he needed no appeal. Leaving Lieutenant Thorn and the larger part of his crew with the prize, Decatur shoved off with a crew of eleven. Decatur searched for the treacherous captain's gunboat and when he thought he spied it in behind the line of enemy

At length Decatur was able to single out the treacherous commander, conspicuous no less by gigantic size, than by the ferocity with which he fought, and to meet him face to face. Decatur was armed with a cutlass, the Turk with a heavily ironed boarding-pike. As the latter made a thrust at Decatur, he struck it violently with his cutlass, in the hope of severing the head; but his cutlass, coming in contact with the iron, broke at the hilt, and left him without a weapon. Many a brave man thus disarmed might have turned to seek another weapon. But Decatur stood his ground, and attempting with his right arm to parry the next thrust of his antagonist, received the point of it in his arm and breast. Tearing the weapon from the wound, he succeeded likewise, by a sudden jerk, in wresting it from the hands of his adversary, who immediately grappled him; and, after a fierce and prolonged struggle, both fell with violence on the deck, Decatur being uppermost. During this time, the crews, rushing to the aid of their respective commanders, joined in furious conflict round their persons. A Tripolitan officer, who had got behind Decatur, aimed an unseen blow at his head, which must have decided his fate, had not a young man, by the name of Reuben James, who had lost the use of both arms by wounds, rushed in, and intercepted the descending cimeter with his own head, thus rescuing his beloved commander by an act of heroic self-sacrifice which has never been surpassed.

Just then the Tripolitan, exerting to the uttermost his superior strength, succeeded in turning Decatur, and, getting upon him, held him to the deck with an iron clutch of his left hand, whilst, thrusting his right beside him, he drew from his sash the shorter of two yataghans, which, for the very purpose of such close work, he carried in the same sheath. The moments of Decatur's existence seemed numbered; scarce an interval remained to breathe a prayer for mercy in another world; a second brother was about to perish beneath the rage of the fierce Tripolitan. But the cool courage and fertile resources of Decatur came to the rescue in this extremity. Disengaging his left hand, he caught the right of the Tripolitan, stayed the yataghan as it was about to drink his blood, and, thrusting his own right hand into his pantaloons' pocket, succeeded in cocking a pistol, which he had there, and, giving it the proper direction, fired. The Tripolitan relaxed his hold, and Decatur, disengaging himself from the heap of wounded and slain, which the struggle had gathered around him, stood again that day a victor on the enemy's deck.

(Mackenzie, *Life of Stephen Decatur*, p. 291

Surgeons Report of wounded on board the Gunboat No. 4, Lt: Decatur, junr: Esqr: Commander. Augt. 3d. 1804.
Capt: Decatur, wounded slightly in the arm.
Sjt. Sal: Wren burnt & slightly wounded in the hand.
Thos. James, superficial puncture in the face.
Dnl. Frashier, two incised wounds on the head, one of them severe; one bad wound across the wrist & seven slightly about his hands.
*   Lewis Heermann.*

gunboats, he sailed straight in and attacked with a vengeance. (Anthony, pp. 143–145)

Decatur quickly closed on his targeted gunboat and coming alongside he immediately boarded followed by the gallant Midshipman Macdonough and the rest of his crew. The Americans quickly found themselves in a desperate hand to hand battle with the Tripolitans and the outcome was uncertain. *(See MacKenzies' description at left)*

The quoted version of this celebrated struggle, which has in other places been narrated somewhat differently, is derived from Messrs. J. K. Hamilton and Francis Gurney Smith, early companions of Decatur, who, feeling a natural curiosity to learn the true history of the adventure, drew from Decatur himself the statement embodied in the text. On the body of the Tripolitan, or rather Turk, (for the officers, like the Bashaw, were from Constantinople,) a devotional work was found, containing Arabic prayers and passages from the Koran. This work has, since the death of Decatur, been presented by Mrs. Decatur to the library of the Catholic College in Georgetown, where it may now be seen by the curious. (Knox, Naval Documents, vol. 4, pp. 347–348)

The Mackenzie description of seaman Reuben James saving Decatur's life is one of those often strange ironies of history that is still debated to this day. Was it seaman Reuben James or seaman Daniel Frazier, as recorded by Irvin Anthony. (Anthony, p. 145) One or the other obviously saved the life of their captain. However, Surgeon Heermann's report only lists seaman Frazier with the likely wounds of Decatur's rescuer at left.

After that action Captain Decatur made his report to Captain Preble as shown on the facing page at the top.

(Knox, Naval Documents, vol. 4, p. 348)

Gun Boat No. 4 off Tripoli
August 3rd. 1804
Commodore Edward Preble

Sir In obedience to your directions to state the proceedings of the 2nd. division of boats that you did me the honor to place under my command,—I beg leave to acquaint you, that after the Signal was displayed to advance and engage the enemy I led in with my boats; finding it impossible to bring their weather division to close action, I bore down on their line of boats consisting of seventeen, which were moored within two cables length of their Batteries,—I boarded and carried two of them, and was successfull in bringing them off,—I was supported in the handsomest manner by Lieutenants Tripp and Bainbridge, Lieutenant Jonathan [John] Tripp who commanded No. 6, Boarded, carried, and got off one of the enemies Boats, I regret that Lieutenant Bainbridge's boat No. 5 being disabled prevented him being equally Successful, I now feel it my duty to Assure you that nothing could surpass the zeal, courage, and readiness of Lieutenant John [Jonathan] Thorn & Mr. Thomas Macdonough and every description of Officers & Men under my command, and I am sorry that my words fall short of their merits,—The Prizes taken by No. 4 are new boats and well fitted, the first captured mounted a long Brass peice carrying a Ball of 27 lb & 2 brass swivels, her crew consisted of 36 men & Officers, 16 of whom were killed, 15 wounded & 5 well Prisoners, the second Boat mounted a long brass 18 Pounder & 2 brass howets her crew consisted of 24 men & Officers, 17 of whom were killed, 4 wounded & 3 well Prisoners,—The Boat captured by No. 6 was of the same dimentions, mounted the same metal, and had the same number of men as the largest Boat captured by No. 4, she had 14 men killed, and 22 made Prisones, 7 of whom were wounded,—I am happy to mention the damage sustained on our part was triffling, No. 4 has 4 wounded Including myself slightly, No. 6 Lieutenant Tripp and 2 men wounded,—I have the honor to be

> *Sir*
> *with great Respect*
> *Your Obedt. humble Servt.*
> *Stephen Decatur Jr.*

Following the action of August 3, 1804, Lt. Richard Sommers also reported to Captain Preble, below.

Above: (Knox, Naval Documents, vol. 4, p. 345) Below: (Knox, Naval Documents, vol. 4, pp. 344–345)

United States Schooner Nautilus
At Anchor Off Tripoli Augt. 4th. 1804

SIR, Agreeable to your orders I send you herewith a statement of the proceedings of the Gun Boats of the 1st. Division under my Command on the 3rd. Inst.—At 2 P.M. when the signal was made to cast off the Gun Boats, I then beeing far to leward, made sail with the Nautilus to Join the rest of the Division which were to windward and advancing with the 2nd. Division under Capt. Decatur; When the Signal for battle was made, I immediately Cast off and advanced with all sail upon a wind with my sweeps out, I found it was impossible to Join the division to Windward which had Commenced firing on the weather line of the Enemy, who lay at Anchor close under the rocks, by this time there was five of the Enemy's Gun Boats of the lee line under way advancing and firing; when within point blank shot I commenced firing on the Enemy with round & grape, they still advanced until within pistol shot when they wore round & stood in for the Batteries I pursued them untill within musket shot of the Batteries which kept up a Continual fire of round & grape, three of their boats had got in behind the rocks, I then wore and stood off—The boats has received no damage and but two of the men slightly wounded.—Gun Boat No. 2, under the Command of Lieut. James Decatur & Mr. Thomas Brown Midshipman Second in Command, engaged one of the Enemy's Gun Boats which after a short conflict haul'd down their Colours to him; the treacherous enemy in the act of Lieut. Decatur's getting on board to take possession, discharged a Volley of Muskettry in which that brave and gallant officer was killed; the enemy then sheered off from a long side and by superior sailing escaped being Captured; Gun Boat No. 2 received no damage and except Lieut. Decatur but one man slightly wounded in the breast by a muskett ball; Gun Boat No.3 was to windward.—Permit me Sir to say that the Officers on board No. 1 Mr. Ridgley & Mr. Miller and the Men behaved with the greatest magnanimity.—

On August 4, 1804, Commodore Preble published the General Orders below in recognition of the gallant conduct of his personnel in the Action of August 3, 1804, shown below.

Preble next worked to reduce the shore batteries. If he could silence them, his fleet was powerful enough to take the Tripolitan Navy. However, in one battle a red-hot shot passed into the magazine of Lt. James R. Caldwell's gunboat. He and his crew of nine were obliterated in a moment. Decatur had served with Caldwell in the *United States* and felt the loss second only to that of his brother James.

During this engagement the *John Adams* under the command of Capt. Isaac Chauncey

Right: Portrait of Edward Preble, Commodore, U.S. Navy by Rembrandt Peale, painted between 1804 and 1807. Naval Academy Museum, Courtesy of Captain Dundas Preble Tucker, USN (Deceased). Photograph courtesy of the Naval Historical Center.

Facing page: Painting of the "Burning of the Frigate *Philadelphia* in the Harbor of Tripoli, February 16, 1804" by Edward Moran, 1897. Print from the U.S. Naval Academy Museum. Courtesy of the Naval Historical Center.

(Knox, Naval Documents, vol. 4, p. 361)

GENERAL ORDERS

The Gallant behaviour of the Officers Seamen & Marines of the Squadron in the Action of Yesterday, with the Enemies Batteries, Gun Boats and Corsairs, claim from the Commodore the warmest approbation and praise he can bestow—

Captain Stewart of the Siren, Captain Hull of the Argus, Captain Smith of the Vixen, will please to accept the Commodores thanks for the Gallant Manner in which they brought their Vessels into action, and for their prompt obedience to Signals, particularly that to cover Gun Boats and prizes—

Captain Somers will please to accept the Commodores thanks for the Gallant Conduct, display'd by him, in attacking five of the enemies Gun Boats, within musket Shot of the Batteries, and obliging them to retreat after a warm conflict—

The very distinguished judgement and intrepidity of Captain Decatur in leading his Division of Gun Boats into Action, in boarding, capturing & bringing out from under the Enemies Batteries, two of their Gun Boats each of superior force, is particularly gratifying to the Commodore, and Captain Decatur will be pleased to accept his thanks—

Lieut. Commandt. Dent, and Lieutt. Robinson, commanding the Two Bomb Vessels, are entitled to the thanks of the Commodore for the judgement & Bravery display'd by them, in placing their Vessels, and for the annoyance they gave the enemy—

Lieutt. Lawrence of the Enterprize and Lieutenant Read of the Nautilus (commanding those Vessels in the absence of their Captains) merit the Commodores thanks for their active exertions in towing out and protecting prizes—

The Commodore deeply regrets the Death of Lieutt. James Decatur, who nobly fell at the moment he had obliged an enemy of superior force to strike to him—

Lieutt. Bainbridge's Conduct in pressing into the Harbour, and engaging the enemy, and his conduct through the action, merits and receives the Commodores thanks—

Lieutt. Trippe will be pleased to accept thanks for the Gallant conduct which distinguished him, in boarding, capturing, and bringing off, one of the enemies Gun Boats of Superior Force—

I have now to tender my warmest thanks to the Lieutenants, Sailing Master, Marine Officers & other Officers of the Constitution, for the prompt support I received from them—

The Conduct of the Officers Seamen and Marines of the Squadron, have not only in the Action of the 3rd. Instant, but on every other Occasion, merited the highest encomiums—

Given on board the United States Ship Constitution at Anchor off
Tripoli the 4th. day of Augt. 1804.
Signed EDWd. PREBLE

. . . The next Action, the Boat I was in, Commanded by Lieut Caldwell, was Blown up. The Lieut, with a midshipman and 14 men, out of 24, were kill'd. I, astonishing to relate, & 6 men escaped. 4 of the men in so wounded a condition that their lives, at first, were despair'd of. It was my Conduct on this occasion that got me my Promotion. I, at the time the shot struck, was forward, taking sight at the Gun; though not a minute before I had been aft, assisting in binding up the woonded. It being a red hot shot, she instantly exploded; I went up some distance in the air, & lighted by the Gun again; the only part remaining was that on which the Gun stood. I found by my side, one man only. Around me lay arms, legs, & trunks of Bodies, in the most mutilated state; though a little confused & bewilder'd by things tumbling on my head, & by the prospect of death before me; for I cannot swim, I had presence of mind sufficient to know my duty, & not to quitt while there was a part remaining. I fired the Gun, & loaded her again. When she went down from under me I gave a cheer and went down—came up again; when I was taken up by one of the other Gun Boats—I cannot describe my sensations, on this melancholy occasion—I felt as though I wish'd to die, because I should die Nobly—This accident will distress my Father much, as Mr. Caldwell he look'd on as a Son, & loved him equally as well as he does me; in fact I never knew so pure, and so strong a friendship to subsist between any two men. He certainly was the most honourable little fellow I ever knew, & the most respected of any young man in the Navy— My Father in a letter from Washington to me says thus; "Remember me to my oldest of all Modern Friends Mr. Caldwell." You may judge from this language how fond he was of him. . . . I made another escape as astonishing as this. I made application, as well as Capt Stew't for me, to go in to the Harbour of Tripoli, in an Infernal, containing 150 Barrels of Powder & 300 shells, for the purpose of blowing the Bashaws Castle up; this expedition was Commanded by Capt Sumers— I received no direct

answer, from the Commodore, & of course, expected to go; but a favorite of the Commodores, persuaded him, to allow him to go. Capt Decatur then made Application for me; But the Commodore reply'd he had already selected the officer, that was to go with Capt Sumers; the Night came—She went in, all were anxious with expectation when Cannon announced her near approach to the Castle. Cannon were fired from all parts of the town. In a few moments she went up—How awfully Grand! Every thing wrapp'd in Dead silence, made the explosion loud, and terrible, the fuses of the shells, burning in the air, shone like so many planets, a vast stream of fire, which appear'd ascending to heaven portrayed the Walls to our view—20 minutes elapsed, without seeing the signal agreed on, between Capt S & the Commodore. Guns were fir'd from the Commodores ship; signals repeated by the different vessels—our small schooners sent to reconnoiter the Harbour—but no Boat appear'd. Poor Sumers a Lieut & a midshipman were gone, no more to return! We conjectured the explosion to have been premature; it has since been confirm'd by information from Tripoli. He was within the Rocks, & only 1/2 mile distant from the Bashaws Castle, when he was boarded by two Gun Boats, 50 men each,—He might have escap'd; but he started with a determination never to let so seasonable a supply fall into their Hands; & never to return alive unless he had, satisfactorily, executed his mission. He touched fire himself to match & she went up, sending 100 Turks and 15 Christians souls to eternity. What a Noble Death, & truly characteristic of that Noble Sumers. He certainly was an extraordinary man. He united every thing that made the man, or the officer—possessing more firmness & determination than any man I ever saw—sought danger in every shape—dangerous undertakings were the most pleasing ones to him. In loosing him we were deprived of one of the Navys most valuable officers. The Lieut with him was a schoolmate of William's his name was Wadsworth, of Portland. . . .

(Knox, Naval Documents, vol. 4, pp 351–353 & USNI Proceedings, April 1923, p. 627)

joined the squadron. Chauncey brought a captain's commission for Stephen Decatur. Also, since the grade had been restored to the Navy, commissions as master commandants for Stewart, Hill, Smith, and Somers as well. Captain Decatur's commission was dated February 16, the date of the burning of the *Philadelphia*. Decatur at the age of twenty-five was the youngest captain ever in the United States Navy.

Chauncey also brought orders relieving Commodore Preble of command of the squadron upon the arrival of Commodore Samuel Barron, who was coming out with four frigates. The Navy was not displeased with Preble. Actually, the president was inspired by his success with such a small force that he was sending out a larger force to bring the war to a close. Preble then made one final attempt to end the hostilities before Barron's arrival by selecting the *Intrepid* to serve as a fire-ship to sail in to the base of the Bashaw's castle and let her explode against the palace walls. On the evening of September 4, 1804, the *Intrepid* sailed in towards Tripoli with an all volunteer crew with Master Commandant Somers in command along with Midshipman Wadsworth as second and Midshipman Israel. They made a valiant attempt to enter the harbor of Tripoli in a ship loaded with explosives, planning to blow up as many of the gun boats as possible. However, something went deadly wrong and Somers and his crew went up with the ship in a mighty explosion just outside the harbor, never to be seen or heard from again. (Anthony, pp. 148–151)

Midshipman Robert T. Spence in a letter to his mother Mrs. Keith Spence, Portsmouth, New Hampshire, dated November 12, 1804, offered an accounting of the incident along with the previous battle with the comments shown on the facing page.

Commodore Samuel Barron arrived with the *President* and *Constellation* on September 9, 1804, and relieved Commodore Preble. On September 11 he directed Preble to take the *Constitution* back to Malta for repairs and turn her over to Decatur before returning home in the *John Adams*. On September 24 Preble wrote his order to Captain Decatur to sail the *Argus* to Malta and upon arrival there to take command of the *Constitution*. It was a

"Blowing Up of the Fire Ship Intrepid commanded by Captain Somers in the Harbour of Tripoli on the night of the 4th Sept. 1804." Line engraving of the USS *Intrepid* (1803–04). Photograph courtesy of the Naval Historical Center.

final tribute of the departing Commodore to his youngest Captain to honor him with a command befitting his new status.

Commodore Preble had reason to be proud of all of his "boys" as he sailed for home. Those gallant officers who gave their lives in the flower of their youth also had to weigh heavily on his mind. Indeed, Congress later resolved that their names should live in the recollection and affection of their country and that their conduct should be regarded as an example to future generations. To this end the Tripolitan Monument stands today at the United States Naval Academy. On it are inscribed the last names of James Decatur, James Caldwell, John Dorsey, Richard Somers, Henry Wadsworth, and Joseph Israel. Although this once beautiful monument is in need of refurbishment and protection from the elements, there is a campaign underway at this writing to accomplish that end. (Johnson, "Shall We Let It Crumble?" *Shipmate,* May 1996, pp. 25, 45–47)

On October 28 Decatur relieved Preble of command of the *Constitution*. After completing her repairs in Malta, Decatur sailed for Syracuse to rejoin the blockade, where he arrived on November 4, 1804. Captain Rodgers relieved Decatur of command of the *Constitution* on November 9 and Decatur subsequently took command of the *Congress*. (Martin, *A Most Fortunate Ship,* pp. 115–117)

In March 1805 Commodore Barron turned over command of the squadron to Commodore John Rodgers because of his failing health. On June 3, 1805, a peace treaty was signed with the Bashaw and the prisoners were released for $60,000. Tripoli raised the American flag and twenty-one gun salutes were exchanged.

Painting of Decatur boarding the Tripolitan gun boat by Dennis Malone Carter. Stephen Decatur is seen in lower right center, in mortal combat with the Tripolitan captain. The action occurred during the U.S. Navy bombardment of Tripoli, August 3, 1804. Photograph courtesy of the Naval Historical Center.

United States Ship Congress
Tunis Bay Jany 9th' 1804 [1805]

DEAR FRIEND I had the satisfaction of receiving yours of 2nd. of November, with a letter for Captain Stewart and one for Robert, which I shall keep until their return, which is expected shortly. Your son (Midshipman Robert T. Spence) has displayed a Manliness of Conduct, that will make every American proud of him as a Countryman. After the accidents which befel his boat, he served in the boat with me, his Conduct with me was such, as you would have wished; as to his being confirmed there can be no doubt as Commodore P. has given me his word that he will have it done.

I have requested Captain Bainbridge to show you some papers I have enclosed to him, You will see in my report to Commodore P. on 7th. August, your son is mentioned in a way, that will not be dipleasing to you. I shall be happy to have him with me, and I know he wishes it, but Capt. (James) Barron wishes him to sail with him in the Essex, R has more than my friendship if possible, and by Sailing with Captain Barron he will insure his, for he is already attached to him, therefore by sailing with B. [two words illegible] when I see R, I will speak to him upon the Subject, Pray let me Know your opinion respecting it. You see he is in great demand—

You will observe I am in the return of the wounded on the 3rd. of August. My wounds were slight and as follows, in the arm by a sword and in the breast by a pike. I find hand to hand is not childs play, 'tis kill or be killed.

You no doubt recollect a conversation we had when in the City of Washington, I then informed you 'twas my intention to board, if ever I had an opportunity and that 'twas my opinion that there could be no doubt as to the issue. You will not doubt me I hope, when I say, I am glad the event has proved my ideas to be correct. I have always thought we could lick them their own way and give them two to one. The first boat they were 36 to 20 we carryed her without much fuss, the second was 24 to 10, they also went to the leeward—

I had eighteen Italians in the boat with me, who claimed the honor of the day, While we fought they prayed. They are convinced we could not have been so fortunate, unless their prayers had been heard. This might have been the case, therefore we could not contradict it Some of the Turks died like men, but much the greater number like women—

I leave this tomorrow for Tripoly, if you are suffered to walk out, you will know my Ship by her having stump top G1 Masts

Believe me to be yours
Sincerely Stephen Decatur jr.

P.S. If I do not write often do not attribute it to neglect. I need not tell you I dislike writing, you know it, and my reason, for fear you should have forgotten, I will tell you, I have always thought, that they who write badly should write little or by the way of practice a great deal. Now as I know I can never become an adept, I know you will think me prudent for not writing much.

(Knox, Naval Documents, vol. 3, p. 346)

40

Decatur was ordered to Tunis with the *Congress* and *Vixen* to observe and check on Tunisian hostility. Rodgers soon joined him with the rest of the squadron and they quickly gained assurances from the Bey that he would honor the existing treaty. Decatur was ordered to prepare the *Congress* to serve the Tunisian Ambassador to the United States, who was awaiting passage to the states. They sailed from Tunis on September 5, 1805, and after a brief and uneventful passage entered Hampton Roads and anchored. (Anthony, pp. 152–158) In early January of 1805, prior to these closing events of the Tripolitan War, Decatur had written the following letter to Purser Keith Spence, father of Midshipman Spence, shown on the left.

As the frigate *Congress* lay at anchor in Hampton Roads while Decatur and the Tunisian Ambassador were ashore, a schooner with a sailing party of guests of the mayor of Norfolk aboard anchored nearby. The young ladies in the party, including the mayor's daughter Miss Susan Wheeler, requested a visit to the *Congress* and were graciously welcomed aboard to see all of the Tunisian presents from the Bey destined for Washington. However, Miss Wheeler was most intrigued by an Italian miniature of Captain Decatur. Coincidentally, the very next day Captain Decatur and the Tunisian envoy called on the mayor, who invited them to dinner followed by a ball in their honor. Susan Wheeler was, therefore, granted a most favorable opportunity to meet and become acquainted with this youngest captain in the Navy, hero of the Tripolitan War, and eligible bachelor.

Following their introduction Susan Wheeler and Stephen Decatur soon found themselves falling in love. Susan was charmed by this tall curly haired young Captain, who presented himself with a quiet dignity, while Stephen was captivated by this beautiful, well educated young lady, who moved about with such social grace and elegance. They were soon engaged, as Decatur was ordered to bring the *Congress* with the Tunisian Ambassador embarked up the Chesapeake and the Potomac to Washington. (Lewis, pp. 81–83)

Decatur soon took leave from Washington to return home to his family in Frankford, Pennsylvania, about six miles from Philadelphia. During this visit his proud father was honored to present to his son the sword that Congress had awarded him for the capture and destruction the Tripolitan fri-gate of forty-four guns, the ex-American frigate *Philadelphia*. They also attended several dinners given in honor of Captain Stephen Decatur, Jr. At one of these dinners the presiding officer gave this toast to Decatur's father: "The gallant father of a gallant son."

Everyone present knew of Capt. Stephen Decatur, Sr.'s, record during the Revolutionary War and the Quasi-War with France and how he had patriotically served his country. They also knew how he had just recently lost one of his sons in battle against the Tripolitans. Therefore, it was quite an emotional event when the senior Decatur rose to present a responding toast as follows: "Our children are our country's property."

After this relatively short visit with his family young Stephen Decatur returned to Norfolk and his betrothed Susan Wheeler toward the end of January. They were married a little over a month later by the Reverend Mr. Grigsby on March 8, 1806. As the *Norfolk Gazette* and *Public Ledger* of March 10 chronicled it, "the gallant Captain Stephen Decatur, Junior of the United States Navy "was married "to the accomplished and much admired Miss Susan Wheeler, only daughter of Luke Wheeler, Esquire, Mayor of this Borough." The newlyweds spent the next few months with Mayor Wheeler in Norfolk and then visited the Decatur family in Frankford. On June 10, 1806, Decatur was ordered by the Secretary of the Navy to superintend the construction of four gunboats to be built in Newport, Rhode Island, and four others in Connecticut. Soon after the Decatur's took up residence in Newport. When the four gunboats were completed in November 1806, Decatur was ordered to Norfolk to oversee the construction of ten additional gunboats there. (Lewis, pp. 83–89)

The Decaturs moved back to Norfolk and Stephen took command of the naval shipyard at Gosport to manage the building of the new gunboats. It was here that the seeds of his ultimate demise were sown. While Decatur was in command of the Gosport yard, he received a letter from the British Consul that demanded the delivery of three U.S. Navy sailors that were purportedly deserters from HMS *Melampus*. The three men had been recruited for the USS *Chesapeake*, which was preparing to sail for the Mediterranean to relieve the USS *Constitution*. Decatur refused to interfere, since the recruiting party was not under orders from him. The British Consul then took his complaint to Mr. Erskine, the British minister in Washington, who in turn went to the U.S. Secretary of State. The demand came back to Commodore James Barron, the flag officer accompanying the *Chesapeake* to the Mediterranean. When Barron determined that the three men were all Americans who had been forcibly impressed, he refused to give them up. The *Chesapeake* under the command of Master Commandant Charles Gordon reached Norfolk after sailing down the Potomac River from Washington. Commodore Barron came on board on June 6, 1807, and hoisted his flag. Still recovering from an illness, the Commodore went back ashore, where he remained except for one visit. He finally embarked the day before sailing.

On June 22, 1807, the *Chesapeake* got underway and stood out of Hampton Roads. She was barely ready for sea and in no way ready for action. Many of her guns were not fully mounted and all kinds of equipment, including cables and timber and passengers' belongings were not properly stowed. As the *Chesapeake* approached Lynnhaven Bay, one of four British ships anchored there also got underway and proceeded out to sea ahead of her. She was the fifty-gun frigate HMS *Leopard* under the command of Capt. S. P. Humphreys. (Anthony, pp. 167–169)

Above: Tripolitan Monument (originally the Navy Monument). U.S. Naval Academy. Photograph by the author.

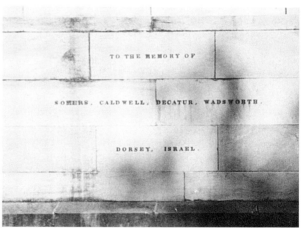

Close-up of the Tripolitan Monument inscription. U.S. Naval Academy. Photograph by the author.

Portrait collage of Decatur meeting the *Macedonian* by Marty Reed Vinograd, 1997. Photograph from the Artist. Currently on loan to Decatur House to be presented to the USS *Decatur* (DDG- 73).

Sketch of Stephen Decatur by Fred S. Cozzens. Photograph
courtesy of the Naval Historical Center.

CHAPTER 3

COMMODORE DECATUR IN THE WAR OF 1812

At about half past three on the afternoon of June 22, 1807, the *Chesapeake* with the *Leopard* out ahead were approximately nine miles east southeast of Cape Henry, when the *Leopard* luffed up into the wind. As the *Chesapeake* came closer to pass, she was hailed by the *Leopard*, saying they had messages for the commodore. The *Leopard's* gunports were open and the tompions ominously out of her guns, but neither Commodore Barron nor Captain Gordon seemed suspicious. The *Chesapeake* heaved to and awaited the British boat bringing her dispatches. A British officer, Lieutenant Meade, came on board with a note from Captain Humphreys that enclosed an order from Vice Admiral G. C. Berkeley, commander-in-chief of his majesty's squadron on the North Atlantic station. The order required the British commander to search the *Chesapeake* for deserters from the *Belisle*, *Bellona*, *Triumph*, *Chichester*, *Halifax*, and *Zenobia* upon meeting her on the high seas. Commodore Barron replied in writing that he knew of no such deserters and that his orders did not permit his crew to be mustered by other than his own officers. After Lieutenant Meade returned to the *Leopard* with the reply, Barron requested that Captain Gordon send his men quietly to quarters, so the British could not claim that the Americans made the first show of hostility. However, the drummer first started a beat to quarters, which Gordon quickly subdued. Therefore, there was much confusion aboard the *Chesapeake*. No guns were primed. Charges, wads, powder horns, loggerheads, and matches were not at hand and the crew was green and untrained. The *Leopard* came within half a pistol shot and Humphreys hailed again. With no response he fired a gun or two and then a broadside. In the brief fifteen-minute engagement the *Leopard* fired three broadsides, while the *Chesapeake's* only response was to fire one gun that First Lieutenant Allen managed to ignite with a coal from the galley. Barron then struck his colors. The *Chesapeake* had three sailors killed and eighteen wounded. Her mizzenmast and mainmast had been shot away and her hull and rigging badly cut up.

The British came on board the *Chesapeake*, mustered the crew, and took away four sailors. Three they claimed from the *Melampus* and one from the *Halifax*. Barron notified Humphreys that the *Chesapeake* was his prize, but Humphreys refused. The *Chesapeake* limped back into Norfolk, arriving there the next day. (Anthony, pp. 169–171; Lewis, pp. 92–93; Tucker & Reuter, pp. 6–11)

Commodore Barron prepared his report, which expressed no fault on the part of his officers. Convalescing from his splinter wound to the calf, Barron dispatched Captain Gordon to Washington to deliver his report to Secretary of the Navy Smith. However, Gordon also carried a letter from the ship's lieutenants requesting Barron's arrest on two charges. The first was for failing to clear his ship for action and the second was for not doing his utmost to take or destroy the other vessel. On June 26, 1807, Secretary Smith ordered Decatur to take command of the *Chesapeake* and prepare her for sea. Gordon was to stay on board as flag captain. (Tucker & Reuter, pp. 99–102)

Print of a portrait of Stephen Decatur in dress uniform wearing the blue Medal of the Cincinnati by James A. Simpson, circa 1846. Courtesy of Decatur House, photograph by John Ballou.

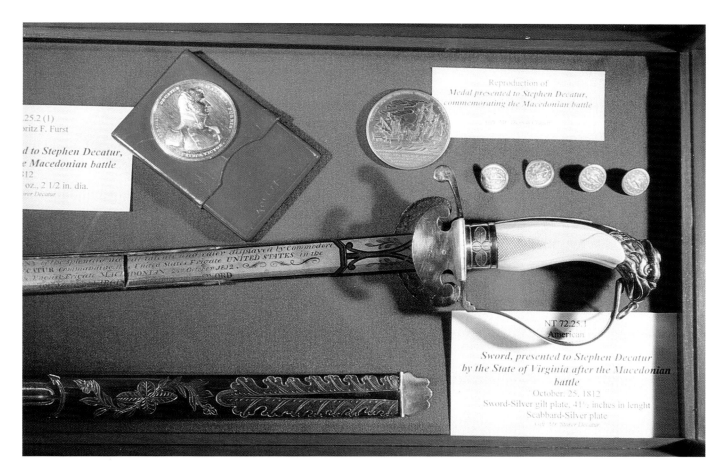

Above: *Macedonian* figurehead monument. U.S. Naval Academy. Photograph by the author.

Above: Sword, presented to Stephen Decatur by the State of Virginia after the *Macedonian* battle. Inscription on the blade of the sword: "In testimony of the splendid naval talent and valor displayed by Commodore Stephen Decatur commanding the United States Frigate United States in the capture of the English Frigate Macedonian twenty-fifth [of] October 1812, the State of Virginia bestows this sword." Courtesy of Decatur House, photograph by John Ballou.

Below: Print of Decatur's Order of the Cincinnati Citation. Courtesy of Decatur House, photograph by John Ballou.

A protest was sent to Great Britain and on July 2 President Jefferson forbade British warships from entering American harbors and prohibited citizens from supplying them. Public feeling was definitely anti-British and excitement was running high around Norfolk over the hostile attitude of the British. (Anthony p. 171; Lewis, p. 93)

Secretary Smith also took action to convene a Court of Inquiry on June 26, the same day he relieved Barron of command. However, Capt. Edward Preble declined to serve as president due to illness. Preble died on August 25 and Smith subsequently named Capt. Alexander Murray as court president on September 12, 1807. Smith then chose Capt. Isaac Chauncey and Capt. Isaac Hull as the other two members and hired Littleton Waller Tazewell, a civilian, to act as judge advocate.

Following delays due to Barron's ill health the court was convened on October 5, adjourned because of Barron's health, and finally reconvened on October 16. The court met with Barron present until November 5, 1807. (Tucker & Reuter, pp. 142–143)

The Court of Inquiry came to the conclusion that "the *Chesapeake* was prematurely surrendered, at a time when she was nearly prepared for battle, and when the injuries sustained either in the Ship or Crew did not make such a surrender then necessary." (Tucker & Reuter, p. 162) This finding was an Article 6 violation of the Navy Regulations of April 23, 1807. (Tucker & Reuter, p. 162; Minutes of the Proceedings of the Enquiry, p. 185, National Archives RG 45, Series 464, Box 328, Folder "0–1859" NO—Courts of Enquiry)

Based on the Court of Enquiry findings President Jefferson ordered a general court martial for Barron, Gordon, marine Captain Hall, and Gunner Hook. On December 7, 1807, Secretary Smith ordered Capt. John Rodgers, as president, to convene the court on January 4, 1808. The eleven court members consisted of Rodgers, Capts. William Bainbridge, Hugh Campbell, Stephen Decatur, and John Shaw, Master Commandants John Smith and David Porter, and Lts. Joseph Tarbell, Jacob Jones, James Lawrence, and Charles Ludlow. Decatur asked Secretary Smith to excuse him, because he had already formed the opinion that Barron had failed to do his duty. Smith refused Decatur's request or he would not otherwise have been able to form a court. Although Decatur provided Barron's counsel a record of his correspondence with Secretary Smith, Barron never formally objected to Decatur's appointment. (Tucker & Reuter, pp. 162–164)

The court convened on the *Chesapeake* on January 8, 1808, and held Barron's trial first on four charges as follows: "for negligently performing the duty assigned him" (ie; preparing for sea); "for neglecting on the probability of an engagement to clear his ship for action"; for failing to encourage in his own person, his inferior officers and men, to fight courageously"; and "for not doing his utmost to take or destroy the *Leopard*, which vessel it was his duty to encounter." (Tucker & Reuter, pp. 162–164; SECNAV to Rodgers, December 7, 1807; Full Specifications, M149, 7)

After all of the testimony was heard the court went into closed session ashore on February 4, 1808. On February 8 the court announced its findings as follows: on the first, third, and fourth charges, it found for Barron; however, on the second charge it found against Barron for "failing to clear for action." (Tucker & Reuter, pp. 181–182)

The court then sentenced Barron "to be suspended from all command in the Navy of the United States, and that without Pay or official emoluments of any kind, for the period and term of five years" from February 8, 1808. When sentence was confirmed by the president, Secretary Smith announced the sentence to Barron on May 7, 1808. (Tucker & Reuter, p. 183; SECNAV to Barron. May 7, 1808, M149, 8.) In the following trials Gordon and Hall were reprimanded by the Secretary of the Navy and Hook was dismissed from the service. (Tucker & Reuter, pp. 186–187)

Meanwhile, Decatur, in command of the *Chesapeake,* also had a squadron of gunboats and became the commodore of naval forces on the southern coast of the United States. To him fell the unwelcome duty of enforcing the embargo to injure Great Britain with these wholly inadequate naval forces. During this time Stephen Decatur, Sr., passed away on November 11, 1808. Commodore Stephen Decatur, Jr., saw his father buried in St. Peter's Episcopal Churchyard in Philadelphia. (Anthony, p. 175)

On March 4, 1809, James Madison was sworn in as president. Later that year non-intercourse with Great Britain replaced the embargo and Decatur was given command of the frigate *United States.* He brought Lt. William Henry Allen from the *Chesapeake,* as his first lieutenant. Together, they drilled the crew of the *United States* to a smart and efficient team. (Anthony, pp. 176–177)

During this time James Barron finally gained command of a small brig merchantman, the *Brazilian,* in April 1809, which he sailed to Pernambuco, Brazil, and back. After his return Barron did not get another ship until 1812. Then on April 5, 1812, Barron became master of the brig merchantman *Portia* and sailed her to Europe, where he took up residence in Copenhagen, Denmark. (Tucker & Reuter, p. 199)

Throughout 1810 foreign affairs became chaotic. French imperial decrees answered British Orders of Council and both antagonists preyed on American commerce. Even Madison could see that the United States was heading for war. Decatur continued to train his crew to the highest proficiency in serving the twenty-four pounders of his frigate, the *United States.* (Anthony, pp. 178–179)

During the months of 1810 and 1811 the British Navy continued visits to Norfolk and the American and British naval officers mingled, seemingly untouched by the increasing national hatred. Capt. John Carden, in command of the British frigate HMS *Macedonian,* was one of the more frequent visitors to Norfolk. Decatur was often the host for Carden and his officers. On one of these occasions Carden promised to take the *United States* should they ever meet in war. Legend has it that a beaver hat was wagered on any such future match.

Later in 1811 the British sloop *Little Belt* started a night engagement against the American frigate *President.* On September 13, 1811, Decatur presided over the inquiry that substantiated Commodore Rodger's report on

"The armaments of the two ships were as follows:

UNITED STATES: 478 men

No. of guns.		Weight of shot
32 long 24-pounders		768 pounds
22 42-pounder carronades	924	"
1 18-pounder carronade	18	"
55		1710

MACEDONIAN: 297 men and boys (James); 306 (Emmons)

28 long 18-pounders		504 pounds
2 long 12-pounders		24 "
2 long 8-pounders	16 "	
16 32-pounder carronades	512 "	
1 18-pounder carronade	18 "	
49		1074 "

(Soley, p. 317)

(Dudley, The Naval War, vol. 1, pp. 552–553)

the matter and found that the *Little Belt* incurred more damage than had the *Chesapeake* in the earlier affair with the *Leopard.* (Anthony, pp. 179–181)

Just prior to the start of the War of 1812 Commodore Stephen Decatur set forth his recommendations for executing a war with Great Britain in a letter to Secretary of the Navy Hamilton from Norfolk on June 8, 1812. In this letter Decatur recommended a plan by which "our little Navy" could "annoy the Trade of Great Britain" to the greatest extent, while exposing it the least to the "immense naval force of that Government." His plan envisaged sending our frigates out singularly or no more than two in company without specific instructions on where to cruise, but relying on the "enterprise of the officers." Decatur noted that the French had been recently deploying their ships in this mode with the "greatest success."

Decatur continued with his rationale that two frigates would not be as easily traced as a greater number, that they could move more rapidly, and could still be sufficiently strong enough to attack a convoy. He doubted that they would meet a superior force; but if they did, our Navy would not be crushed with "one blow." Decatur went on to note that the greatest risk was getting in and out of port. Therefore, they should be well provisioned to stay out as long as possible and cruise long distances. This would not only relieve our own coast by requiring the British to withdraw ships to search for ours, but also possibly compel them to detach another force from Europe in search of ours.

Decatur went on to discuss the relative safety of our ports. Most he considered safe unless we massed too many ships in one to make it attractive enough to attack in force in order to destroy a significant portion of our Navy. He gave preference to "Boston, New London, and Norfolk" because of their narrow entrances that were more easily defended. Decatur further argued that "Boston, Portsmouth, N.H., and Portland" were the "safest Harbours" to return to from cruising, "particularly in the winter season." He also noted that during the Revolution the British had proven for themselves the "impracticability of blockading our Eastern coast during that season."

In conclusion, Decatur recommended that if war came, they should have their instructions and be sent out before the declaration was known to the enemy. This was justified by the greater number of British cruisers ready and waiting in Bermuda. (Dudley, *The Naval War* , vol. 1, pp. 122–124)

On June 16, 1812, just two days before the declaration of war, Decatur sent a report to Secretary of the Navy Hamilton concerning the British Bermuda station from the US Frigate *United States.* In this report Decatur noted that the British admiral only permitted two ships to cruise at a time. They were also not to approach our coast or continue out more than fifteen days. Decatur further noted that the British Consul at Norfolk and other places had licenses for those that applied that would protect vessels against capture if that vessel were trading with British ports or those of their allies. (Dudley, *The Naval War,* vol. 1, pp. 134–135)

On June 18, 1812, Congress declared war on Great Britain and Secretary of the Navy Hamilton started to warn his officers of the event and the duties they would assume. He urged Capt. Isaac Hull to take the USS *Constitution* to New York when ready and join Commodore John Rodgers, who was assembling his cruising squadron there. However, Commodore Rodger's squadron left Sandy Hook in a northeasterly direction on June 21 and Captain Hull did not sail from the Chesapeake until July 12. The subsequent success of the USS *Constitution* under Captain Hull in taking HMS *Guerriere* under Capt. Richard Dacres on August 19, 1812, increased the credibility of independent cruising. After the return of the squadrons of Commodore Rodgers and Decatur, Secretary of the Navy Hamilton wrote the letter at right to Commodore Rodgers, an identical one to Commodore Decatur, and a similar one to Commodore Bainbridge.

Having put to sea on October 8, 1812, with Commodore Rodgers' squadron, the *United States* and *Argus* left the squadron four days later. Commodore Stephen Decatur wrote a letter to Secretary of the Navy Hamilton on October 12, 1812, from the USS *United States* at sea at Latitude 41, Longitude 60. This letter noted that on that morning he "fell in with the American Ship *Mandarin* William Baker Master from London bound to Philadelphia." When Decatur examined her papers he found "that a large portion of the Merchandize on board her was for British account," so he put an officer on to sail her to Norfolk.

Decatur also noted that he discovered "a number of licenses from the British Government to Citizens of the United States granting them protection in the transportation of Grain &c to Spain & Portugal." These he forwarded to the secretary for disposal. (Dudley, *The Naval War*, vol. 1, p. 527)

Then *Argus* detached and the *United States* was sailing independently farther and farther to the east in hopes of meeting some East India Company merchantmen or an escort. Decatur, perhaps still mourning his mother who had died on March 27 of that year, was in a generally somber mood during this cruise. He gave up some of his nautical smartness and, not unlike the more casual attire of his Midshipman days, he began wearing homespun and an old straw hat.

Then on October 25, 1812, the *United States* came upon the British forty-nine-gun frigate, HMS *Macedonian*. Although the men on board the *Macedonian* were in good spirits, they would have rather been facing a Frenchman than a Yankee. They had a consciousness of superiority over the French and the Americans on board had told the British seamen that American frigates carried more metal. The Americans on board the *Macedonian* were quite disconcerted at having to fight against their own coun-

Comre Rodgers Nav: Dapt 9 Septr 1812
Boston

It has been determined that our vessels of war shall be divided into three small Squadrons to be commanded by yourself in the frigate President, Comre Bainbridge in the frigate Constitution & Comre Decatur in the frigate United States; for the present, each Squadron will consist of two frigates, & a small brig. When ready for sea each Squadron will be instructed to pursue that course, which to the commanding officer, may, under all circumstances, appear the most expedient to afford protection to our trade & to annoy the enemy; returning into port, as speedily as circumstances will permit, consistently with the great objects in view & writing to the Department by all propere oppertunities

In arranging these Squadrons reference must be made to the relative rank of the respective commanding officers, & to the properties of the respective vessels—In paying every proper respect to rank we must not forget the great importance of selecting vessels for each of the squadrons, as nearly equal in the property of sailing & in the capacity of burthen, as may be practicable: The three small vessels that will be attached to the squadron, will be commanded by Capt [Jacob] Jones Capt [James] Lawrence & Capt [Arthur] Sinclair; & they are to be attached to the Squadrons in the order of their rank. That is to say—Capt Jones will join Comre Rodgers; Capt Lawrence will join Comre Bainbridge—& Capt Sinclair will join Comre Decatur. The three frigates to be attached to the Squadrons (besides those to be commanded by the commodores themselves) will be the Chesapeake-the Congress & the Essex- & with respect to these frigates the commanders will consult the good of the Service & decide for themselves, if found necessary, & the good of the service will permit, they will choose in the order of their relative rank; that is Comodore Rodgers will choose first, Comre Bainbridge next & Comre Decatur will take the third-In making the arrangement, You will also have proper reference to the periods when the respective vessels will probably be ready for service, it being important that the whole should proceed to sea, as early as may be practicable.

The Essex & the Wasp are expected in daily—& unless they should meet with some untoward accident, they will, in a day or two, after their arrival be again prepared for service.

The commanders will give every requisite order for carrying into effect the objects of these instructions & having made the necessary arrangements, each will give every attention to the outfit of his Squadron.
P. Hamilton

(Dudley, *The Naval War*, vol. 1, pp. 471–472)

Commodore Stephen Decatur To
Secretary of the Navy Hamilton
USS United States at sea October 30 1812

Sir,

I have the honour to inform you that on the 24th Inst. being in the Lat. 29. N. Long. 29. 30. W., We fell in with, & after an action of an hour & an half, captured his Britannic Majesty's ship Macedonian commanded by Captain John Carden, and mounting 49. carriage guns (the odd gun shifting)—She is a frigate of the largest class—two years old—four months out of dock, and reputed one of the best sailers in the British service. The enemy being to windward had the advantage of engaging us at his own distance, which was so great, that for the first half hour we did not use our carronades, & at no moment was he within the complete effect of our musketry or grape—to this circumstance & a heavy swell which was on at the time I ascribe the unusual length of the action. The enthusiasm of every officer Seaman & marine on board this ship on discovering the enemy, their steady conduct in battle & the precision of their fire could not be surpassed—where all have met my fullest expectations it would be unjust in me to discriminate. Permit me however to recommend to your particular notice my first Lieutenant Wm H. Allen, who has served with me upwards of five years & to his unremitted exertions in disciplining the crew is to be imputed the obvious superiority of our gunnery exhibited in the result of this contest.

Subjoined is a list of the killed & wounded on both ships our loss compared with that of the enemy will appear small. Amongst our wounded you will observe the name of [Acting] Lieutenant Funk, who died a few hours after the action he was an officer of great gallantry & promise and the service has sustained a severe loss in his death. The Macedonian lost her mizzenmast, fore & maintopmasts and mainyard & was much cut up in her hull. The damage Sustained by this Ship was not such as to render her return into port necessary, and had I not deemed it important that we should See our prize [in?] should have continued our cruise. With the highest consideration and respect I am [&c.]

Stephen Decatur

I was much struck with the appearance of Decatur that evening, as he sat in full uniform, his pleasant face flushed with the excitement of the occasion. He formed a striking contrast to the appearance he made when he visited our ship on the passage to New York. Then, he wore an old straw hat and a plain suit of clothes, which made him look more like a farmer than a naval commander.

(Leech, p. 161)

Dudley, *The Naval War,* vol. 1, pp. 552-553. A list of killed and wounded on board the *United States* is delineated in Appendix A.

trymen. One of them, John Card, even presented himself to the captain as a prisoner, but was sent to his quarters under pain of being shot. He was later killed by a shot from the *United States.* British seaman Samuel Leech later described it as "more disgraceful to the captain of the *Macedonian,* than even the loss of his ship." (Leech, *Thirty Years,* pp. 127–128)

There then ensued a gallant battle on both sides which became one of the greatest single-ship actions of naval history. The fire of the *United States* was exceedingly rapid and accurate and soon cut up the *Macedonian* aloft. Samuel Leech noted a strange noise that caught his attention "like the tearing of sails, just over our heads." He "soon ascertained [it] to be the wind of the enemy's shot." (Leech, p. 129–130)

Then, at Decatur's command, his gunners began to go for the hull. The heavy twenty-four-pound shot battered the *Macedonian's* sides and the canister from the carronades on the quarterdeck entered the *Macedonian's* gun ports and began cutting down the crews. Samuel Leech heard the shots striking the sides of the ship "like some awfully tremendous thunder-storm." He saw "blood suddenly fly from the arm of a man stationed at our gun." He "saw nothing strike him; the effect alone was visible." Leech continued, noting that "cries of the wounded rang through all parts of the ship." He stated that the wounded "were carried to the cockpit as fast as they fell" but those who were killed, "were immediately thrown overboard." (Leech, p. 130–131)

Suddenly the firing stopped, as the *United States* moved off and ahead of the now crippled *Macedonian.* Captain Carden held counsel with his officers. Although the first lieutenant, Mr. Hope, advised continuing the fight, on advice from the others, Carden made the decision to strike the colors. (Leech, pp. 135–136)

The *Macedonian's* captain, John Carden, somewhat dazed, surrendered his *Macedonian* on the quarterdeck of the *United States* to this man dressed in homespun and wearing a straw hat. British seaman Samuel Leech later best described Decatur's appearance contrasting it with that during the New York celebration of the taking of the *Macedonian* as shown to the left.

As Captain Carden extended his sword, Decatur declined it, saying: "Sir, I cannot receive the sword of a man, who has so bravely defended his ship." (Mackenzie, p. 176)) Carden was dismayed "that his name should go down in history as the first and assuredly only British frigate captain to surrender to an American." Decatur to no avail even tried to console Carden with the fact that Capt. James Dacres of HMS *Guerriere* had indeed preceded him in surrendering to Captain Hull of the USS *Constitution* on August 28, 1812. (Anthony, p. 190)

Perhaps the best descriptions of the encounter of the USS *United States* with HMS *Macedonian* are the individual after-action reports of Capt. John S. Carden and Commodore Stephen Decatur, respectively. They narrated the battle from their own points of view in the letters, shown below and on the facing page, to their superiors.

Captain John S. Carden, R.N., To
Secretary of the Admiralty John W. Croker
        American Ship United States at Sea 28th October 1812

Sir,
        It is with the deepest regret I have to acquaint you for the information of my Lords Commissioners of the Admiralty that His Majesty's late Ship Macedonian was Captured on the 25th Instant by the United States Ship, United States, Commodore Decatur Commander, the detail is as follows.
        A short time after daylight steering NW b W with the Wind from the Southward in Latitude 29 00 N and Longitude 29 30 W in the execution of their Lordships orders, a sail was seen on the lee Beam, which I immediately stood for, and made her out to be a large Frigate under American Colours, at 9 OClock I closed with her and she commenced the Action, which we returned, but the Enemy keeping two points off the Wind I was not enabled to get as close to her as I could have wished; after an hours Action the Enemy back'd and came to the wind, and I was then enabled to bring her to close Battle, in this situation I soon found the Enemys force too superior to expect success, unless some very fortunate chance occur'd in our favor, and with this hope I continued the Battle to two hours and ten minutes, when having the mizen mast shot away by the board, Topmasts shot away by the caps, Main Yard shot in pieces, lower Masts badly wounded, lower Rigging all cut to pieces, a small proportion only of the Foresail left to the Fore Yard, all the Guns on the Quarter Deck and Forecastle disabled but two, and filled with wreck, two also on the Main Deck disabled, and several shot between wind and water, a very great proportion of the Crew Killed and wounded, and the Enemy comparitively in good order, who had now shot ahead, and was about to place himself in a raking position without our being enabled to return the fire, being a perfect wreck, and unmanagable Log.
        I deemed it prudent th'o painful extremity to surrender His Majesty's Ship, nor was this dreadful alternative resorted too till every hope of success was removed even beyond the reach of chance, nor till I trust their Lordships will be aware every effort has been made against the Enemy by myself, my brave Officers

and Men, nor should she have been surrendered whilst a man lived on board, had she been managable. I am sorry to say our loss is very severe, I find by this days muster, thirty six killed, three of whom linger'd a short time after the Battle, thirty six severely wounded, many of whom cannot recover, and thirty two slight wounds, who may all do well, total one hundred and four.
        The truly noble and animating conduct of my Officers, and the steady bravery of my Crew to the last moment of the Battle, must ever render them dear to their Country.
        My first Lieutenant David Hope was severely wounded in the head towards the close of the Battle, and was taken below, but was soon again on deck displaying that greatness of mind and exertion, which th'o it may be equalled, can never be excelled; the third Lieutenant John Bulford was also wounded, but not obliged to quit his Quarters, second Lieutenant Samuel Mottley and him deserves my highest acknowledgements, the cool and steady conduct of Mr [James] Walker the Master was very great during the Battle, as also that of Lieutenants Wilson and [George] Magill of the Marines.
        On being taken onboard the Enemys Ship, I ceased to wonder at the result of the Battle; the United States is built with the scantline of a seventy four gun Ship, mounting thirty long twenty four pounders (English Ship Guns) on her Main Deck, and twenty two forty two pounders, Carronades, with two long twenty four pounders on her Quarter Deck and Forecastle, Howitzer Guns in her Tops, and a travelling Carronade on her upper Deck, with a complement of four Hundred and seventy eight pick'd Men.
        The Enemy has suffered much in masts, Rigging and Hull, above and below water, her loss in killed and wounded I am not aware of, but know, a Lieutenant and six Men have been thrown overboard.
        Enclosed you will be pleased to receive the names of the Killed and wounded on board the Macedonian, And have the Honour to be [&c.]
        Jno S. Carden

J. W. Croker Esqr
Secretary to the Admiralty
London

(Dudley, *The Naval War,* vol. 1, pp. 549–552)

Extracting from these two after action reports amongst others, Professor J. Russell Soley provided an excellent summary of the battle. Even Theodore Roosevelt admitted that Professor Soley's diagram of the battle was more accurate than his. The ships first sighted each other at daylight at twelve miles. The *Macedonian* was sailing to the NNW before the wind, which was from the SSE. The *United States* was north of her sailing to the SW close hauled on a port tack. They continued to close until approximately 7:30, when the *United States* wore and stood off to assess the enemy's force. The

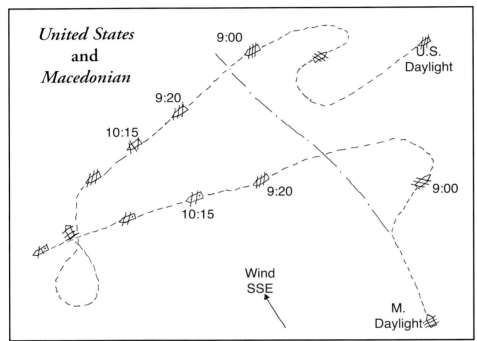

United States versus *Macedonian* battle sequence by the Author. Taken from sketches by Professor Soley and President Theodore Roosevelt.

Macedonian continued on course and the *United States* again wore and started to close. If Carden had kept his course as Lieutenant Hope advised, he would have crossed the bow or "T" of the *United States*. This is noted on the diagram by the dot-and-dash line crossing the bow of the *United States*. However, Carden chose to keep the weather gauge and passed to windward of the *United States*, where they exchanged the first broadsides at approximately 9:00 o'clock. The *Macedonian* then wore and followed the *United States* on the same tack. At approximately 9:20 the first broadsides carried away the mizzen-togallant-mast of the *United States* and the mizzen-topmast and gaff-halliards of the *Macedonian*. In this running battle the diagonal fire of the *United States* guns was very effective. However, at approximately 10:15 the *United States* backed her main-topsail and let the *Macedonian* catch up. As the ships came abreast the disabling fire of the *United States* began to take its toll. In approximately half an hour the *Macedonian* lost her mizzen-mast, fore and main-topmasts, and what was left of her masts and rigging were badly cut up. The *Macedonian's* upper battery was disabled with the exception of two guns, a third of her crew were killed or wounded, and there were a hundred shot in her hull. The *United States* drew off to refill cartridges and make minor repairs before returning to a commanding position off the stern of the *Macedonian*. By then Carden had decided to strike his colors. (Soley, *The Naval Campaign of 1812*, pp. 317–318, *see list above*)

In summary Soley states: "The accurate and careful gunnery of the Americans and the great rapidity of their fire quickly disable the enemy, carry away his masts, shatter his hull, silence his battery; while in return he inflicts little or no injury. The inequality in the loss of men is still more striking. The Americans have only seven killed and six wounded; while the English loss foots up to the comparatively enormous total of thirty-six killed and sixty-eight wounded." (Soley, p. 319) As Roosevelt summed it: "That is, the relative force being about as three is to two, the damage done was as nine to one!" (Roosevelt, *The Naval War of 1812*, p. 112)

Seaman Samuel Leech of the HMS *Macedonian* offered a brutal first-hand account of the carnage that he witnessed as shown on facing page.

After putting Lieutenant Henry Allen aboard the *Macedonian* in charge of the prize crew and a herculean effort on their part to patch her up, jury rig the sails, and regain her seaworthiness, Decatur decided to stay with her and see his prize safely into port. The *United States* and her prize *Macedonian* then slowly worked their way west to the American East Coast, where upon arrival they were separated in a fog. The *United States* anchored off New London, while the *Macedonian* made her way into Newport temporarily. While off New London, Commodore Stephen Decatur wrote the following letter to Secretary of the Navy Hamilton on December 4, 1812, in which he noted that the *United States* had arrived that morning and referred to an enclosed letter "for the details of an action between this ship & His Britannic Majesty's ship *Macedonian*," which was probably his report of October 30, 1812. He continued, stating that the last night was very dark and that they unavoidably parted with their prize off Montauk point. Decatur ended by saying that with a pilot on board he was sure that the *Macedonian* would be in as soon as the thick weather and visibility allowed. (Dudley, *The Naval War*, vol. 1, p. 616)

The *Macedonian* under the command of Lt. William Allen did make it into Newport that day and upon seeing the wounded ashore managed to make it into New London a short time later. (Leech, pp. 151–153) Decatur sent Lt. Archibald Hamilton to Washington with his dispatches, as well as the captured colors of the *Macedonian*. Following the news of the capture, on December 8, 1812, Mrs. B. H. Latrobe in Washington, D.C., wrote a letter to her friend Mrs. Juliana Miller describing the news of the *Macedonian* defeat as shown on the next page.

Decatur finally escorted his prize back to New York where they received a tumultuous welcome. The city was virtually theirs for days and the crew enjoyed their popularity with great festivity. As the *Macedonian* proceeded to Wallabout Bay and the Navy Yard for repair and refit, the surrounding hills were full of spectators staring at the shot holes in her sides and the cannon balls still buried in her planking. (Dye, *Naval History*, p. 36) Decatur and his crew earned the thanks of Congress and several state legislatures for this victory.

The overwhelming superiority and accuracy of the USS *United States* gunfire is not only attributed to the drilling of First Lieutenant Allen, but also to Commodore Decatur's style of leadership that showed great consideration for his crew. Indeed, this combination of leadership and discipline led to one of the first battles won by gunfire alone without any need to board. Therefore, Commodore Decatur is also remembered as one of the leading proponents of the ultimate employment of accurate tactical naval gunfire.

The first object I met was a man bearing a limb, which had just been detached from some suffering wretch. . . . The surgeon and his mate were smeared with blood from head to foot: they looked more like butchers than doctors. Having so many patients, they had once shifted their quarters from the cockpit to the steerage; they now removed to the wardroom, and the long table, round which the officers had sat over so many a feast, was soon covered with the bleeding forms of maimed and mutilated seamen. . . .

Our carpenter, named Reed, had his leg cut off. I helped to carry him to the after wardroom; but he soon breathed out his life there, and then I assisted in throwing his mangled remains overboard. . . . It was with exceeding difficulty I moved through the steerage, it was so covered with mangled men and so slippery with streams of blood.

We found two of our mess wounded. One was the Swede, Logholm. We held him while the surgeon cut off his leg above the knee. The task was most painful to behold, the surgeon using his knife and saw on human flesh and bones, as freely as the butcher at the shambles does on the carcass of the beast! (Leech, *A Voice from the Main Deck*, pp. 141–143)

. . . On Tuesday a very splendid ball was given to the Navy Officers, Hull, Morris[,] Stewart &c. My husband could not be absent as he holds an office in the Navy Department, and I was not sorry we went, as it is not likely I shall ever witness such another scene. At about five in the evening my husband came home and informed me that we must immediately illuminate our house, as the account of a victory gained by Commodore Decatur had just arrived. My house in ten minutes was prepared for lighting up and we prepared for the ball. The Avenue was very brilliant on our way to the Capital Hill, and, the company assembling, the crowd was immense. Mrs. Madison was there, but not the President. The evening went on with crowding as usual upon the toes and trains of those that did not dance; when about ten o'clock, a loud huzza announced the arrival of young Archibald Hamilton, who had at that moment appeared with the colors of the Macedonian. He was borne into the room by many officers. Good little Mrs. Hamilton, his mother, stood by me, and was so much agitated at the sight of her son, that she must have fallen, had I not stepped forward and offered my arm. The young man sprung into her arms; his sisters threw their arms around him, and the scene was quite affecting. The colors were then held up by several gentlemen over the heads of Hull, Morris, and Stewart, and Hail Columbia played and there were huzzas until my head swayed.

The aforesaid colors were then laid at the feet of Mrs. Madison. Oh tempora. Oh mores. This was rather overdoing the affair. I forgot to say that the flag of the Guerriere was festooned on one side of the room, and some other vessel. Now, between ourselves, I think it was wrong to exalt so outragiously over our enemies. We may have reason to laugh on the other side of our mouths some of these days; and, as the English are so much stronger than we are with their Navy, there are ten chances to one that we are beaten. Therefore it is best to act moderately when we take a vessel; and I could not look at these colors with pleasure, the taking of which had made so many widows and orphans. In the fullness of my feelings, I exclaimed to a gentleman who stood near me, "Good Heavens—I would not touch that color for a thousand dollars", and he walked quickly away, I hearing the gentleman say, however, "is it possible Mrs. Latrobe." I looked around, and it was a good staunch Federalist from Rhode Island, Mr. Hunter, so that I shall escape hanging after so treasonable a speech. I came home with a raging headache at 12, and went, the next evening, to the drawing room by way of curing it. I must not fail to leave room to announce the marriage of Commodore Tingey who was united to Miss Dulany, on Wednesday evening after they had been engaged three weeks. She is 28 and he 61. He gives a ball tomorrow evening. . . .

(Partial Manuscript, Decatur House Museum, source unknown at 15 August 1990, believed to have originated from Heather Palmer-White at Decatur House)

Commodore Stephen Decatur was still bothered by the licenses he had seized from the *Mandarin* and like other Navy commanders thought that Congress should prohibit them. He wrote again to Secretary of the Navy Hamilton about them in a letter from New York dated December 28, 1812. In this letter Decatur reminded Secretary Hamilton of the "number of British licenses addressed to Citizens of the United States," which he had found "on board the Ship *Mandarin* Baker Master-from London bound to Philadelphia" and forwarded to the secretary for his disposal. Decatur continued, stating that the licenses had been diverted from their original destinations, because he believed then that "the Government of the United States would interdict the use of such protections to their citizens." He went further to say that he thought too that "it might be of some service to have the Government apprised of the extent to which this trade seemed enlarging itself under the protection of the Enemy, and of the individuals concerned in it." Decatur went further by saying that since the trade had not been made illegal, he wished that "the licenses should be transmitted to their owners unless the Government think proper to dispose of them otherwise." He ended by asking to be advised of any other disposition, so he might "satisfy owners" who were "becoming importunate in their applications" to him for their licenses. (Dudley, *The Naval War*, vol. 1, p. 638)

On the other hand Secretary of the Navy Paul Hamilton was more concerned about compensation of Decatur and his crew for the prize ship *Macedonian*. Almost simultaneously he wrote the letter on the facing page to Commodore Stephen Decatur.

Meanwhile James Barron's suspension from the Navy ended on February 8, 1813, and he sent two letters from Denmark to then Secretary of the Navy Jones on July 22, 1813. However, Barron never received a reply and remained abroad for the duration of the war. (Tucker & Reuter, *Injured Honor*, pp. 200–201)

After losing the frigates *Guerriere*, *Macedonian*, and *Java* and sloops *Frolic* and *Peacock*, the British realized that the Americans were determined to wage an aggressive war. Therefore, by the spring of 1813 the British in response had established an effective blockade of all of the important Atlantic ports from New York southward. In May of 1813 Decatur attempted to break out of the blockade with his squadron, consisting of the frigates *United States* under his command and the *Macedonian* under the command of Capt. Jacob Jones and the sloop *Hornet* under the command of James Biddle. After a delay from unfavorable winds through the sound they tried to elude the British off Montauk Point and get to sea on June 1, 1813. However, they found their way blocked by two British ships of the line and two frigates. Decatur was forced to retire to New London, where the British established an even tighter blockade. Decatur made preparations for one night escape on December 12, 1813, but canceled it when told that blue signal lights were burning on both sides of the river mouth. On January 14, 1814, Decatur wrote to Sir Thomas Hardy commanding the blockade and challenged the *Endymion* to fight the *United States* and the *Statira* to engage the *Macedonian*. However, Hardy rejected the challenge of the *United States* on the grounds that she was stronger than the *Endymion*. Decatur then rejected the single engagement between the *Macedonian* and the *Statira* on the grounds that they would be able to select their crew from the whole British squadron. Finally, on April 4, 1814, the Secretary of the Navy ordered the *United States* and *Macedonian* to be dismantled and moved to the head of navigation above New London to keep them safe from enemy attack. Decatur was given his choice of command of the *President* or the *Guerriere* and he chose the *President*. By May 7, 1814, Decatur had completed securing the safety of the two frigates *United States* and *Macedonian* fourteen miles above the mouth of the river with ample protection and departed for New York to assume command of the *President*. (Lewis, pp. 133–140)

During the summer and early fall of 1814 the British invaded the Chesapeake and burned the Capitol in Washington, but were repulsed at Baltimore. There was fear of further attacks on Philadelphia and New York and Decatur was ordered to take command of the entire naval defenses at New York. Macdonough's Lake Champlain victory on September 11, 1814, was the

*Comr Decatur Nav: Depm't
N York 29 Decem 1812*

The President of the U.S. desires me to express to You & to Lt. [William H.] Allen through You. to the officers & crew, of the frigate U.S. his warmest thanks & highest approbation of Your & their conduct on the defeat & capture of his Britanic Majesty's frigate the Macedonian. I assure You, sir, that it affords me real happiness to be the Medium of Conveying to You the expression of his feelings & sentiments upon this subject. Permit me also to congratulate You upon this brilliant achievement which adds another laurel to those already justly earned by You.

With respect to the prize, two points namely, her relative force & her value must be immediately ascertained. This can best be done by the appointment of referees on the part of the Department. I nominate Jacob Lewis Esqr now at New York as one of the referees. You will be pleased to appoint another & should the two so appointed disagree, they will choose a third whose decission shall be conclusive.

The objects to be particularly attended to by the referees, are 1. the relative force of the two frigates, the United States & the Macedonian including her rigging, apparel, armaments, & everything belonging to her-at such valuation the Navy Depmt will purchase her & put her in commission. Should She be considered equal in force to the United States, the Department will pay to the Captors the whole amount of her valuation—if of inferior force, one moiety only unless Congress should vote the whole to the captors.

Be pleased to apprise Capt Lewis of his appointment as a referee, & give to the referees a Copy of such parts of this letter as belongs to the Subject.
P. Hamilton

(Dudley, *The Naval War*, vol. 1, pp. 638–639)

only significant American naval achievement of that year. After it became apparent that the British were not going to attack New York, Decatur wrote to the secretary on November 17 concerning a projected cruise, which was subsequently approved.

When the blockading squadron, consisting of the fifty-six-gun razee *Majestic*, the forty-gun frigate *Endymion*, and the thirty-eight-gun frigates *Pomone* and *Tenedos*, were forced out to sea during a severe snowstorm on January 14, 1815, Decatur took his opportunity and set sail in the *President* along with a merchant store-ship. However, due to pilot error, the *President* struck a bar, where she pounded for an hour and a half and sprung her masts before being freed. The westerly gale prevented Decatur from putting back into the harbor and after coasting Long Island for fifty miles, he turned to the southeast. On January 15 at daylight three of the British ships were seen to the east-southeast. Decatur immediately turned to the north with the British in pursuit. The *Majestic* and *Endymion* were astern with the *Pomone* on the port and the *Tenedos* farther away on the starboard quarter. By midday *Endymion* outsailed *Majestic* and was gaining on the *President* due to her sprung masts. As *Endymion* yawed to fire broadsides at the *President*, Decatur endeavored to increase speed by lightening ship. Anchors, spare spars, cables, boats, and provisions were thrown overboard to no avail. By five o'clock *Endymion* reached point-blank range off the *President's* starboard quarter, where Decatur's stern and quarter guns could not bear. Decatur hoped the *Endymion* would come to close quarters, so that he could attempt to board her. He laid out his plan to the officers and then the crew. Hearty cheers followed his speech to the crew, but the *Endymion* yawed and stayed off. Decatur then changed course to the south, hoping to put the *Endymion* out of action before the others could come up. As the two ships headed south on parallel courses, the *President's* fire succeeded in stripping the *Endymion's* sails from her yards. *Endymion* was technically defeated as she dropped astern of the *President*. Decatur could have easily taken her, if it were not for the other British ships.

By eleven o'clock that evening the *Pomone* and *Tenedos* overtook the *President*. The *Pomone* opened fire on the starboard bow and the *Tenedos* took a raking position off the *President's* quarter. The *President* was too extensively damaged to escape. Decatur, twice wounded and having lost twenty-four men with another fifty-five wounded reluctantly surrendered to save his crew from further bloodshed. When Decatur offered his sword to Captain Hayes of the *Majestic*, he returned it with almost the same words that Decatur had addressed to Carden after the defeat of his *Macedonian*. The *Endymion* was so badly damaged that she did not arrive until two hours after the surrender. The *President* had been taken by the entire squadron and the prize money was divided equally among all of the ships.

The *President* was sent to Bermuda as a prize under convoy of the *Pomone* and *Endymion*. Decatur was given passage on the *Endymion* under Captain Hope, who had been Carden's first lieutenant on the *Macedonian*. Remembering their kind treatment by Decatur during their captivity, Captain Hope and the other British officers exhibited great kindness and courtesy towards Decatur. The naval authorities at Bermuda returned Decatur to New London under parole on the frigate *Narcissus* under command of Capt. Alexander Gordon. They arrived off New London on February 22, 1815, and

British Admiral Hotham wrote Decatur congratulating him on his arrival home along with the rejoicing over the establishment of peace. The Treaty of Ghent had been signed on December 24, 1814, and ratified by Great Britain on December 28 and the United States on February 17, 1815. The Admiral also enclosed a letter from Mrs. Decatur. (Lewis, pp. 142–151)

When Decatur landed in New London, he was treated as a hero and when he arrived in New York on February 28, he learned that the carpenters at the Brooklyn Navy Yard had volunteered sixteen hundred work days towards building a new frigate for him. Nevertheless, Decatur wrote to Secretary of the Navy Crowninshield on March 6, 1815, requesting a court of inquiry to investigate his conduct in the loss of the *President*. The secretary appointed Commodore Alexander Murray and Capts. Isaac Hull and Samuel Evans to the court. On April 17 they reported that they were convinced that the damage the *President* sustained grounding on the bar led to her capture and that this was caused by improperly placed boats serving as beacons in the dangerous channel. The court further reported that ". . . the *Endymion* was subdued; and if her friends had not been at hand to rescue her, she was so entirely disabled that she soon must have struck her flag . . ." The court concluded that Decatur ". . . evinced great judgement and skill, perfect coolness, the most determined resolution and heroic courage,—that his conduct, and the account of his officers and crew are highly honorable to them and to the American navy, and deserve the warmest gratitude of their country; that they did not give up their ship till she was surrounded and overpowered by a force so superior that further resistance would have been unjustifiable, and a useless sacrifice of the lives of brave men."

Secretary Crowninshield sanctioned the court proceedings and on April 20 wrote the letter below to Decatur.

> *I* have, therefore, sir, to express to you in the fullest manner the high sense of approbation which the President of the United States and this department entertain for your professional character as an officer, who in every instance has added lustre to the stars of the Union; and whose brilliant actions have raised the national honor and fame even in the moment of surrendering your ship to an enemy's squadron of vastly superior force, over whose attack, singly, you were decidedly triumphant; and you will be pleased to present to each of your gallant officers and crew the thanks of your government, for their brave defense of the ship and the flag of the United States.

(Lewis, pp. 152–154)

Print by Stapco of portrait of Susan Wheeler Decatur by Gilbert Stuart, circa 1803. Courtesy of Decatur House, photograph by John Ballou.

Print of engraving of Stephen Decatur profile by A. B. Durand. Courtesy of Decatur House, photograph by Johm Ballou.

CHAPTER 4

COMMODORE DECATUR, THE
FINAL YEARS

Encouraged by the British in early 1812, the Algerian Dey, Hadji Ali, claimed an arrearage of $27,000 had accumulated on his annual tribute payments from the treaty of 1796. The Dey said it was due to the shorter 354-day Mohammedan year. When the Dey threatened war, the American consul paid the debt and then departed for Gibraltar. During the War of 1812 American ships stayed out of the Mediterranean, but the Dey was able to capture the American brig *Edwin* and hold the crew in slavery. Attempts to ransom them failed.

As the war with Great Britain was concluded, President Madison focused on Algiers, recommending a declaration of war, which Congress approved on March 2, 1815. On March 24 Decatur was given command of a squadron, which was to sail to the Mediterranean and bring the Dey to terms. Decatur accepted on condition that when Bainbridge, who was senior to him, arrived with a second squadron, he would be allowed to return home. Prior to the outcome of the court of inquiry Decatur did not want a subordinate position that might look like the Navy had lost confidence in him because of the loss of the *President.*

Decatur's flagship was the frigate *Guerriere* commanded by Capt. William Lewis. The rest of the squadron included the following: the frigates *Macedonian* under Capt. Jacob Jones and *Constellation* under Capt. Charles Gordon, the sloop *Ontario* under Master Commandant Jesse D. Elliott, the brig *Epervier* under Lieutenant Commandant John Downes, the fourteen-gun brigs *Firefly, Spark,* and *Flambeau,* and the twelve-gun schooners *Torch* and *Spitfire.* Decatur was also allowed to take many of his old officers and men from the *President* and *United States* that wanted to accompany him in the *Guerriere.* Decatur's squadron sailed from New York on May 20, 1815, and except for the *Firefly,* which sprung her masts in a gale and returned to New York, arrived off Gibralter on June 15. Decatur learned that he might find the Algerian admiral off Cape de Gat, Spain, and immediately sailed in search of the Algerians.

On the morning of June 17 the *Constellation* sighted a sail to the southeast and gave chase followed by the rest of the squadron. As *Constellation* opened fire the now fleeing ship wore and headed for the Spanish coast, hoping for a neutral port. The ship was the Algerian forty-six-gun frigate *Mashuda* under command of Admiral Hammida. When the *Guerriere* closed and fired a broadside, Hammida was killed. The *Epervier* then came up and fired nine broadsides into the Algerian before she finally surrendered. Thirty of her crew were killed and many of the remaining 406 prisoners were wounded. Two days later the Algerian twenty-two-gun brig *Estedio* was run aground off Cape Palos and captured by the *Epervier* with assistance from the *Spark, Torch,* and *Spitfire.* The *Estedio* lost twenty-three killed and eighty were taken prisoner. Decatur sent both ships into Cartegena, Spain, as prizes and proceeded to

Print of painting of Decatur House by Mr. E. Vaile, 1822. Courtesy of Decatur House, photograph by John Ballou.

Algiers to intercept any other returning Algerian cruisers. Decatur's squadron arrived off Algiers on June 28, 1815. Mr. William Shaler, the newly appointed American consul-general of the Barbary States, was on board the flagship *Guerriere* with Decatur, as they received the Swedish consul, Mr. Norderling, and the Algerian port captain the next morning. The Algerian refused to believe that Admiral Hammida was dead and the *Mashuda* and *Estedio* captured until Decatur brought forward Ham-mida's Lieutenant as a witness. Decatur then gave them a letter from the president to the new Dey Omar, stating that Congress had declared war, but hoping that the Dey would choose peace. Dey Hadji Ali had been killed by his own soldiers a few months before and Omar now ruled. Decatur and Shaler also presented a letter stating that they were instructed to deal from the principle of perfect equality and on terms of most favored nation. There would be no form of tribute.

On June 30 the Swedish consul and Algerian port captain returned with authority to negotiate and a treaty was presented to them. The treaty provided for the abolition of all tribute, the release of all Americans held by the Dey and all Algerians held by the Americans, and payment of $10,000 by the Dey for the *Edwin*. The Algerian requested restoration of the two recently captured ships and after some deliberation the

Commemorative pitcher with Decatur's bust on the front with flags, ships, and cannons. Courtesy of Decatur House, photograph by John Ballou.

Americans agreed. When the Algerian asked for a truce until the Dey signed the treaty, Decatur refused. However, they did agree that hostilities would cease, when a boat flying a white flag was seen heading out with the signed treaty and all of the freed Americans. (Lewis, pp. 159–165)

Omar the Terrible was in a bind. He was besieged by locusts devouring his crops and American guns, if he refused to give up piracy. He could at least save face by getting his ships back. Upon seeing a familiar ship on the horizon heading home the Dey knew the Americans would take her too, if he did not sign. Conversely, Decatur was in an excellent position. He awaited the Dey's reply in full uniform wearing the badge of Cincinnatus. His blue flag flew at the masthead bearing an olive branch and a sword with the motto, "The one or the other." Decatur was ready for war, if the treaty was not signed. Accordingly, he sent his crew to quarters and stood ready to challenge the incoming Algerian ship. At the last moment a boat was seen heading out flying a white flag. The treaty had been signed and all of the American prisoners were freed and in the boat. (Anthony, pp. 248–250)

Decatur then sailed for Tunis on July 8, 1815, where the Bey had allowed the British to regain two prizes taken by the American privateer *Abaellino* during the war. After stopping at Sardinia for water and provisions, Decatur arrived off Tunis on July 26. He immediately sent a demand to the Bey through the American consul for a $46,000 indemnity for the two ships. When the Bey learned from the American consul that his admiral was Decatur, who had burned the frigate *Philadelphia* and taken the *Macedonian* from the British, he conceded.

Decatur next went to Tripoli, where two other prizes of the same American privateer had been retaken by the British. After learning what Decatur had gained from Algiers and Tunis, the Bey decided to accept Decatur's terms of a $25,000 indemnity and the release of two Danish and eight Sicilian captives. With peaceful relations now restored with Algiers, Tunis, and Tripoli Decatur took his squadron to visit the Kingdom of the two Sicilies to allow his officers and men some rest and recreation. Following additional visits to Naples, Cartagena, and Malaga, Decatur learned that Bainbridge's squadron was at Gibraltar. He sent his squadron ahead to Gibraltar and then joined them there on October 6, 1815. Bainbridge had arrived at Cartegena on August 5 and learned of the treaty with Algiers, but according to his orders he proceeded there and then on to Tripoli and Tunis.

Poem on satin to honor Decatur with biographical sketch at bottom, circa 1820. Courtesy of Decatur House, photograph by John Ballou.

The effect of the appearance of a second American squadron was not lost on the Barbary rulers. Leaving a small squadron composed of the *United States, Constellation, Erie,* and *Ontario* in the Mediterranean, Bainbridge sailed for home on October 7 with the rest of the two squadrons except *Guerriere*. Decatur departed later that same day in *Guerriere* and arrived in New York on November 12, 1815. (Lewis, pp. 168–174)

Decatur returned triumphantly to the United States that fall of 1815 following his successful diplomacy in the Mediterranean. The Secretary of the Navy was well pleased with Decatur's performance to the extent that he offered him a position on the Board of Navy Commissioners that had just been vacated by Capt. Isaac Hull's retirement. Decatur accepted the nomination in a letter to Secretary Crowninshield on December 9, 1815. While still in Philadelphia, Decatur was informed of the confirmation of his appointment by the Senate and his commission was dated December 20, 1815. (Lewis, pp. 176-177)

When Stephen and Susan Decatur moved to Washington following acceptance of his commission, he purchased a house in one of the "Seven Buildings" on Pennsylvania Avenue between Nineteenth and Twentieth Streets next door to the Madisons. Using some of his prize money, Decatur then purchased a lot on the northwest corner of Lafayette Square (then President's Square), which is now at the corner of H Street and Jackson Place. Later he engaged Benjamin H. Latrobe, an architect for the Capitol, St. John's Church, and other Washington buildings, to design the Decatur's permanent home for the site. (Lewis, p. 185; Bullock and Morton, *Decatur House,* pp. 9 and 46)

Print of engraving of Stephen Decatur standing by a classical column and holding the hilt of his sword in his right hand by A. B. Durrand, circa 1835. Courtesy of Decatur House, photograph by John Ballou.

Decatur settled into his new position on the Board of Navy Commissioners with his old friends of many years, John Rodgers and David Porter. Their duties were similar to those of the British Lords of the Admiralty and were considered the highest in the American Navy. They were tasked with almost every important decision under the secretary of the Navy from determining the various classes of ships to be built to the necessary naval material requirements, to establishing naval regulations and to determining personnel requirements. In April 1816 Congress authorized the construction of nine ships of the line and twelve forty-four-gun frigates, which the Commissioners were to superintend. (Lewis, pp. 178–180)

In April 1816 Decatur traveled to Norfolk on duty accompanied by his wife Susan. In her native city they were received with great cordiality and a public dinner was held in his honor at which 120 gentlemen were present.

Following a number of noteworthy toasts Decatur responded with his more famous toast: "Our country! In her intercourse with other nations, may she always be in the right; and always successful, right or wrong." (Lewis, pp. 182–183; Bullock and Morton, p. 46)

Using his prize money, Decatur purchased eleven lots that stretched a block between today's H Street and Pennsylvania Avenue, and Seventeenth Street and Jackson Place. Stephen and his well-educated wife Susan engaged the architect Benjamin H. Latrobe to design their house. The socializing Decaturs specified a house that was "suitable for foreign ministers" and "impressive entertainments." (Keister, *Influence and Ambition*, Reprint for Decatur House, p. 4) Although the Decaturs had no children of their own, the daughters of his sister spent considerable time in Washington with their uncle and aunt, since their father, Captain McKnight of the Marines, had been killed in a duel in 1802. Decatur's niece, Priscilla Decatur McKnight, then fourteen years old, spent that first winter of 1816 in Washington with the Decaturs. Her sister, Anna Pine McKnight when she was about eighteen years old, spent the winter of 1818 with the Decaturs. Then both Anna Pine and her oldest sister, Mary Hill McKnight, came to Washington to stay with the Decaturs in December 1819 following the untimely death of their mother in September of that year. By this time the Decaturs were comfortably settled in their new Benjamin Latrobe-designed permanent residence on the northwest corner of Lafayette Square.

The earliest surviving correspondence between Latrobe and Decatur is the letter at right.

Although the house as constructed is only fifty-one feet facing Lafayette Square and forty-five feet deep, it contains a full basement with three stories and garret above. Additionally, there were servants' quarters and a carriage house at the rear.

Meanwhile, James Barron had finally returned to the United States and requested a naval command, but was turned down. Barron then met with Secretary of the Navy Smith Thompson in February 1819. However, he was rebuked by Thompson for remaining in a foreign country after expiration of his suspension and particularly during the war. On March 6, 1819, Barron wrote to President Monroe pleading his case, but to no avail. Decatur was strongly opposed to giving Barron a command because of his absence during the war and as a member of the Board of Navy Commissioners, made his feelings known.

Although most of the other captains agreed with Decatur, Capt. Jesse Elliott supported Barron. As Barron's strongest supporter during his court-

Washington, June 4, 1817
Commodore Decatur

Dear Sir:
The sickness of one of my children, & the badness of the weather, prevented my sending to you the enclosed yesterday morning, agreeably to my promise.—The two proposals are from Men, one of whom (Mr. Meade) has built Mrs. Casenave's [Casanove's] house, & the house now occupied by Congress,—perfectly to the satisfaction of all parties,—the other, (Mr. Skinner) built St. John's Church, & Mr. McDaniel's house. Both may be relied upon, I believe, to execute well & promptly what they undertake.

I have not opened their proposals, but I believe that they amount to from 10 to 11,000$ dollars, from what they said to me before they were sent in.—They were not required to include fencing, stabling, or pavements;—which may be rated at from 1500 to 1800$ more.—If the house should be occupied by a foreign Minister, I would also recommend the addition of a slight one store-room, back, for a servant's hall.—

I believe the drawing & description are sufficient to enable any other intelligent Mechanic to contract.

respectfully yrs
B. H. Latrobe
Papering, & the 3 principal Chimney pieces are omitted, the latter can be better procured from Italy.—

(Bullock and Morton, p. 13)

Right: Front view of Decatur House. Courtesy of Decatur House, photograph by Robert McClintock of PhotoAssist.

Below: Decatur House downstairs family parlor. Courtesy of Decatur House, photograph by Robert McClintock of PhotoAssist.

Above: Decatur's office in downstairs Decatur House. Courtesy of Decatur House, photograph by Robert McClintock of PhotoAssist.

Left: Decatur House downstairs entrance hallway. Courtesy of Decatur House, photograph by Robert McClintock of PhotoAssist.

Norfolk, January 16th, 1820

Sir,—Your letter of the 29th ultimo I have received. In it you say, that you have now to inform me that you shall pay no further attention to any communication that I may make to you, other than a direct call to the field; in answer to which, I have only to reply, that whenever you will consent to meet me on fair and equal grounds, that is, such as two honorable men may consider just and proper, you are at liberty to view this as that call. The whole tenor of your conduct to me justifies this course of proceeding on my part. As for your charges and remarks, I regard them not; particularly your sympathy. You know not such a feeling. I cannot be suspected of making the attempt to excite it.

(Sabine, Notes on duels & Dueling, p. 162)

Washington, January 24, 1820

Sir,

I have received your communication of the 16th, and am at a loss to know what your intention is. If you intend it as a challenge, I accept it, and refer you to my friend Commodore Bainbridge, who is fully authorized by me to make any arrangements he pleases, as regards weapons, mode or distance.
Your obedient servant
Stephen Decatur

(Anthony, p. 293; Sabine, p. 163)

martial, Elliott also blamed Decatur for stopping an inquiry into his feud with Commodore Perry, stemming from Elliott's failure to close with the enemy at the Battle of Lake Erie. So it was Elliott who continued to incite the animosity between Barron and Decatur by reporting Decatur's continuing criticism of Barron. (Tucker & Reuter, pp. 201–202)

Thus began a correspondence of some thirteen letters. The letters raised accusations and refutations, point and counterpoint, and became more intransigent and deadly as they grew. One of the last letters from Barron to Decatur read as shown at left. Decatur responded to Barron with the letter below:

It was now left for the seconds, Bainbridge for Decatur and Elliott for Barron to work out the arrangements. Once this was done, the place was set as Bladensburg, Maryland, a well known dueling ground not far from the District of Columbia line. A date of March 22, 1820, was established. On that fateful morning of March 22 several other Navy gentlemen were close by, including Captains Rodgers and Porter.

Bainbridge measured out the distance of eight paces between Barron and Decatur, as had been chosen by Decatur because of Barron's nearsightedness. It would be difficult for either to miss at that range. Decatur had already declared that he did not care to kill Barron and would shoot for the hip only to wound. As Bainbridge gave them their pistols Barron told Decatur "if we meet in the other world, let us hope that we may be better friends." Decatur answered with "I have never been your enemy, sir." Under dueling etiquette this exchange could have been used by seconds to attempt a reconciliation, but neither second attempted. As Elliott ordered them to their places, each took aim at the other's hip. Their shots were fired simultaneously and both men went down shot in the hip. Although Barron's wound was not fatal, Decatur's was. As the two men lay not ten feet apart, they apparently made peace with each other.

After the duel, Elliott, perhaps fearing arrest, fled the scene in Barron's carriage. Bainbridge helped get Decatur into a carriage to take him back to his house at President's square. Porter hailed a carriage and helped Barron in. As they crossed the District line they ran into Elliott slowly returning to the scene. Porter then insisted that Elliott take charge of Barron in his place. That night Decatur died at his house in great pain, while Barron recovered after a lengthy convalescence. Several days later Decatur was honored with an impressive funeral attended by the president, chief justice, Senate and House delegations, and many ranking naval officers. (Tucker & Reuter, pp. 202–203; Sabine, pp. 141–142)

Ironically, Decatur was opposed to dueling. According to Mr. Wirt, then attorney-general of the United States, Decatur told him that "Fighting, he said, was his profession, and it would be impossible for him to keep his station and preserve his respectability, without showing himself ready, at all times, to answer the call of any one who bore the name of a gentleman." (Sabine, p. 143) Decatur had actually said as much in his October 31, 1819, letter to Barron, when he stated: "I do not think that fighting duels, under any circumstances, can raise the reputation of any man, and have long since discovered, that it is not even an unerring criterion of personal courage. I should regret the necessity of fighting with any man; but, in my opinion, the man who makes *arms his profession* is not at liberty to decline an invitation from any person, who is not so far degraded as to be beneath his notice." (Sabine, p. 150)

Following the funeral procession to Kalorama, Decatur's body was deposited there in the Barlow's family vault. Kalorama was situated in a beautiful grove overlooking Washington and Georgetown. The text below was inscribed on the tomb:

Decatur's treatment of the sailors who served with him had been exceptionally humane at a time when brute force and the cat-o'-nine were more the rule of discipline on a man-of-war. As the old sailor at his funeral had weepingly declared, "He was the friend of the flag, the sailor's friend; the navy has lost its mainmast." (Lewis, p. 235; Mackenzie, p. 332)

Some years later Decatur's remains were reinterred in St. Peter's Episcopal Churchyard in Philadelphia, where his parents were buried. Friends then erected a monument there in his honor. When she died, his beloved wife Susan was buried there with him.

Here lie the remains of Stephen Decatur of the United States Navy, who departed this life on the 22nd of March, 1820, aged 41 years. His public services are recorded in the annals of his country, his private virtues in the hearts of his friends, and above all in her heart who was fourteen years the happy partner of his life, and the delighted witness of his exalted worth, and who can with truth inscribe upon this tablet that he possessed every virtue of which the human character is susceptible and each carried to its highest perfection.

(Lewis, pp. 233–234)

Decatur House upstairs library. Courtesy of Decatur House, photograph by Robert McClintock of PhotoAssist.

Right: Decatur House downstairs dining room. Courtesy of Decatur House, photograph by Robert McClintock of PhotoAssist.

Facing page: Decatur House upstairs south parlor. Courtesy of Decatur House, photograph by Robert McClintock of PhotoAssist.

Top left, middle left, bottom left and right top: St. Peter's Episcopal Church Bell Tower, Philadelphia, 1997. Decatur is buried in the Churchyard. Photograph by the author.

Decatur Monument in St. Peter's Episcopal Church yard, Philadelphia, 1997. Photograph by the author.

STEPHEN DECATUR
BORN JANUARY 5TH 1779,
ENTERED THE NAVY OF THE UNITED STATES
AS MIDSHIPMAN
APRIL 30TH 1798,
BECOME LIEUTENANT,
JUNE 3, 1799
MADE CAPTAIN
FOR DISTINGUISHED MERIT,
PASSING OVER THE RANK OF COMMANDER
FEBRUARY 16TH 1804,
DIED
MARCH 22, 1820.

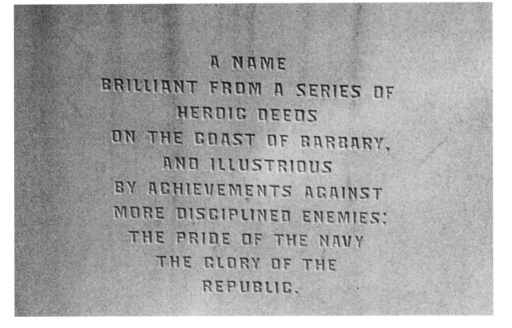

A NAME
BRILLIANT FROM A SERIES OF
HEROIC DEEDS
ON THE COAST OF BARBARY,
AND ILLUSTRIOUS
BY ACHIEVEMENTS AGAINST
MORE DISCIPLINED ENEMIES;
THE PRIDE OF THE NAVY
THE GLORY OF THE
REPUBLIC.

Above: Detail of the St. Peter's Episcopal Church big window, Philadelphia, 1997. Photograph by the author.

Left: Headstone of Susan Wheeler Decatur in St. Peter's Episcopal Churchyard, Philadelphia, 1997. Photograph by the author.

US Frigate Constitution Off Boston Light, August 28th 1812

Sir

    I have the Honour to inform you that after leaving Boston Light on the 2d inst, the date of my last letter to you I stood to the Eastd along the Coast, in hopes to fall in with one of the Enemy's Frigates, which was reported to be cruising in that direction the day before I left Boston. I passed near the Coast, as far down as the Bay of Fundy, but saw nothing. I then run off Halifax, and Cape Sables, and remained near there, for three, or four days, without seeing any thing, which made me determine to change my situation to the Eastd, towards Newfoundland, I accordingly bore up, and run to the Eastd under all sail, passing near the Isle of Sables, and hauling in, to take a Station off the Gulph of St Lawrence near Cape Race, to intercept the Ships of the Enemy, bound either to, or from Quebec, or Halifax, and to be in a situation to recapture such of our vessals, as they might be sending in.

    On the 10th inst being off Cape Race I fell in with a light Merchant Brig bound to Halifax, from Newfoundland, and as she was not worth sending in, I took the crew on board, and set her on fire. On the 11th I fell in with the British Brig Adeona from Nova Scotia, bound to England loaded with Timber I took the crew out of her, and set her on fire, and made sail to take station nearer Cape Race; Where we continued cruizing until the morning of the 15th at daylight when five sail were in sight ahead of us, apparently a small convoy, I gave chace under a press of sail, and soon found that we gained on them very fast, and discovered that one of them was a Ship of War, at sunrise they tacked, and stood on the same tack with us, by this time we could plainly discover that the Ship of War had a Brig in tow. At 6 coming up very fast with the Ship and could see that she had cast off the Brig, that she had in tow, and had set her on fire, and had ordered a second Brig to stand before the wind, to separate them. The Ship of War making sail to Windward I gave chace to a ship wich appeared to be under her convoy but when we came up with her, she proved to be a British Ship, Prize to the Dolphin Privateer of Salem she had been Spoken by the Ship of War, but we came up with them before they had time to put men on board, and take

charge of her, whilst our boats were boarding this vessel the Ship of War got nearly Hull down from us, and understanding from one of the prisoners that she was a very fast sailer, I found it would not be possible to come up with her before night, or perhaps not then, I therefore gave chace to the Brig that run before the Wind, determined to destroy all his convoy, we soon found we came up fast with the Brig and that they were making every exertion to get off by throwing overboard all the Lumber, Water Casks &c &c.

    At 2 PM we brought too the chace and found her to be the American Brig Adeline, from Liverpool, loaded with dry goods &c Prize to the British Sloop of War Avenger, I took the British Prize Master, and crew out and put Midshipman Madison (John R. Madison), and a Crew on board, with Orders to get into the nearest Port he could make. From the prize master of this vessel I learnt that the Brig burnt by the Sloop of War, belonged to New York, and was loaded with Hemp, Duck &c last from Jutland, having gone in ther in distress.

    Having chaced so far to the Eastd as to make it impossible to come up with the Sloop of War, I determined to change my cruizing ground, as I found by some of the Prisoners that came from this vessel that the Squadron that chaced us off New York were in the Western Edge of the Grand Bank, not far distant from me. I accordingly stood to the Southd intending to pass near Bermuda, and cruize off our Southern Coast. Saw nothing till the night of the 18th at 1/2 past 9 PM, discovered a Sail very near us it being dark, made Sail and gave chace, and could see that she was a Brig. At 11 brought her too, and sent a boat on board, found her to be the American Privateer Decatur belonging to Salem, with a crew of One Hundred and Eight Men, and fourteen guns, twelve of which, he had thrown overboard whilst we were in chace of him. The Captain came on board, and informed me that he saw the day before a Ship of War standing to the Southward, and that she could not be far from us. At 12 PM, made sail to the Southd intending if possible to fall in with her. The Privateer Stood in for Cape Race intending to cruize there, and take Ships by boarding as he had lost all his Guns but two. The above is a Memorandum of what took place on board the Constitution under my Command from the time we left Boston, up to the 18th inst, which I hope will meet your approbation. I have the honour to be (&c.)

    Isaac Hull

(Dudley, *The Naval War*, vol. 1, pp. 231–232. The *Decatur* was out of Newburyport vs Salem, p. 233)

CHAPTER 5

THE DECATUR PRIVATEERS

During the War of 1812 there were three American privateers with the name *Decatur*. One of these was a schooner manned by twenty-three men and armed with four guns, although she had ports for sixteen. The schooner was sent to sea in hopes of completing her armament from prizes. This was often done in those days, when the owners were unable to obtain all of the desired ordnance. (Maclay, *A History of American Privateers,* p. 309) The owners were Richard H. Douglass, William Douglass, and Cumberland D. Williams. This schooner *Decatur* was built in Somerset County, Maryland, in 1811 and was 99.6 feet in length, 27 feet at the beam, had a draft of 10.6 feet, and her displacement was 248 tons. She was first commissioned on March 1, 1813, and sailed out of Baltimore with a Letter of Marque under her first captain, Thomas N. Lane. Her first lieutenant was Henry Graham and the four guns were twelve-pounders. (Cranwell and Crane, *Men of Marque,* p. 379) Captain Lane was a New Englander from Maine. (Maclay, p. 309)

The schooner *Decatur* was again commissioned on February 2, 1814; then with a single owner, Richard Douglass. She sailed out of Baltimore with a Letter of Marque under a new captain, George Montgomery. Her lieutenant was then Moses Bears and on this cruise the *Decatur* captured the brig *William* and took her into Elizabeth City, North Carolina. (Cranwell and Crane, p. 379) However, this *Decatur's* luck ran out on the next cruise under Capt. E. Brown. On September 3, 1814, she was captured by a British squadron and subsequently was lost at sea. (Maclay, p. 309) A second *Decatur*, a brig with fourteen guns and 160 men under Capt. William Nichols, sailed out of Newburyport. This *Decatur* was one of the most successful privateers from the Eastern ports, capturing four ships, six brigs, two barks, and two schooners.

On the night of August 18, 1812, *Decatur* was chased for two hours by the USS *Constitution* under Capt. Isaac Hull. During the chase Captain Nichols jettisoned twelve of his fourteen guns to lighten ship in his attempt to escape. However, *Constitution* still succeeded in catching up to *Decatur* and it was only after Captain Hull sent one of his boats over that he learned the true identity of this privateer. Ironically, only the day before *Decatur* had been chased by HMS *Guerriere,* but had easily outsailed her. These incidents offered a perfect example of the sailing superiority of the American frigates over their British counterparts. While *Decatur* had easily eluded *Guerriere,* she was unable to get away from *Constitution* even after throwing most of her guns overboard.(Maclay, pp. 309–310)

Capt. Isaac Hull reported this incident along with others in the letter to Secretary of the Navy Hamilton shown at left. Following her encounter with the USS *Constitution* the *Decatur* returned to port. *Decatur* then cruised in the West Indies with replenished armament, where off Barbadoes she was captured by the British frigate *Surprise* on January 16, 1813. On arrival in Barbadoes, Captain Nichols was recognized by the captain of the British frigate *Vestal,* as the earlier captain of the American merchantman *Alert* before she was converted to the privateer *Decatur.* The *Vestal* had captured the *Alert* only to have Captain Nichols succeed in recapturing her and escape. The captain of the *Vestal* accordingly ensured that Captain Nichols was harshly treated by confining him in a five-by-seven foot cell before shipping him out to England. (Maclay, pp. 310–311)

The third and last *Decatur* privateer was a schooner out of Charleston, South Carolina,

So: Carolina. Augt., 24th: 1813.

Sir.

I have the pleasure to inform you, that by the Capture of his Britannic Majesty's Sloop of War Dominica, command by the Late George Wilmot Barrette Esqr. the British Naval Signals, & various military Orders And other important informations have come into my hands, as prize of the Court of Admiralty of this State: and which I now have the honor & satisfaction of forwarding, for the information of the President of the United States—.

The above Vessel was taken after a severe engagement by, the Privateer Decatur of this Port, Commanded by Captain Dominique Diron. It is with pleasure I announce him to the notice of Government: as it appears, that he & his whole Crew fought nobly: took the Sloop by boarding: and treated the prisoners with the utmost humanity—

The prize is completely fitted up as a Sloop of War; 14 twelve pound Carronades 1 thirty pounder Carronade midships, & one brass four pounder— Coppered up to the beams, and would be an useful addition to the navy of the United States— As the Capture was by boarding, little or no damage by cannon shot has occurred—

With congratulations on this occasion I have the honor to subscribe myself in haste Sir respaectfully yr. ob. st.
John Drayton
Judge of the District Court
of South Carolina.

Letters above and facing page: (Dudley, The Naval War, vol. 2, pp. 214–217)

armed with six twelve-pounders and one long eighteen-pounder amidships. *Decatur* had a complement of 103 men and boys and was commanded by Captain Diron, who was one of the most celebrated privateersmen of the time. (Maclay, p. 311)

This *Decatur* was built in the Pritchard and Shrewsbury shipyard in Charleston. She was launched on March 13, 1813, the largest privateer to sail out of Charleston at 240 tons. *Decatur* departed Charleston on her maiden voyage on May 27, 1813. (Dudley, *War of 1812*, vol. 2, p. 213) One of *Decatur's* first prizes was the *Nelson*, "a monstrous three-decked vessel" of six hundred tons, with an immensely valuable cargo. She was bound for Jamaica and was sent into New Orleans. *Decatur* also took the brig *Thomas*, of two guns.

On August 5, 1813, a little to the south of the Bermudas, *Decatur* sighted two vessels at about 10:30 A.M. and began to close. By 11:00 A.M. they were determined to be a ship and a schooner and at 12:30 P.M. the schooner showed the British colors. *Decatur* managed to maintain the weather gauge and at about 1:30 P.M. the British schooner fired the first shot which fell short. The British opponent was the *Dominica*, a three-masted schooner carrying twelve short twelve-pounders, two long six-pounders, one brass four-pounder, and a short thirty-two-pounder. She was under the Command of Lieutenant Barrette and had a complement of eighty-eight men and boys. Captain Diron knew that the *Dominica* had heavier armament, but believed he had more crew and determined to fight at the closest quarters in order to carry the Englishman by boarding. After clearing for action Captain Diron wore ship at about 2:00 P.M. in an attempt to pass under the *Dominica's* stern for a raking fire, but the *Dominica* luffed and let go a broadside that passed over the *Decatur*. At 2:15 P.M. the *Decatur* began to use her long tom with accurate and murderous effect. Conversely, the *Dominica's* fire was erratic and inaccurate, such that by 3:00 P.M. Captain Diron ordered his boarders to assemble. However, the *Dominica* sailors managed to get in one effective broadside that foiled the *Decatur's* attempt to board. The American's renewed action with their long tom and twelve-pounder as they followed the Englishmen and soon made another attempt to board. However, this attempt was frustrated similar to the first. Captain Diron continued to follow his opponent and gradually began to overhaul her. At 3:30 P.M. Captain Diron once again called for his boarders as *Decatur's* bowsprit ran over the enemy's stern and her jib boom pierced the *Dominica's* mainsail. This was the signal to board. While some of the Americans covered the boarders with a heavy fire of musketry, Vincent Safitt, the prize master, and Thomas Wasborn, the quartermaster, led the boarders over the bowsprit and onto the *Dominica's* deck. The scene quickly turned into one of a bloody slaughter, as nearly two hundred men and boys went at one another with muskets, pistols, and cutlasses in a space approximately twenty feet wide by eighty long.

One of the first casualties was the gallant British commander, Lieutenant Barrette. He was wounded twice in the left arm early in the action, but remained at his post. Although urged several times by his officers to surrender, he refused to do so. The sailing master, Isaac Sacker, and the purser, David Brown, of the *Dominica* were also killed. Midshipmen William Archer and William Parry were wounded. In all eighteen of the *Dominica's* crew were killed and forty-two were wounded. Even with this heavy a list of casualties, the British cannot be said to

Charleston,—South Carolina
24 August, 1813

Sir,

My attention has been So Compleetly engaged in attending to the Wounded, obtaining Paroles for the officesr and permission for the Surgeon, and Secretary to Land with other matters incidental to the unfortunate occurrence it is now my painfull Duty to Communicate, and not being myself a Resident in the City that I have not before had time to make Known to you the Capture of His Majestys Late Sloop (a Phildelphia Schooner formerly called Glee I believe, Captured on an Illegal Voyage) Dominica commanded by George Wilmote Barrett Esquire on the 5 inst by the American Privateer Decatur, Capt Dominique Diron belonging to this Port and the arrival of both Vessels, with the British Ship London Trader of London from Surinam bound to London, on the morning of the 20 inst.—Mortifying as is the Result of this unfortunate Affair. I trust His Majestys Government will never for a moment doubt that the Crew of the Dominica which consisted of 85 Men, amoung whom a Sergeant & Corporal and Thirteen Marines, did their Duty, when they are informed that when this Vessel was taken possession of there were not more than Three Men able to do Duty. and Every officer Killed or Mortally Wounded excepting Mr. Nichols a Midshipman, slightly wounded and a Young Gentleman of the Name of Lindo a Volunteer and Supernumerary—. I have not yet seen Mr. Nichols in consequence of his being on board of one of the United States Schooners appointed for the defence of this harbor. and laying at a Considerable Distance from the City so that I have been able to learn no particulars from him, but from those I have seen it seems very evident that the Loss of this vessel is to be attributed entirely to the Want of Knowledge of and Experience in the Management of a Schooner, on the part of Captain Barrette, who had been Second Lieutenant of the Dragon and made in the West Indies. and immediately appointed to the Dominica. and the Vessel herself being extremely difficult to Work.—. of these two very Serious disadvantages Capt. Diron. a Frenchman. and complete Privateersman. with a very large Crew consisting Chiefly of his own Countrymen who amounted in Number I believe to 93 chiefly if not all Blacks, & Mulattoes. and in Ferocity and cruelty *exceeded by none*. as will be Shewn on the Return of the remainder of the crew to His Majestys Dominions, more fully availed himself and after a most desperate Discharge of Musketry succeeded in Boarding when a Scene of Cruelty was exhibited which has perhaps been never equalled. the Boarders Killing in the most merciless manner all the Wounded on the Decks.— I have requested the Surgeon Mr. David Watson an officer whose *whom* anxious Care of and Generous to His Majestys Government, in Case of his Seeing Mr. Nichols before I should to Solicit him to write to the Admiral a Letter communicating the Fate of this unfortunate Vessel. and to convey it to me that I may forward it to you to be transmitted by the earliest opportunity. of which request I hope you will not be disapprove.— I have the pleasure to inform you that Since their arrival the Wounded have been taken every Care of. and all are excepting Two or three, very desperately Wounded. and of whose recovery there is some doubt. but great hopes, in a fair Way of Recovery. For the Surgeon and Clerk. I have obtained permission to land. and to return to His Majestys Dominions. by the earliest Conveyance, and I am very hopefull of Soon finding one for them for Bermuda in a Neutral. I have not yet Obtained *for* Paroles for Messrs. Nichols and Lindo. but hope to do So to day. although I find much difficulty in So doing in Consequence of there being no Such provision in the Agreement. and so with Masters & Merchantmen. who think it very hard to be Confined in a Prison Ship which is at this moment the Case with Mr. Lindo. and Capt. Sinclair of the London Trader.—. I should be much obliged to be made acquainted with the Custom of Nations on these occasions.—. I have been at Some loss how to act in Consequence of the Privateersmen having retained all the Bedding belonging to the Dominica, and the prisoners being entirely without it. and its Cost being now so very extravagant. but in order to be as economical as possible. I propose if I cannot obtain it Gratis, to endeavor to buy the Bedding from the Privateersmen.— As the number of Prisoners in the Prison Ship is now considerable. you would do me a great favor by reminding General Mason of the Repairs it requires. and also. and particularly of the Awning or Shed over the Deck which it so very much wants. and I would most earnestly Solicit the favor of you to expedite as much as possible their Return to His Majesty Dominions. I observe Two cartels are hourly expected at the Northward from Halifax and should be much pleased if you could order one of them here. or obtain permission for an American vessel to proceed. which I little doubt I could procure on Good Terms. I have the honor to be Sir Your most obedient humble Servant

Charles R. Simpson

have surrendered for it was the American's who hauled down the colors with their own hands.

The *Decatur* crew for its part suffered five men killed and fifteen wounded. This disparity in casualties, however, has to be attributed to the superior seamanship of Captain Diron and the better marksmanship of the Americans, both with their cannon and small arms. This was later attested to by the surviving officers of the *Dominica*. They also acknowledged that during their captivity they were treated with great kindness and humanity by Captain Diron, his officers and crew, and that the utmost care and attention were given to the sick and wounded. (Maclay, pp. 309–319)

Two letters give a somewhat different perspective to the action after the fact. Perhaps the after action report depends somewhat on the point of view. District Court Judge John Drayton wrote to Secretary of State James Monroe the letter at left.

On the other hand Charles R. Simpson, who was probably one of the numerous agents employed by Thomas Barclay at U.S. seaports to protect British prisoners, reported to Barclay, who was the principal agent for British prisoners in the U.S. Simpson's letter to Barclay on this page.

Beating round "Cape Freward" Straits of Magellan. Dec: 1854.

USS *Decatur* (1838–1865) (Sloop of War) beating around "Cape Freward," Straits of Magellan, December 1854. Sketch by "J.Y.T." Courtesy of the Naval Historical Center.

CHAPTER 6

USS DECATUR, SLOOP-OF-WAR

The first *Decatur* was built as a sloop-of-war from 1838 to 1839 at the New York Navy Yard. She was 117 feet long with a beam of 32 feet and a draft of 15 feet 6 inches. Decatur could sail at nine and a half knots on a wind and eleven knots free. Her complement was 150 officers and crew and she was armed with sixteen guns. *Decatur* was first commanded by Commander H. W. Ogden. She served with the Brazil Squadron on her first cruise from March 1840 to February 1843.

Decatur set sail on her second cruise on August 5, 1843, to join the African Squadron, arriving on station in September 1843. She cruised under the command of Commodore Matthew C. Perry in suppression of the slave trade, returning to Norfolk on January 3, 1845. *Decatur* was then placed in ordinary where she remained through 1846.

Decatur then served in the Mexican War, arriving off Castle Juan de Uloa, Mexico, on April 14, 1847. Although she was too large to go up the Tuxpan River, fourteen officers and 118 of the crew accompanied Commodore Perry's expedition to attack Tuxpan. Eight officers and 104 of the crew then participated in the capture of Tobasco from June 14 to 16, before *Decatur* returned to Boston on November 12.

Returning to the African Squadron under Commodore Benjamin Cooper, *Decatur* again served as a deterrent to the slave trade from February 1848 to November 1849. She was then placed in ordinary at Portsmouth, New Hampshire, during 1850.

Decatur next cruised with the Home Squadron under Commodore Foxhall A. Parker off the Atlantic Coast and in the Caribbean until August 1852. On August 21 she arrived at the Boston Navy Yard and was decommissioned in preparation for heavy repairs.

After being recommissioned July 12, 1853, *Decatur* served with a Special Squadron in the North Atlantic under Commodore William B. Shubrick to protect American fishing interests from July to September 1853. *Decatur* then helped search for the missing merchantman *San Francisco* in the Caribbean in January and February 1854.

Decatur sailed from Norfolk June 16, 1854, for duty with the Pacific Squadron. After transiting the stormy Straits of Magellan she visited Valparaiso, Chile, on January 15, 1855 and Honolulu, Hawaii, from March 28 to June 23. Under Commander Isaac Sterett, *Decatur* then sailed for duty in the Washington Territory to deter Indian outbreaks, where she served from July 1855 to June 1856. Commander Guert Gansevoort relieved Commander Sterett while in Seattle December 10, 1855. In January 1857 *Decatur* sailed for Panama, Nicaragua, Peru, and Chile, where she served to protect American interests until March 1859. *Decatur* was decommissioned on June 20, 1859 at Mare Island, but was refitted as a harbor battery in March 1863 and stationed off San Francisco until finally sold in August 1865 at Mare Island for $5,600 in gold. (Sloop of War *Decatur*, Ship's History, pp. 1–3)

USS *Decatur* (DD-5). Fleet Admiral Chester W. Nimitz, USN, served as her commanding officer from November 1, 1907, to July 29, 1908, and he has signed the photograph. Courtesy of the Naval Historical Center.

CHAPTER 7

USS *DECATUR* (DD-5)

The second *Decatur* (DD-5), a Bainbridge Class Torpedo Boat Destroyer, was built by the William R. Trigg Shipbuilding Company of Richmond, Virginia, which was a brand new shipyard organized by Mr. Trigg in October 1898 by converting the Talbott Iron Works on the Richmond dock into a shipyard. The Trigg shipyard quickly earned a reputation for turning out some of the finest and fastest ships and boats on American waters, securing contracts for two torpedo boats, the *Stockton* and the *Dale*. When the *Stockton* was launched on November 1, 1899, President McKinley made a stirring address in front of 30,000 people. Contracts for two of the new Torpedo Boat Destroyers followed and the first built in the South, the *Dale*, was launched on July 24, 1900. (Richmond, *Her Past and Present,* pp. 462-471)

Decatur, the second of these Torpedo Boat Destroyers, was launched on September 26, 1900. Miss Maria Ten Eyck Decatur Mayo of Norfolk, the great-grandniece of Commodore Decatur, was the ship's sponsor. (*Richmond Times,* September 27, 1902)

The USS *Decatur* (DD-5) was commissioned on May 19, 1902, and Lt. L. H. Chandler assumed command, as the first commanding officer. *Decatur* was 250 feet long with a beam of 23 feet 7 inches and a draft of 6 feet 6 inches. Her displacement was 420 tons and her trial speed was 28.10 knots. *Decatur* had a complement of 4 officers and 69 crew and was armed with two 18-inch Whitehead torpedo tubes, two 3 inch/50 rapid fire and five six-pounder rapid fire guns.

Decatur was designated as the lead vessel of the first Torpedo Flotilla conducting drills and maneuvers along the East Coast and in the Caribbean until December 1903, when the Flotilla departed for the Asiatic Station. She arrived at Cavite, Philippine Islands, on April 14, 1904, and exercised along the China and Philippine coasts until placed in reserve on December 5, 1905, at Cavite.

Ensign Chester W. Nimitz, in USS *Panay*, arrived in Cavite on July 8, 1907. Reporting to the commandant of the Navy Yard on July 9, he was handed orders of immediate detachment from *Panay* to place *Decatur* in commission. A war scare with Japan had suddenly come up. Although in dress whites, he was directed to proceed directly to *Decatur* without returning to the Panay for his gear which would be sent to him.

The future fleet admiral was carried straight out to the *Decatur* by the commandant's launch. *Decatur* was anchored in Canacao Bay, red lead colored from stem to stern, completely empty of any stores or equipment whatever, and without a drop of water or a pound of coal.

Ensign Nimitz reached the deck of the destroyer, greeted only by two native watchmen and with orders for *Decatur* to be in Olongapo for drydocking within seventy-two hours. While still making up his mind what to do, he observed two boats pulling out from a group of ships some two miles distant. In one was his classmate Ensign John M. Smeallie with two or three other men. In the other was Midshipman Hugh Allen with a few men. The officers, under temporary orders, became respec-

VIEW OF THE WM. R. TRIGG CO., SHIP-BUILDING PLANT,

View of the Wm. R. Trigg Company Ship Building Plant from *Richmond, The Pride of Virginia, An Historical City,* Illustrated, p. 35. Progress Publishing Company, Philadelphia, 1900. Courtesy of the Virginia Historical Society.

tively, chief engineer, executive officer and navigator. Twenty-seven men soon reported as crew, later being joined by eleven men of the engineering force of USS *Chauncey* to assist in the run to Olongapo.

Ensign Nimitz commandeered one of the boats that had brought the officers to the ship and contacted his friends, the warrant officers in the yard, who had helped him fit out *Panay.* They pointed out all of *Decatur's* gear stored in a warehouse with latticed sides and open to the weather. Here were guns, torpedoes, spare parts and other equipage which were sent out in lighters along with a working party before sundown. Fifty tons of coal also came to *Decatur* and a water barge. All hands worked through the night and into the next afternoon to get supplies, guns, torpedoes, ammunition, and other equipage on board.

When the flotilla commander approached in *Chauncey* about 2:00 on July 10, Nimitz was ordered to clear the buoy and follow him to Olongapo. At this time there were lighters full of heavy gear on each side and *Decatur's* compass and binnacle stores were still on the lighters. Everything was on board by 5:55 when Ensign Nimitz was on the bridge, ordering "cast loose." He rang one-forth speed astern on both engines and must have had an anxious moment as the ship forged slowly ahead. Before he could act, the wind had drifted the destroyer clear of the buoy and it was safe and convenient to proceed ahead. So he ordered "full speed astern" and *Decatur* went ahead at twelve knots to take position astern of *Chauncey* on the way to Olongapo. It turned out that *Decatur's* engine telegraphs had been reversed, a situation Nimitz had experienced when he had commissioned the *Panay.*

Decatur arrived off the entrance of Olongapo at 2:00, July 11, 1907, plagued by a heavy rain squall and total darkness in which contact was lost with *Chauncey.* Nimitz anchored off Olongapo until daylight and entered the Floating Drydock, *Dewey* at 8:40. The destroyer remained in drydock until the afternoon of July 26, emerging ready for a fight, but found the war scare with Japan had evaporated. After practice on the torpedo target range in Manila Bay, the destroyer departed Olongapo on January 21, 1908, for a cruise to the southern Philippines. She returned from this cruise to Cavite on February 29, repaired at Olongapo, then set course on May 17 for Saigon, Indo-China, where she remained from May 20 to 24, 1908.

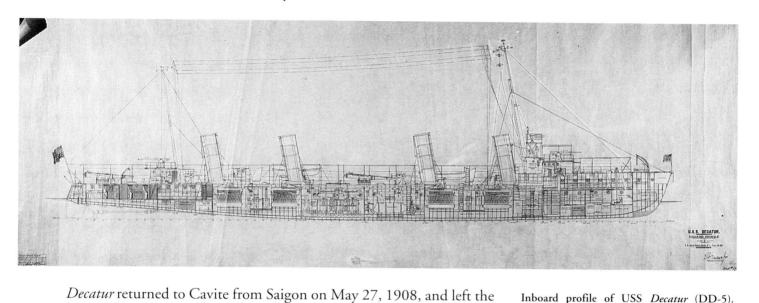

Inboard profile of USS *Decatur* (DD-5). Courtesy of the National Archives II. Photograph by King Visual Technology, Hyattsville, Maryland.

Decatur returned to Cavite from Saigon on May 27, 1908, and left the afternoon of July 7 for a run to Batangas Bay. As she approached her destination the light at Banan was not visible and the Batangas light was mistaken for the proper navigational light the night of July 7. As a result *Decatur* found herself aground on a sand bar at the mouth of the Batangas River at 9:52 P.M., July 7, 1908. After attempts to back off the bar failed, she passed a six-inch manila hawser to the U.S. Army transport *Wright*, but the cable parted in four tries. Finally, at 2:30 A.M., July 8, SS *Buena Lurte*, pulling on a bow cable that had been passed to her by *Decatur*, pulled the destroyer free. She suffered no damage, but Ensign Nimitz had the misfortune to report the incident to the Asiatic Fleet commander at a time when the pressure was on for court martial action in the case of two other officers. This probably had some influence on the ordering of a General Court Martial in his case on board the *Denver*. Ensign Nimitz, who found himself detached from *Decatur* on 28 July 1908, was "admonished" for his navigational error.

This incidence apparently had little effect on his career, as he rose to become Fleet Admiral Nimitz. As Commander-in-Chief Pacific Command in World War II, he masterminded the Battle of Midway and the Central Pacific drive through to the Japanese home island of Okinawa.

Ensign John M. Smeallie took command of *Decatur* on July 28, 1908, and made infrequent cruises for the next two years before placing her out of commission on February 18, 1909. *Decatur* was then placed in commission in reserve on April 22, 1910. Placed back in full commission on December 22, 1910, *Decatur* resumed operations with the Torpedo Flotilla cruising in the

USS *Decatur* (DD-5). Photograph of the Ship's Crew, 1907. The center officer is Ensign Chester W. Nimitz, commanding officer. Courtesy of the Naval Historical Center.

Fleet Admiral Nimitz khaki uniform shirt with the five stars of a Fleet Admiral and accompanying khaki cap. Courtesy of the U.S. Naval Academy Museum. Photograph by the author.

Fleet Admiral Nimitz dress blue blouse with the five stripes of a Fleet Admiral. Courtesy of the U.S. Naval Academy Museum. Photograph by the author.

Picture of Fleet Admiral Nimitz in khakis. Courtesy of the U.S. Naval Academy Museum. Photograph by the author.

southern Philippines and between ports in China and Japan for the next seven years. (Ship's History, pp. 4 -6)

While anchored off Cavite on September 9, 1915, an explosion occurred in *Decatur's* ordnance workshop and storeroom. Immediately following the explosion, Chief Watertender Eugene P. Smith entered the compartments at great personal risk several times, locating and rescuing his injured shipmates.

When asked by the Navy Board of Inquiry to describe the main features of the explosion, Chief Watertender Smith replied as quoted on the following page from the Board Report

The final casualties from this mishap were later reported as three killed and six injured. Both Hayden and Bell later succumbed from their multiple injuries, as corroborated by the Board of Inquiry Report. (Navy Board of Inquiry, USS *Decatur*, p. 6) The probable cause of the explosion was later determined to have been a spontaneous or extraneous ignition of heavier-than-air vapor which had collected at or under the hatch, between compartments, but again is not corroborated by the Board Report.

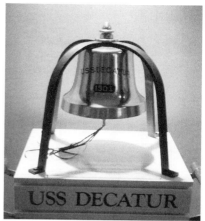

USS *Decatur* (DD-5) ship's bell. The Bell is on loan to the Decatur House from the Naval Historical Center Curator Branch. Courtesy of the Decatur House, photograph by John Ballou.

On February 8, 1916, Chief Watertender Eugene P. Smith was awarded the Medal of Honor for his heroic efforts that night of September 9, 1915, with the following Citation: "Attached to U.S.S. *Decatur*; for several times entering compartments on board of Decatur immediately following an explosion on board that vessel, 9 September 1915, and locating and rescuing injured shipmates." (U.S. Congress, Senate, Medal of Honor Recipients, 1863–1968, p. 428)

On August 1, 1917, *Decatur* departed for the Mediterranean and was assigned to U.S. Patrol Squadrons after arriving at Gibralter on October 20, 1917. During passage, on the afternoon of October 8, 1917 she twice sent a salvo from her forward 3-inch gun towards a submarine which appeared astern. She performed patrol and convoy duty in the Atlantic and the Mediterranean. On several occasions *Decatur* reported sighting submarines and dropped depth charges without any visible results.

USS *Decatur* (DD-5) deck scene, circa 1905, showing a torpedo partly withdrawn from the tube. Courtesy of Capt. D. W. Knox, 1932. Courtesy of the Naval Historical Center.

On November 9, 1918, *Decatur* and HMS *Defender* were escorting HMS *Britannia* when the *Britannia* was torpedoed. *Decatur* promptly charged in dropping depth charges to keep the submarine down, but as other ships arrived to assist, the *Britannia* sank.

On December 8, 1918, *Decatur* departed for the United States via Lisbon, Portugal, the Azores, and Bermuda and arrived in Philadelphia on February 6, 1919. *Decatur* was decommissioned there on June 20, 1919, and sold on January 3, 1920. (DD-5, Ship's History, p. 7)

When I heard the report of the explosion I was on deck alongside #2 stack, I went aft and told the fireman on watch to start the pumps on the fire main. Callahan came aft calling "fire in the forecastle." I grabbed the hose and ran forward, not knowing where the fire was, but saw white smoke coming out of the hatch of the paint locker, and the gunner's mate's storeroom. Some one said there was someone down there. The smoke was so thick I could not breathe. I went down from five to eight times. Part of the flooring was gone, as one of my legs went through as I went down. We took turns going down; Corrigan, machinist's mate, first class; Fiske, quartermaster, first class; Barksdale, quartermaster, third class; Clemmer, seaman, and McGlothlen, gunner's mate, first class. Hayden was the first man found and taken out. Bell was found after Hayden and taken out; Elkins was found on the starboard side forward in the compartment and was brought out by Corrigan and myself, ten or fifteen minutes after the explosion.
(Navy Board of Inquiry, USS Decatur, p.4)

The completed list of casualties was as follows:
DEAD:

Elkins, L.J. Gunner's Mate, second class. Multiple burns sustained from, and the traumatic effects of, the explosion.
INJURED.

Hayden, W.U. Chief Gunner's Mate. Burns, multiple. Both extremities, head, face, neck, parts of both legs and 3rd degree.

Bell, E. Gunner's Mate, third class. Burns, multiple. Both upper extremities, head, face, neck, parts of body and parts of both legs. Also scalp wound about 3-1/2" in length.

Santos, C. DeLos, Seaman. Fracture, compound (comminuted) both bones right leg, 2nd degree burns of face and left arm and fore arm and left ankle.

Brashear, E.L. Fireman, second class. Fracture, simple, of femur. Bruises about lower chest. No burns.

Meikle, O.S., Ordinary Seaman. Wound, lacerated (scalp) unqualified.

Sagner, C.E., Fireman, second class. Sprain, of joint, left ankle.

Young, B.P. Hospital Apprentice, 1st. class. Minor Burns, both hands and fore arms.

CHIEF WATERTENDER EUGENE P. SMITH, UNITED STATES NAVY

BY DIRECTION OF CONGRESS, THE MEDAL OF HONOR IS PRESENTED TO CHIEF WATERTENDER EUGENE P. SMITH, UNITED STATES NAVY. CITATION: WHILE ATTACHED TO U.S.S. DECATUR; FOR SEVERAL TIMES ENTERING COMPARTMENTS ON BOARD OF DECATUR IMMEDIATELY FOLLOWING AN EXPLOSION ON BOARD THAT VESSEL, 9 SEPTEMBER 1915, AND LOCATING AND RESCUING INJURED SHIPMATES.

ENTERED SERVICE:	CALIFORNIA
PLACE OF BIRTH :	QUINCY, ILLINOIS
DATE OF BIRTH :	8 AUGUST 1871
DATE OF DEATH :	24 MARCH 1918
PLACE OF BURIAL :	CYPRESS HILLS NATIONAL CEMETERY BROOKLYN, NEW YORK

NATIONAL MEDAL OF HONOR MUSEUM - CHATTANOOGA, TENNESSEE

Above: Medal of Honor Citation of Chief Watertender Eugene P. Smith, USN. Courtesy of Ann Moyer of the National Medal of Honor Museum, Chattanooga, Tennessee.

Below: Photograph of the headstone of CWT Eugene P. Smith in the Cypress Hills National Cemetery, Brooklyn, New York. Courtesy of the Veteran's Administration.

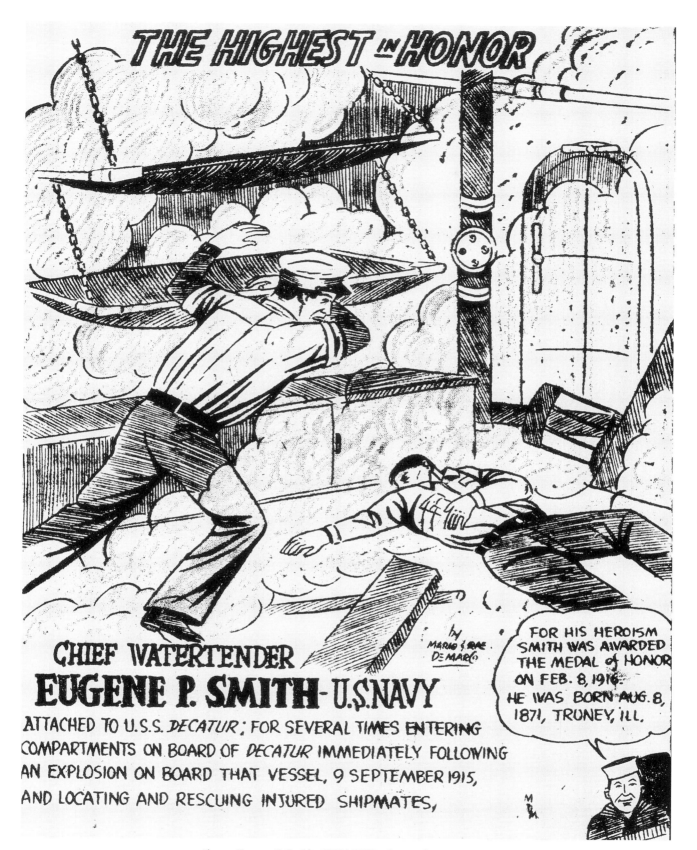

Above: Eugene P. Smith, CWT, USN, vignette by Mario Demarco for "Navy Times," giving details on how CWT Smith won the Medal of Honor on board USS *Decatur*, September 9, 1915. Courtesy of the Artist, 1978. Courtesy of the Naval Historical Center. Note: Chief Smith was born in Quincy, Illinois, not Truney, Illinois.

USS *Decatur* (DD-341). Courtesy of the Naval Historical Center.

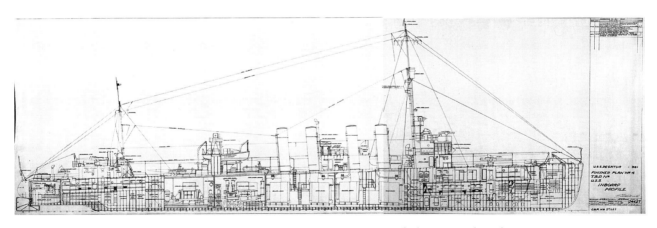

Inboard profile of USS *Decatur* (DD-341). Courtesy of the National Archives II.
Photograph by King Visual Technology, Hyattsville, Maryland.

CHAPTER 8

USS *DECATUR* (DD-341)

The third *Decatur* (DD-341), a Clemson Class Destroyer, was launched on October 29, 1921, at Mare Island Navy Yard and commissioned there on August 9, 1922, sponsored by Mrs. J. S. McKean. She was 314 feet 4 1/2 inches in length with a 30 foot 8 1/2 inch beam and 9 foot 3 inch mean draft. Her displacement was 1,215 tons and trial speed was 35 knots powered by two boilers and two geared turbines with each providing 25,200 Shaft Horsepower (SHP). *Decatur's* complement was 9 officers and 117 crew. Her armament was four 21-inch triple torpedo tubes and four 4 inch/50 and one 3 inch/23 anti-aircraft guns.

Lt. C. K. Osborne was assigned as the first commanding officer. After completing trials *Decatur* sailed to San Diego where she was placed out of commission on January 17, 1923. She was recommissioned on September 26, 1923, and served as flagship of Destroyer Squadron 11, Battle Fleet. *Decatur* operated along the West Coast and in Caribbean and Hawaiian waters until February 22, 1937, when she arrived in Norfolk for Training Detachment duty.

On September 14, 1941, *Decatur* arrived in Argentia, Newfoundland, and served on convoy escort and patrol to ports in Iceland until May 17, 1942, when she returned to Boston. From June 4 to August 25, 1942, she performed convoy duty between Norfolk and Key West and from August 30 to October 13 between New York and Guantanamo Bay. From October 1942 until January 1943 she escorted ships out to sea and from New York to Boston. One of those trips from New York to Boston on December 8, 1942, found *Decatur* escorting the *Queen Mary* at 25 to 28 knots, which was considerably faster than the normal convoy speed. Since The *Queen* was being employed as a primary troop transport, she made the most of her speed capability to out run any potential German submarine.

Decatur departed for the Mediterranean on February 11 by way of Aruba, Netherlands West Indies, in company with USS *Roper* and USS *Dickerson*, escorting the Fleet Oilers, USS *Mattaponi* (CTG 21.5) and USS *Chirrano*. From Aruba they picked up convoy DT-2 and headed for the Mediterranean. *Decatur* made four more voyages from New York and Aruba to the Mediterranean until October.

On Tuesday, November 16, 1943, *Decatur* was operating out of NOB Hampton Roads off the Virginia Capes for aircraft training exercises. While three F4F planes were simulating low altitude strafing attacks, two of the three planes collided in making a turn and crashed into the sea. *Decatur* proceeded immediately to the approximate crash zone at 20 knots and lowered the ship's boat with Crash Party aboard. After patrolling the vicinity and only finding an oil slick and a few pieces of debris, the boat returned to *Decatur*. No survivors were located.

Decatur joined the *Card* (CV-11) task group, sailing from Norfolk on November 24, 1943, for an antisubmarine sweep and returned to New York on January 3, 1944. From January 26 to February 17, she escorted a convoy to Panama and returned with another to Hampton Roads. On March 13, *Decatur* departed Norfolk as flagship of TF 64 with a large convoy of seventy-two merchant ships and

General Statistics

Standard Displacement................1,090 tons
Length Over-all ....314' 4"
Beam ....30' 6"
Maximum Draft.............................12'
Main Battery ....4-4"/50
Antiaircraft Battery ....1-3"/23
Torpedo Battery ....12-21" torpedo tubes
Antisubmarine Weaponry...not in original design
Boilers 4
Machinery ....2 geared turbines, 25,200 SHP
Designed Speed....................... 35 knots
Quarters Available ....9 officers, 144 men

These figures, from *Ships' Data U. S. Naval Vessels 1935*, are for the *Wickes* (DD-75). The statistics for any one ship might vary slightly from those for any other.

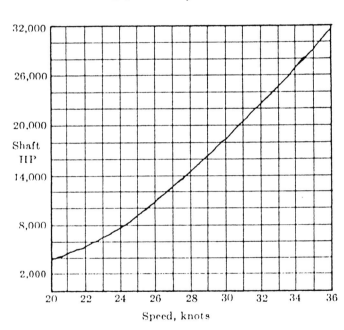

Horsepower vs Speed Curve *USS Hamilton* (DD-141) (Displacement 1,250 tons)

Data on *Hamilton* and other destroyers indicates the following variation in horsepower required to make 35 knots for different displacements:

1,163 tons—25,100 SHP
1,250 tons—29,300 SHP
1,305 tons—32,400 SHP

Data adapted from "Full Scale Trials on a Destroyer" by H. E. Saunders and A. S. Pitre in Society of Naval Architects and Marine Engineers *Transactions*, Vol. 41, 1933, pp. 243-295.

USS *Decatur* (DD-341) General Statistics

90

eighteen LSTs to Bizerte, Tunisia. On March 31, TF 64 successfully fought off a coordinated German submarine and plane strike between Oran and Algiers. Some twenty German planes participated in the strike, first dropping a string of flares over the column. Every gun of the Task Force opened fire and splashed three and possibly a fourth enemy torpedo bomber. *Decatur* experienced one personnel casualty believed to have been from a 20mm shell dropping from the convoy's barrage rather than by a strafing attack from one of the planes. The attack appeared to develop on the quarters of the convoy away from *Decatur's* van position. The only damage sustained was to the SS *Jared Ingersoll*, which was hit by an aircraft torpedo on her port bow. However, she was salvaged and much of her cargo saved. The convoy arrived at Bizerte on April 3, 1944.

Decatur returned to Boston on May 2, for a brief overhaul and then to Norfolk on July 2, 1944, from where she performed escort and training duty in the Caribbean until June 30, 1945. She was decommissioned on July 28, 1945, at the Philadelphia Naval Shipyard and sold on November 30, 1945. *Decatur* received two battle stars for her World War II service. (DD-341, Ship's History, pp. 7–9)

USS *Decatur* (DD-341) off the New York Navy Yard August 7, 1943. Courtesy of A. D. Baker III. Courtesy of the Naval Historical Center.

USS *Decatur* (DD-936) at Sea, April 1963.
Photographer; PH2 Joel S. Cary. Courtesy of
the Naval Historical Center.

Insignia of USS *Decatur.*
This emblem was in use in
1960. Courtesy of Capt. G.
F. Swainson and the Naval
Historical Center.

CHAPTER 9

USS *DECATUR* (DD-936)

The fourth *Decatur* (DD-936) was built by the Bethlehem Steel Company of Quincy, Massachusetts, as a Forest Sherman Class Destroyer. She was launched on December 15, 1955, and sponsored by Mrs. W. A. Pierce and Mrs. D. J. Armsden, both descendents of Commodore Decatur. USS *Decatur* (DD-936) was commissioned on December 7, 1956, and Commander John J. Skahill, USN took command, as her first commanding officer. *Decatur* was homeported at Newport, Rhode Island and participated in the NATO Operation "Strikeback" in September and October 1957. Following local operations she sailed to the Mediterranean for a tour of duty with the 6th Fleet from February to August 1958. While in the Mediterranean, Comdr. Seymour Dumbroff relieved Commander Skahill as commanding officer of the USS *Decatur* (DD-936) on July 10, 1958.

Decatur returned to the Mediterranean for another 6th Fleet tour from August 1959 to February 1960. During this cruise Comdr. Alpine W. McLane relieved Commander Dumbroff of command of *Decatur* on October 15, 1959.

After her return from the Mediterranean *Decatur* joined in antisubmarine exercises and a Midshipman cruise from March to September 1960. This was followed by a cruise north of the Arctic Circle through the Mediterranean, Suez Canal, Arabian Sea, and Indian Ocean before returning to the Mediterranean and 6th Fleet and then home to Newport in December 1960.

On May 12, 1961, Comdr. Royal T. Daniel, Jr. relieved Commander McLane of command of *Decatur*. In September of 1961 *Decatur* was serving as flagship of Destroyer Squadron 20, when one of the highlights of her relatively brief career occurred. *Decatur* recovered the first orbital spacecraft which carried a "robot astronaut" and was the first NASA spacecraft launched with the intention of having it recovered.

After an overhaul in the Boston Naval Shipyard from October 11, 1961, to February 1, 1962, and refresher training in the Caribbean, *Decatur* continued antisubmarine warfare training with USS *Lake Champlain* (CVS-39) along the Eastern Seaboard until November 1962. Decatur then participated in the Cuban crisis with this task group into December. (DD-936, Ship's History, pp. 10–13)

In preparation for deployment Decatur sailed to the Caribbean in January 1963. While performing various exercises, *Decatur* lost steering control on the bridge at 1:30 P.M. on January 22, 1963. (*Decatur* Deck Log of January 22, 1963)

Following the Caribbean exercises *Decatur* was moored starboard side to USS *Cascade* (AD-16), berth 152, pier 1, U.S. Naval Base, Newport, in a nest of five ships on February 13, 1963. While making her approach to berth 132, pier 1, at 9:10 A.M. HMCS *Gatineau* (DD-236) struck USS *Decatur* (DD-936) and USS *Purvis* (DD-709). Damage to the *Decatur* was as follows: two to four feet of the port side of the fantail on the main deck was sheared off; the degaussing cable was partially severed; after steering and shipfitter's shop after bulkheads were slightly buckled; gasoline racks for p-500 and p-250 pump gas cans were smashed; and the flagstaff, several stan-

Comdr. Alpine W. McLane relieving Comdr. Seymour (n) Dombroff as commanding officer of USS *Decatur* on October 15, 1959. Courtesy of the Decatur Mediterranean Cruise Book, 1959–1960, as provided by Mr. Larry Lee, Jr. Cruise book photographed by John Ballou.

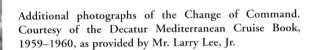

Additional photographs of the Change of Command. Courtesy of the Decatur Mediterranean Cruise Book, 1959–1960, as provided by Mr. Larry Lee, Jr.

chions, and two cleats were sheared off. There were no personnel casualties and there was no apparent underwater hull damage. (*Decatur* Deck Log for February 13, 1963)

On March 7, 1963, *Decatur* departed Newport for the Mediterranean leading a Destroyer Squadron. There she participated in exercises in the Middle East off Jidda, Saudi Arabia, as well as in the Mediterranean with the French throughout the spring and summer of 1963. On May 21, 1963, while steaming in company with USS *Saratoga* (CVA-60), *Decatur* again lost steering control on the bridge at 6:36 A.M. The problem turned out to be a burned out coil in the starboard motor. (*Decatur* Deck Log for May 21, 1963) On May 22, 1963, at 9:05 A.M., Comdr. Thomas F. Booker relieved Comdr. Royal T. Daniel, Jr., as commanding officer of USS *Decatur* (DD-936) (*Decatur* Deck Log for May 22, 1963)

Decatur was enroute to Newport in company with a unit of Task Force 26, including USS *Enterprise* (CVA (N) 65) on September 1, 1963. At 2:32 P.M. *Enterprise* Helo No. 62 was over the *Decatur* fantail to receive movies, when it lost engines, crashed into the starboard side of the fantail, and fell into the water at latitude 36–41'N, longitude 52–00'W. *Decatur* immediately maneuvered to recover Helo personnel. By 2:42 *Decatur* recovered the Helo pilot, Lieutenant Commander Sharpe and crewman RD3 Green. There were no personnel injuries. Damage to the *Decatur* fantail included five stanchions and 40 feet of shaking and lifeline carried away. (*Decatur* Deck Log for September 1, 1963) *Decatur* returned to her home port of Newport that fall of 1963 and after a few weeks of rest and relaxation continued local operations into the spring of 1964.

On the morning of May 6, 1964, at 7:00, USS *Decatur* (DD 936) had just completed refueling operations with the USS *Lake Champlain* (CVS 39) on *Decatur's* port side at Latitude 86 degrees–18 minutes North, Longitude 73 degrees–49 1/2 minutes West. All lines were cleared and the *Decatur* Officer of the Deck Lt. (jg) Charles J. McKenna, USNR, ordered "All Ahead Full, RPMs for 22 knots." The last ordered heading was 198, which had been given shortly before all lines were clear. In coming to that course the ship's head swung left past 198.5 and the helmsman, QM3 A. J. Smulling, attempted to take off the left rudder. He was steering on the combination of port motor, port cable. When the rudder failed to respond, Smulling placed the wheel right, left, and then right 18–20 degrees. Realizing that he had lost control, he announced twice "Bridge has lost steering control." His first report came almost at the same time that the engine rooms were answering the all ahead full bell. Smulling then sounded the steering alarm and announced that the rudder was at 10 degrees left.

USS *Decatur* (DD-936) in formation heading to the Western Mediterranean and Fleet Exercises in the summer of 1959. Courtesy of Decatur Mediterranean Cruise Book, as provided by Mr. Larry Lee, Jr.

Above: Spacecraft in the water alongside USS *Decatur* (DD-936) with recovery line attached, September 1961. Sequence of photographs of *Decatur*'s recovery of the first orbital spacecraft carrying a "robot astronaut." This was the first NASA spacecraft launched with the intention of having it recovered. Photograph by and courtesy of GMGC Gilbert A. Freihoffer, USN (Ret), as provided by Larry Lee, Jr.

Right: Spacecraft being hoisted aboard USS *Decatur*. Photograph by and courtesy of GMGC Gilbert A. Freihoffer, USN (Ret), as provided by Larry Lee, Jr.

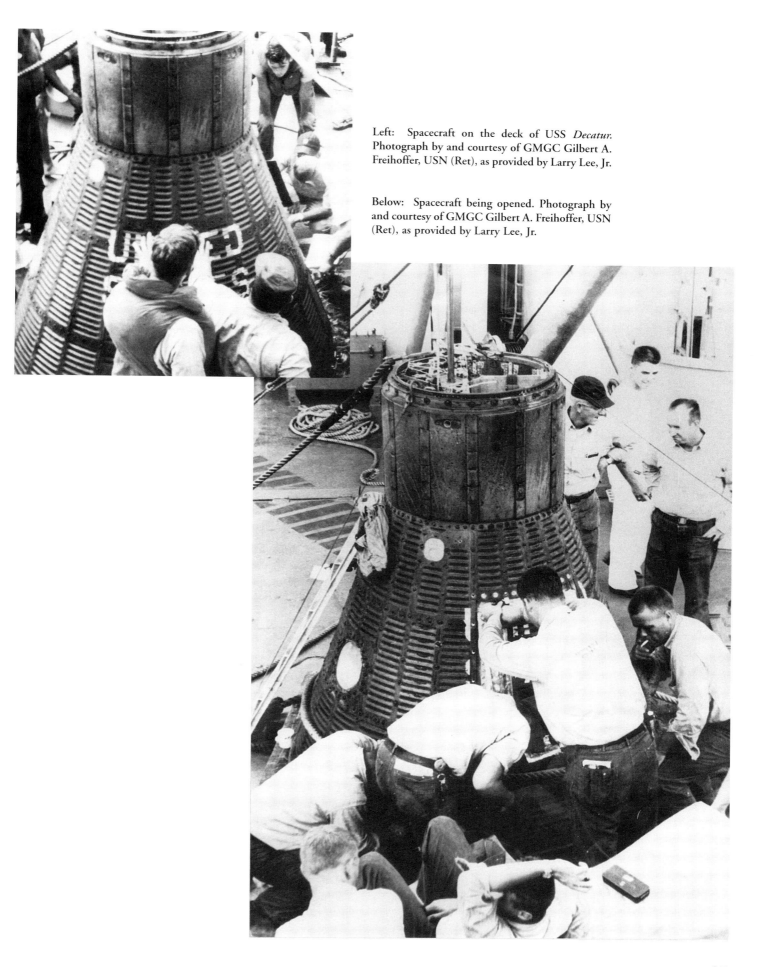

Left: Spacecraft on the deck of USS *Decatur*. Photograph by and courtesy of GMGC Gilbert A. Freihoffer, USN (Ret), as provided by Larry Lee, Jr.

Below: Spacecraft being opened. Photograph by and courtesy of GMGC Gilbert A. Freihoffer, USN (Ret), as provided by Larry Lee, Jr.

Above: USS *Decatur* collides with the USS *Lake Champlain* (CVS-39) on the morning of May 6, 1964. View showing the Decatur's mast toppling to the water. Photograph taken by AN Thomas J. Parrett, USN. Courtesy of the Judge Advocate General, Department of the Navy.

From the time of the first "Lost Steering Control" announcement Lieutenant (jg) McKenna issued the following orders and instructions:

To the Helmsman: "Repeat or What."

To the 1JV Phone Talker: "Does after steering have control?"

To the Junior OOD (JOOD): "Tell the carrier we have lost steering control."

To the Helmsman: "Port Engine Ahead Full; Starboard Engine Stop. Starboard Engine Back two thirds."

To All Concerned: "Clear the Port Wing–Get in the Pilot House."

Just prior to the steering alarm sounding, the after steering watch heard an unusual noise from the port unit. However, everything appeared normal. At the sounding of the alarm, the six-way valve was shifted to activate the starboard unit. QM3 Carolus J. Davis promptly engaged the trick wheel and brought the rudder from its locked position of 7–8 degrees left to amidships and requested instructions from the bridge. The time required to make the shift was estimated to be between 3 and 7 seconds.

The back 2/3 bell was received in engineering before the starboard shaft had built up to 182 RPMs in response to the "All Engines Ahead Full."

Aerial view showing port side of the USS *Decatur* after the collision with the USS *Lake Champlain*. Photograph by PHC James R. Avery, USN. Courtesy of the Judge Advocate Gene-ral, Department of the Navy.

The back 2/3 bell was answered as if it were an emergency (ie; the astern throttle was being opened as the ahead throttle was being closed). At the time of impact the starboard shaft had begun to reverse.

The commanding officer of the *Lake Champlain* observed the *Decatur* clearing, sheering in towards him, steadying on a parallel course momentarily, then sheering in again at an accelerated rate. He ordered "All Engines Back Emergency Full" just as his officer of the deck announced that *Decatur* had reported loss of steering control on the Primary Tactical Circuit (.). The commanding officer subsequently ordered "Left Full Rudder."

The collision occurred between 15 and 30 seconds after the first "Lost Steering Control" announcement at approximately 7:30 **Q**. The collision alarms were sounded on both vessels prior to the collision. The two ships were in physical contact for approximately 2 to 3 minutes.

The *Decatur* commanding officer (CO), Comdr. T. F. Booker gave the order for "All Engines Stop" and it was executed while the two ships were in contact. The officer of the deck and CO *Decatur* gave orders for all personnel to clear the bridge and pilot house. *Decatur's* forward electrical switchboard was stripped, deenergizing circuits forward of the Number One Fireroom and above the main deck.

The only personnel casualty was the *Decatur* OOD, Lieutenant (jg) McKenna, who, while directing evacuation of the bridge, was struck by the MK 56 Gun Director, which fell from its mounting onto the starboard wing of the Bridge. McKenna requested a morphine shot before being transported to sickbay. The Deck Log indicated that he had injured his hip.

Following the accident *Decatur* set course for Norfolk under her own power, but accompanied by the USS *Gearing* (DD 710). Enroute, the fleet tug, USS *Sukori* (ATF 162) took *Decatur* in tow in the early morning of the 7th of May for the final leg of the trip. *Decatur* arrived in Norfolk later that day and tied up alongside the destroyer tender, USS *Shenandoah* (AD 26).

Witnesses reported several impacts between the *Decatur* and the *Lake Champlain* characterized as crushing downward blows from the carrier's overhang to the forward superstructure of the *Decatur*. Both of *Decatur's* masts were broken off, the MK 56 gun director was toppled, the pilot house roof

Above: Overall three-quarter stern view of the USS *Decatur* showing damage caused by the collision with the USS *Lake Champlain*. Photograph by PHC James R. Avery, USN. Courtesy of the Judge Advocate General, Department of the Navy.

crushed, and both stacks were raked off. No fires or flooding occurred on *Decatur*. Cost of repairs to *Decatur* were estimated at $2.7 million dollars.

Damage to the *Lake Champlain* in comparison was relatively minor. Catwalks were damaged and some holes were punched through the skin of the ship. An S2F aircraft was damaged by the main yard arm of *Decatur*. Cost of repairs to the *Lake Champlain* were estimated at $100 thousand dollars and at $25 thousand to the aircraft.

No material defects were found in *Decatur's* steering system and there was no evidence of a material failure or a maintenance mal-practice. The Office of Naval Investigation (ONI) found no culpability on the part of any *Decatur* after steering personnel.

Opinions in the basic final investigative report concerning the collision of the USS *Decatur* (DD 936) and the USS *Lake Champlain* (CVS 39), which occurred on May 6, 1964, included the following:

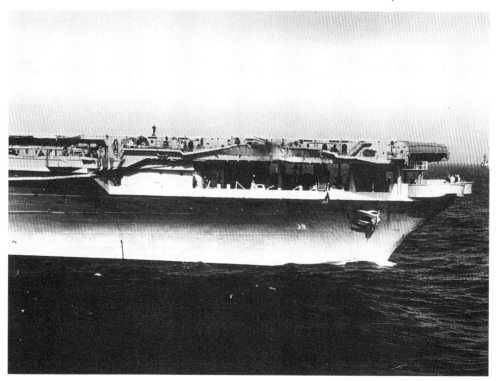

Above: Aerial view showing the starboard bow setion of the USS *Lake Champlain* damaged after the collision with the USS Decatur. Photograph by PHC James R. Avery, USN. Courtesy of the Judge Advocate General, Department of the Navy.

"The proximate cause was a malfunctioning of the *Decatur's* port steering unit in after steering . . ."
"The prompt action taken by both ships was logical . . ."
"Resulting damage was not due to fault, negligence or culpable inefficiency of any person or persons in the naval service . . ."
"Prompt action in stripping the *Decatur's* electrical switchboard prevented additional personnel injuries and material damage from shock and fires . . ."

Recommendations in the final investigative report included the following:

"No disciplinary action should be taken against any individual as a result of this collision . . ."
"Cutler-Hammer steering motor control switches installed in *Decatur* Class ship's after steering spaces, and other Navy ships if applicable, should be redesigned to prevent inadvertent movement . . ."
(JAG Manual Investigative Report on the collision of *Decatur* (DD-936) and Lake Champlain (CVS-39) on May 6, 1964, pp. 1–10)

Left: Damage done to a forward section stateroom on the USS *Lake Champlain* by the collision with the USS *Decatur*. Photograph by PH1 Arthur W. Giverson, USN. Courtesy of the Judge Advocate General, Department of the Navy.

Above: Part of the signal bridge of the USS *Decatur* lodged on the USS *Lake Champlain* after their collision at sea. Photograph by SN F. L. Radford, USN. Courtesy of the Judge Advocate General, Department of the Navy.

Left: Close up of damage to the starboard elevator of the VS-22 S-2 aircraft damaged by the radar mast of the USS *Decatur* during the collision with the USS *Lake Champlain*. Photograph by PH3 Lawrence E. Le Tourneau, USN. Courtesy of the Judge Advocate General, Department of the Navy.

Temporary repairs were soon completed and on May 21, 1964, *Decatur* in company with USS *Northampton* (CC 1) got underway for Newport arriving there on May 23rd. *Decatur* was then placed In Commission In Reserve to await conversion to a Guided Missile Destroyer (DDG 31), as the lead ship of a new class. The other ships of the new class to be similarly converted were the USS *John Paul Jones* (DDG 32), the USS *Parsons* (DDG 33), and the USS *Somers* (DDG 34). (USS *Decatur* [DD 936] Ship's History, pp. 1–5)

CHAPTER 10

USS *DECATUR* (DDG-31)

The conversion of USS *Decatur* (DD-936) to Guided Missile Destroyer USS *Decatur* (DDG-31) commenced on June 15, 1965, and culminated with her commissioning almost two years later. The major improvements during this conversion included the installation of the MK 74 Tartar Missile Weapon System, the MK 68 Gun/Missile Weapon System, AN/SQS-23E Sonar upgrade from 23A, the MK 16 ASROC Launcher Group, MK 32 Torpedo Tubes, AN/SPS-48 Radar (three dimensional), and other structural and space rearrangements.

USS *Decatur* was placed in commission on April 29, 1967, by Rear Adm. Roy Stanley Benson, Commandant, First Naval District and Comdr. Lee Baggett, Jr., assumed command as her first commanding officer. Immediately following the commissioning ceremony Rear Admiral Benson awarded the Navy Cross to HM2 William L. Hickey for meritorious service in Vietnam prior to joining the crew of *Decatur.*

She left Boston on August 22, 1967, enroute to her homeport of Long Beach, California. After visits to St. Thomas, Virgin Islands; San Juan, Puerto Rico; and Ocho Rios, Jamaica, she transited the Panama Canal on September 11 and visited Acapulco, Mexico, before arriving in Long Beach on September 26, 1967. After a brief respite in her new homeport, she got underway for the Seattle and Vancouver area to perform Ship Qualification Trials (SQT) for sonar and torpedo launching. *Decatur* then returned to Long Beach for upkeep and the holidays. In early January 1968 *Decatur* sailed to San Diego for refresher training.

According to the ship's log on Monday, January 15, 1968, *Decatur* was moored with her anchor chain bow on to mooring buoy 20 in San Diego Bay with a stern line to buoy 21. After disconnecting water and phone service from buoy 20 the anchor chain mooring to buoy 20 was replaced with a dip rope. At 7:45 A.M. the Section II Special Sea and Anchor Detail was set for completion of exercise Z-5-S, duty section getting the ship underway. At 7:47 the mooring line from buoy 21 was disconnected. At 8:00 all preparations for getting underway were completed. The officer of the deck had the conn and began maneuvering at 8:01 at various engine combinations to clear buoy 20. At 8:15 the Captain took the conn and at 8:18 mooring buoy 20 submerged on the starboard side at approximately frame 32. At 8:28 Sonar reported a leak in the starboard bulkhead of compartment 4-39-O-Q and at 8:32 mooring buoy 20 surfaced on the starboard side at approximately frame 35.

Facing page top: *Decatur* (Ex-DD-936) undergoing conversion to a Guided Missile Destroyer at the Boston Naval Shipyard during the mid-1960s. Photograph by B. D. Sullivan. Courtesy of the USS *Decatur* (DDG-31), The First Year, 1968 Cruise Book, Taylor Publishing Company and the Naval Historical Center.

Facing page bottom left: Comdr. Lee Baggett, Jr., USN, takes command of the USS *Decatur* (DDG-31) on April 27, 1967. Photograph by B. D. Sullivan. Courtesy of the USS *Decatur* (DDG-31, The First Year, 1968 Cruise Book, Taylor Publishing Company and the Naval Historical Center.

Bottom page right: First of a new class of ship, the Decatur Class, joins the Fleet, April 27, 1967. Almost two years since the collision with the USS *Lake Champlain* (CVS-39) the USS *Decatur* (DD-936) is superseded by a new relation, the USS *Decatur* (DDG-31). Photograph by B. D. Sullivan. Courtesy of the USS *Decatur* (DDG-31), The First Year, 1968 Cruise Book, Taylor Publishing Company and the Naval Historical Center. Photographs of cruise book pictures in this cahpter by John Ballou.

Figure 1. Scenario. USS *Decatur* (DDG-31) San Diego Buoy Snagging (fouling), January 1968. Sketch courtesy of Jeffrey V. Wilson, December 22, 1997.

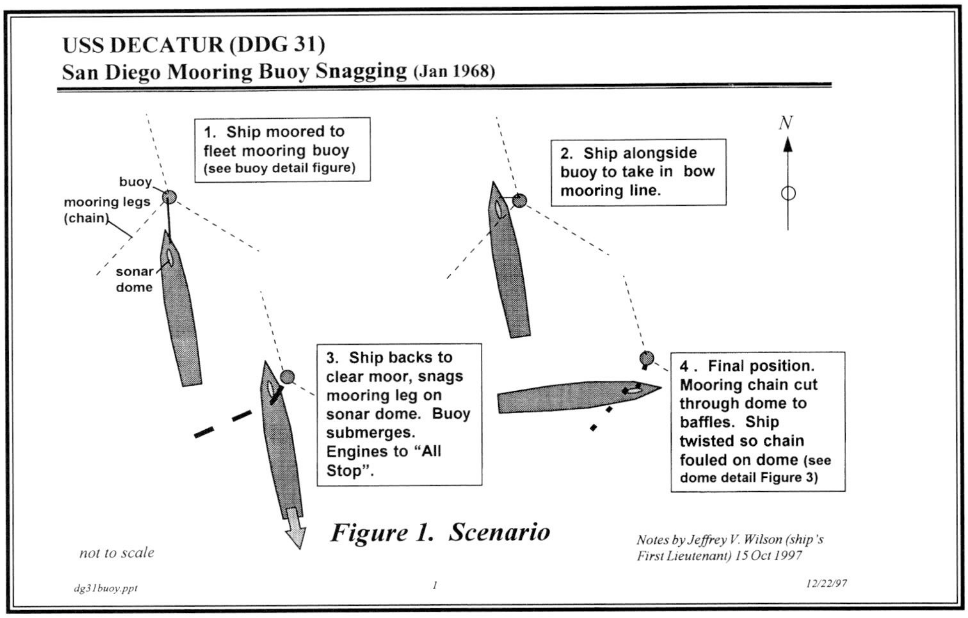

Figure 2. Buoy Detail. USS *Decatur* (DDG-31) San Diego Mooring Buoy Snagging (fouling), January 1968. Sketch courtesy of Jeffrey V. Wilson, December 22, 1997.

Figure 3. Final Snag (fouling) Detail. USS *Decatur* (DDG-31) San Diego Mooring Buoy Snaging (fouling), January 1968. Sketch courtesy of Jeffrey V. Wilson, December 22, 1997.

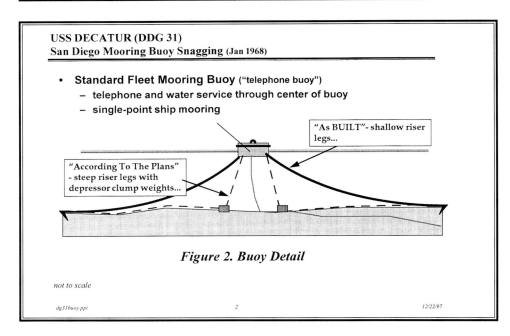

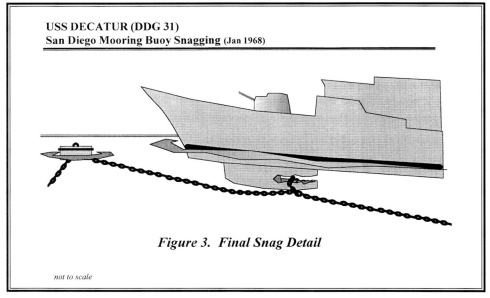

We set the Sea Detail as usual, disconnected the phone and water lines, recovered the motor whale boat and got ready to leave the mooring. The ship moved forward, we slacked the mooring line and, as the ship moved to place the mooring buoy alongside our starboard bow, we recovered the mooring line (step 2, Figure 1).

I then heard someone from the bridge order backing bells and I watched the buoy to be sure we cleared safely as we backed away. For several minutes we didn't seem to move at all. On the foc'sle we waited, assuming the bridge had other business to do. Finally, I could feel the vibrations of heavy backing bells. About that time, I saw the buoy start to submerge alongside the starboard bow and told the phone talker 'Foc'sle recommends All Stop. The buoy's submerging.' (step 3, Figure 1).

Backing immediately stopped. The buoy partially surfaced. Someone called down from the bridge and told me to check out the problem so I got into my wet suit and, along with one of the other swimmers, went into the water to check out the situation.

By the time we got into the water, the ship had moved into the position shown in step 4 of Figure 1. The buoy was now a few yards off the port bow. My buddy and I swam to the buoy and from the surface we could see that the mooring chain was not descending to the bottom but was tending off toward the Decatur. With an appropriate exchange of curses, we snorkeled along toward the port bow. With a couple of short dives we discovered that the mooring chain had sawed through the back side of the sonar dome, producing a slot 13 feet long and 1 foot high. With the ship rotated from its original mooring heading, the mooring leg chain now passed from port to starboard under the dome, then up the starboard side of the dome, through the cut in the dome, down the port side of the dome and then on back under the dome and down toward the mooring chain anchor position, as shown in Figure 3.

I remember surfacing off the starboard bow and seeing LCDR McDaniel's face leaning over the rail. I seem to remember saying 'you're not going to like this, sir'—or words to that effect. I hustled up to the bridge and sketched out the situation for CAPT Baggett while somebody worked to dry me off so I wouldn't drip all over the notes.

We were well and truly fouled, and it was pretty well beyond our own capabilities to get ourselves free without a lot of risk to the crew and ship. CAPT Baggett immediately departed for shore and returned not much later with a crew of salvage divers from the shipyard. They cut the chain to set us free and from there we proceeded directly to the Long Beach Naval Shipyard for drydocking to replace the dome.

JAG Investigative Report opinions:

That when Decatur was maneuvered with engines and rudders on 15 January 1968 between the times of 0801U and 0854U, the chain of mooring leg "E" of buoy 20 penetrated the after end of the sonar dome and continued this penetration of the dome with a "sawing" action for a distance of about 13 1/2 feet on the starboard side and about 10 feet on the port side . . .

That no negligence or other culpability on the part of the Commanding Officer or of any other Decatur personnel has been established by this investigation . . .

That the lack of readily available complete and accurate information concerning the details of the mooring arrangement of buoy 20 is a significant contributing circumstance leading to and connected with the fouling of e sonar dome with a buoy chain from buoy 20 . . .

That assignment of buoy 20 as a mooring for destroyer type ships is not desirable under normal conditions due to its mooring chain arrangement . . .

JAG Investigative Report recommendationss:

That no punitive action or censure be directed against any Decatur personnel . . .

That destroyer type ships not be assigned to moor to buoy 20 or to any other buoys with similar mooring arrangements . . .

(JAG Manual Investigative Report on damage incurred by DECATUR to the sonar dome on January 15, 1968, pp. 1–12)

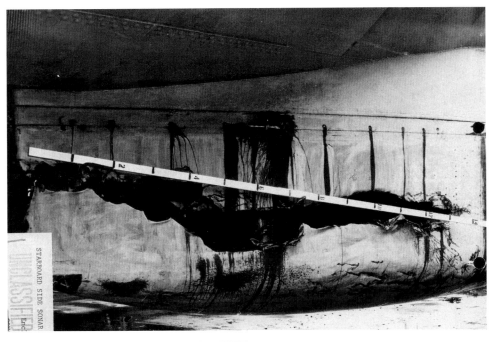

Right: Photograph of the damage to the starboard side of the USS *Decatur* (DDG-31) sonar dome, while in drydock at the Long Beach Naval Shipyard following the mooring buoy snagging (fouling), January 1968. Courtesy of the Judge Advocate general, Department of the Navy.

Below: Photograph of the damage to the port side of the USS *Decatur* (DDG-31) sonar dome, while in drydock at the Long Beach Naval Shipyard following the mooring buoy snagging (fouling), January 1968. Courtesy of the Judge Advocate General, Department of the Navy.

According to Lt. Jeff Wilson, *Decatur's* first lieutenant, who was at his Sea Detail station on the foc'sle and had the closest on-scene view, the incident was described as shown on page 105.

Lieutenant Wilson also provided Figure 1 to describe the mooring positions during the snagging and Figure 2 to describe the bad information available on the buoy design, as opposed to the actual situation with three taut chain legs at very shallow angles from the surface. His Figure 3 depicts how badly the ship was fouled on the buoy anchor chain in the buoy snagging incident. Lieutenant Wilson used sketches similar to these in his statement during the investigation, which assisted considerably in the final determination.

Opinions in the final investigative report concerning circumstances connected with the damage incurred by the *Decatur* to the sonar dome on January 15, 1968, in San Diego Harbor in the vicinity of Buoy 20 included those listed on page 105.

The investigative report also made recommendations that included those listed on page 105.

Similar to his earlier counterpart, Ensign Chester W. Nimitz, Commander Baggett went on to a very distinguished navy career. Among other notable achievements before his retirement, Admiral Lee Baggett, Jr., served as Commander-in-Chief, Atlantic and Supreme Allied Commander, Atlantic.

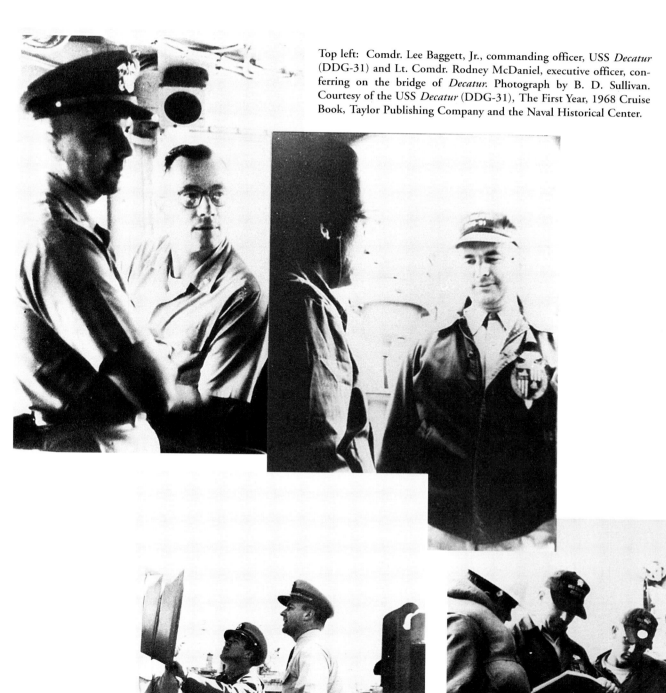

Top left: Comdr. Lee Baggett, Jr., commanding officer, USS *Decatur* (DDG-31) and Lt. Comdr. Rodney McDaniel, executive officer, conferring on the bridge of *Decatur*. Photograph by B. D. Sullivan. Courtesy of the USS *Decatur* (DDG-31), The First Year, 1968 Cruise Book, Taylor Publishing Company and the Naval Historical Center.

Bottom right and top right: Lt. Comdr. Rodney B. McDaniel, USS *Decatur* (DDG-31) executive officer checking records, and inspecting the Watch and material condition of the ship. Photographs by B. D. Sullivan. Courtesy of the USS *Decatur* (DDG-31), The First Year, 1968 Cruise Book, Taylor Publishing Company and the Naval Historical Center.

Above: Lt. Gerald F. Gneckow, weapons officer, USS Decatur (DDG-31). Photograph by B. D. Sullivan. Courtesy of the USS Decatur (DDG-31), The First Year, 1968 Cruise Book, Taylor Publishing Company and the Naval Historical Center.

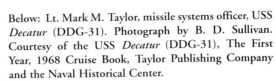

Below: Lt. Mark M. Taylor, missile systems officer, USS Decatur (DDG-31). Photograph by B. D. Sullivan. Courtesy of the USS Decatur (DDG-31), The First Year, 1968 Cruise Book, Taylor Publishing Company and the Naval Historical Center.

Above: Lt. Jeffrey V. Wilson, first lieutenant, USS Decatur (DDG-31), November 1966 to March 1968. Photograph by B. D. Sullivan. Courtesy of the USS Decatur (DDG-31), The First Year, 1968 Cruise Book, Taylor Publishing Company and the Naval Historical Center.

Above: Ens. Larry Meyer, missile officer, 1967. Photograph by B. D. Sullivan. Courtesy of the USS Decatur (DDG-31), The First Year, 1968 Cruise Book, Taylor Publishing Company and the Naval Historical center.

Above: Lt. James Tyng, ASW officer, 1967. Photograph by B. D. Sullivan. Courtesy of the USS Decatur (DDG-31), The First Year, 1968 Cruise Book, Taylor Publishing Company and the Naval Historical Center.

Right: Lt. (jg) T. M. Moore, ASW officer, November 1967 to December 1968. Photograph by B. D. Sullivan. Courtesy of the USS Decatur (DDG-31), The First Year, 1968 Cruise Book, Taylor Publishing Company and the Naval Historical Center.

Lt. (jg) Grant P. Kimball, first lieutenant, March 1968. Photograph by B. D. Sullivan. Courtesy of the USS Decatur (DDG-31), The First Year, 1968 Cruise Book, Taylor Publishing Company and the Naval Historical Center.

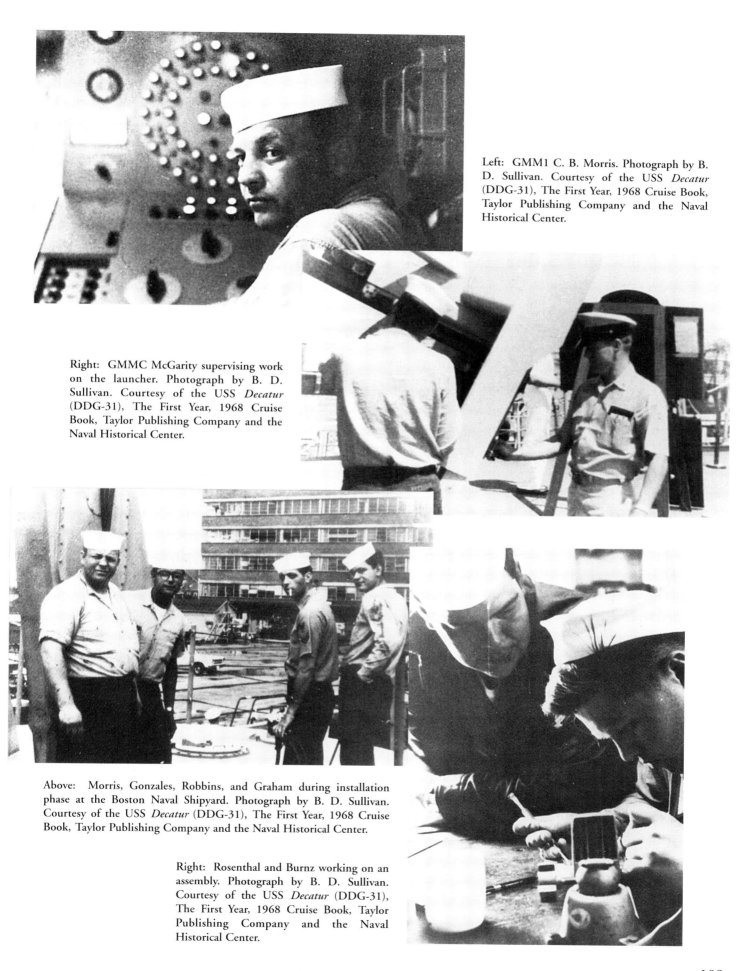

Left: GMM1 C. B. Morris. Photograph by B. D. Sullivan. Courtesy of the USS *Decatur* (DDG-31), The First Year, 1968 Cruise Book, Taylor Publishing Company and the Naval Historical Center.

Right: GMMC McGarity supervising work on the launcher. Photograph by B. D. Sullivan. Courtesy of the USS *Decatur* (DDG-31), The First Year, 1968 Cruise Book, Taylor Publishing Company and the Naval Historical Center.

Above: Morris, Gonzales, Robbins, and Graham during installation phase at the Boston Naval Shipyard. Photograph by B. D. Sullivan. Courtesy of the USS *Decatur* (DDG-31), The First Year, 1968 Cruise Book, Taylor Publishing Company and the Naval Historical Center.

Right: Rosenthal and Burnz working on an assembly. Photograph by B. D. Sullivan. Courtesy of the USS *Decatur* (DDG-31), The First Year, 1968 Cruise Book, Taylor Publishing Company and the Naval Historical Center.

Below left: Schmitz, Lawrence, and Connelly supporting the AN/SPS-48 Radar. Photograph by B. D. Sullivan. Courtesy of the USS *Decatur* (DDG-31), The First Year, 1968 Cruise Book, Taylor Publishing Company and the Naval Historical Center.

Right: Ens. Meyer and FTM1 Petzold comparing notes. Photograph by B. D. Sullivan. Courtesy of the USS *Decatur* (DDG-31), The First Year, 1968 Cruise Book, Taylor Publishing Company and the Naval Historical Center.

Bottom: BMC McMillan and BM1 Manual of the deck division. Photograph by B. D. Sullivan. Courtesy of the USS *Decatur* (DDG-31), The First Year, 1968 Cruise Book, Taylor Publishing Company and the Naval Historical Center.

Left: BM3 Angel and BM3 Copeland on the deck planning ahead. Photograph by B. D. Sullivan. Courtesy of the USS *Decatur* (DDG-31), The First Year, 1968 Cruise Book, Taylor Publishing Company and the Naval Historical Center.

Above: STG3 Robison on watch in sonar. Photograph by B. D. Sullivan. Courtesy of the USS *Decatur* (DDG-31), The First Year, 1968 Cruise Book, Taylor Publishing Company and the Naval Historical Center.

Above: STG2 Madore and STG2 Bauer in underwater battery plot. Photograph by B. D. Sullivan. Courtesy of the USS *Decatur* (DDG-31), The First Year, 1968 Cruise Book, Taylor Publishing Company and the Naval Historical Center.

Above: STG2 Dias and STG2 Madore. Photograph by B. D. Sullivan. Courtesy of the USS *Decatur* (DDG-31), The First Year, 1968 Cruise Book, Taylor Publishing Company and the Naval Historical Center.

Right: ASROC Gunner's Mate Jordan maintaining his launcher. Photograph by B. D. Sullivan. Courtesy of the USS *Decatur* (DDG-31), The First Year, 1968 Cruise Book, Taylor Publishing Company and the Naval Historical Center.

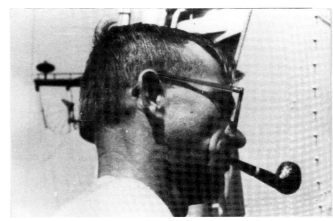

Left: GMG1 Lumby by his gun mount. Photograph by B. D. Sullivan. Courtesy of the USS *Decatur* (DDG-31), The First Year, 1968 Cruise Book, Taylor Publishing Company and the Naval Historical Center.

Below: GMG3 Smith and GMG2 Smits in the gun mount. Photograph by B. D. Sullivan. Courtesy of the USS *Decatur* (DDG-31), The First Year, 1968 Cruise Book, Taylor Publishing Company and the Naval Historical Center.

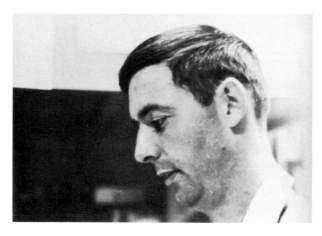

Above: Chief Gunner's Mate Zumbaugh and FTG1 Kincaid in gun plot. Photograph by B. D. Sullivan. Courtesy of the USS *Decatur* (DDG-31), The First Year, 1968 Cruise Book, Taylor Publishing Company and the Naval Historical Center.

Above: Lt. Martin S. Hellewell, operations officer. Photograph by B. D. Sullivan. Courtesy of the USS *Decatur* (DDG-31), The First Year, 1968 Cruise Book, Taylor Publishing Company and the Naval Historical Center.

Left: Lt. James S. Rugowski, CIC officer. Photograph by B. D. Sullivan. Courtesy of the USS *Decatur* (DDG-31), The First Year, 1968 Cruise Book, Taylor Publishing Company and the Naval Historical Center.

Above: Lt. Jack U. Klaas, communications officer. Photograph by B. D. Sullivan. Courtesy of the USS *Decatur* (DDG-31), The First Year, 1968 Cruise Book, Taylor Publishing Company and the Naval Historical Center.

Above: SM3 Hooker awaiting a message. Photograph by B. D. Sullivan. Courtesy of the USS *Decatur* (DDG-31), The First Year, 1968 Cruise Book, Taylor Publishing Company and the Naval Historical Center.

Left: SM2 Morrison rigging a flag hoist. Photograph by B. D. Sullivan. Courtesy of the USS *Decatur* (DDG-31), The First Year, 1968 Cruise Book, Taylor Publishing Company and the Naval Historical Center.

Left: SMSA Munn and SM3 Reed drilling in port. Photograph by B. D. Sullivan. Courtesy of the USS *Decatur* (DDG-31), The First Year, 1968 Cruise Book, Taylor Publishing Company and the Naval Historical Center.

Right: SM2 Morrison and SM3 Gilliland in the signal shack. Photograph by B. D. Sullivan. Courtesy of the USS *Decatur* (DDG-31), The First Year, 1968 Cruise Book, Taylor Publishing Company and the Naval Historical Center.

Above: Chavez, Eagan, and Ream checking messages. Photograph by B. D. Sullivan. Courtesy of the USS *Decatur* (DDG-31), The First Year, 1968 Cruise Book, Taylor Publishing Company and the Naval Historical Center.

Right: RM1 Whitlock in the radio shack. Photograph by B. D. Sullivan. Courtesy of the USS *Decatur* (DDG-31), The First Year, 1968 Cruise Book, Taylor Publishing Company and the Naval Historical Center.

Above: SM3 Reed sending a message. Photograph by B. D. Sullivan. Courtesy of the USS *Decatur* (DDG-31), The First Year, 1968 Cruise Book, Taylor Publishing Company and the Naval Historical Center.

Right: PO2 Rosbury. Photograph by B. D. Sullivan. Courtesy of the USS *Decatur* (DDG-31), The First Year, 1968 Cruise Book, Taylor Publishing Company and the Naval Historical Center.

Left: ETN3 Wilson and ETC Godwin checking in parts. Photograph by B. D. Sullivan. Courtesy of the USS *Decatur* (DDG-31), 1968 Cruise Book, Taylor Publishing Company and the Naval Historical Center.

Below: ETR3 Ketchum at work. Photograph by B. D. Sullivan. Courtesy of the USS *Decatur* (DDG-31), The First Year, 1968 Cruise Book, Taylor Publishing Company and the Naval Historical Center.

Below: ETCS Parker and ETR3 North on watch in Radar. Photograph by B. D. Sullivan. Courtesy of the USS *Decatur* (DDG-31), The First Year, 1968 Cruise Book, Taylor Publishing Company and the Naval Historical Center.

Right: RD3 Alexander maintaining ship's position. Photograph by B. D. Sullivan. Courtesy of the USS *Decatur* (DDG-31), The First Year, 1968 Cruise Book, Taylor Publishing Company and the Naval Historical Center.

Left: RD1 Bunn at the plotter. Photograph by B. D. Sullivan. Courtesy of the USS *Decatur* (DDG-31), The First Year, 1968 Cruise Book, Taylor Publishing Company and the Naval Historical Center.

Below: RD2 Williams and RD2 O'Brien plotting air contacts. Photograph by B. D. Sullivan. Courtesy of the USS *Decatur* (DDG-31), The First Year, 1968 Cruise Book, Taylor Publishing Company and the Naval Historical Center.

Below: RD3 Whiteman and RD3 Kelly reporting contacts. Photograph by B. D. Sullivan. Courtesy of the USS *Decatur* (DDG-31), The First Year, 1968 Cruise Book, Taylor Publishing Company and the Naval Historical Center.

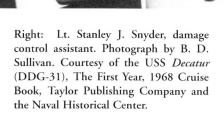

Right: Lt. Stanley J. Snyder, damage control assistant. Photograph by B. D. Sullivan. Courtesy of the USS *Decatur* (DDG-31), The First Year, 1968 Cruise Book, Taylor Publishing Company and the Naval Historical Center.

Above: Lt. Richard H. Renner, engineering officer. Photograph by B. D. Sullivan. Courtesy of the USS *Decatur* (DDG-31), The First Year, 1968 Cruise Book, Taylor Publishing Company and the Naval Historical Center.

Left: Lt. Theodore F. Smolen, main propulsion assistant. Photograph by B. D. Sullivan. Courtesy of the USS *Decatur* (DDG-31), The First Year, 1968 Cruise Book, Taylor Publishing Company and the Naval Historical Center.

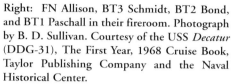

Right: FN Allison, BT3 Schmidt, BT2 Bond, and BT1 Paschall in their fireroom. Photograph by B. D. Sullivan. Courtesy of the USS *Decatur* (DDG-31), The First Year, 1968 Cruise Book, Taylor Publishing Company and the Naval Historical Center.

Left: BT2 Eldington and FN Hodge watching the pressure. Photograph by B. D. Sullivan. Courtesy of the USS *Decatur* (DDG-31), The First Year, 1968 Cruise Book, Taylor Publishing Company and the Naval Historical Center

Above: BT3 Stoffel and BT1 Paschall performing preventive maintenance. Photograph by B. D. Sullivan. Courtesy of the USS *Decatur* (DDG-31), The First Year, 1968 Cruise Book, Taylor Publishing Company and the Naval Historical Center.

Above: BT3 Schmidt and BT3 Bowser preparing to blow tubes. Photograph by B. D. Sullivan. Courtesy of the USS *Decatur* (DDG-31), The First Year, 1968 Cruise Book, Taylor Publishing Company and the Naval Historical Center.

Above: MM2 Millar feeding power to the shaft. Photograph by B. D. Sullivan. Cour-tesy of the USS *Decatur* (DDG-31), The First Year, 1968 Cruise Book, Taylor Publishing Company and the Naval His-torical Center.

Below: MM1 Richardson checking out a steam line. Photograph by B. D. Sullivan. Courtesy of the USS *Decatur* (DDG-31), The First Year, 1968 Cruise Book, Taylor Publishing Company and the Naval Historical Center.

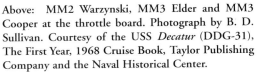

Above: MM2 Warzynski, MM3 Elder and MM3 Cooper at the throttle board. Photograph by B. D. Sullivan. Courtesy of the USS *Decatur* (DDG-31), The First Year, 1968 Cruise Book, Taylor Publishing Company and the Naval Historical Center.

Below: MM2 Shetler watching the gauges. Photograph by B. D. Sullivan. Courtesy of the USS *Decatur* (DDG-31), The First Year, 1968 Cruise Book, Taylor Publishing Company and the Naval Historical Center.

Right: MMCS Dyer maintaining communica-tions. Photograph by B. D. Sullivan. Courtesy of the USS *Decatur* (DDG-31), The First Year, 1968 Cruise Book, Taylor Publishing Company and the Naval Historical Center.

Below: MM2 Hill, FN Gonzales, and IC3 Lyons on watch in the after engine room. Photograph by B. D. Sullivan. Courtesy of the USS *Decatur* (DDG-31), The First Year, 1968 Cruise Book, Taylor Publishing Company and the Naval Historical Center.

Above: FN Allison, FN Schmidt, and FN Terrell at the burners. Photograph by B. D. Sullivan. Courtesy of the USS *Decatur* (DDG-31), The First Year, 1968 Cruise Book, Taylor Pub-lishing Company and the Naval Historical Center.

Below: MR1 Hawkins lending an experienced hand. Photograph by B. D. Sullivan. Courtesy of the USS *Decatur* (DDG-31), The First Year, 1968 Cruise Book, Taylor Publishing Com-pany and the Naval Historical Center.

Right: FN Montoya working on the lathe. Photograph by B. D. Sullivan. Courtesy of the USS *Decatur* (DDG-31), The First Year, 1968 Cruise Book, Taylor Publishing Company and the Naval Historical Center.

Left: SF1 Parker in Repair III. Photograph by B. D. Sullivan. Courtesy of the USS *Decatur* (DDG-31), The First Year, 1968 Cruise Book, Taylor Publishing Company and the Naval Historical Center.

Left: FN Audi working in the shipfitter shop. Photo-graph by B. D. Sullivan. Courtesy of the USS *Decatur* (DDG-31), The First Year, 1968 Cruise Book, Taylor Publishing Compa-ny and the Naval Historical Center.

Below: EM3 Brown and EM3 Kaiser working on one of the shi*p's* circuit boards. Photograph by B. D. Sullivan. Courtesy of the USS *Decatur* (DDG-31), The First Year, 1968 Cruise Book, Taylor Publishing Company and the Naval Historical Center.

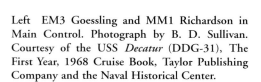

Left EM3 Goessling and MM1 Richardson in Main Control. Photograph by B. D. Sullivan. Courtesy of the USS *Decatur* (DDG-31), The First Year, 1968 Cruise Book, Taylor Publishing Company and the Naval Historical Center.

Keeping the ship's bell shined.

Above: Lt. Ben Birindelli, Supply Officer. Photograph by B. D. Sullivan. Courtesy of the USS *Decatur* (DDG-31), The First Year, 1968 Cruise Book, Taylor Publishing Company and the Naval Historical Center.

Right: SK1 Goebel checking out a requisition. Photograph by B. D. Sullivan. Courtesy of the USS *Decatur* (DDG-31), The First Year, 1968 Cruise Book, Taylor Publishing Com-pany and the Naval Historical Center.

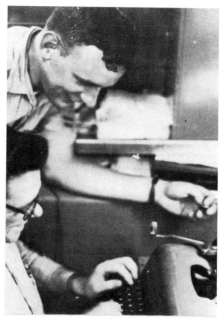

Above: Lt. (jg). Bruce Babbitt, assistant supply officer. Photo-graph by B. D. Sullivan. Courtesy of the USS *Decatur* (DDG-31), The First Year, 1968 Cruise Book, Taylor Publishing Company and the Naval Historical Center.

Right: SK1 Bumber and SK2 Guenther getting out a priority requisition. Photograph by B. D. Sullivan. Courtesy of the USS *Decatur* (DDG-31), The First Year, 1968 Cruise Book, Taylor Publishing Company and the Naval Historical Center.

Below: SN Boehlke re-viewing correspondence. Photograph by B. D. Sullivan. Courtesy of the USS *Decatur* (DDG-31), The First Year, 1968 Cruise Book, Taylor Publishing Company and the Naval

Above: SKSN Hihn posting ship's store receipts. Photograph by B. D. Sullivan. Courtesy of the USS *Decatur* (DDG-31), The First Year, 1968 Cruise Book, Taylor Publishing Company and the Naval Historical Center.

Right: Barber Wilczek trimming away. Photograph by B. D. Sullivan. Courtesy of the USS *Decatur* (DDG-31), The First Year, 1968 Cruise Book, Taylor Publishing Company and the Naval Historical Center

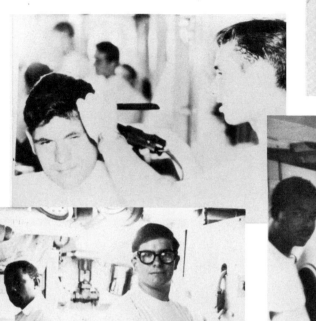

Above: Ship's Store operator Shields. Photograph by B. D. Sullivan. Courtesy of the USS *Decatur* (DDG-31), The First Year, 1968 Cruise Book, Taylor Publishing Company and the Naval Historical Center.

Left: Laundrymen Crowe and Suniga keeping the uniforms smart. Photograph by B. D. Sullivan. Courtesy of the USS *Decatur* (DDG-31), The First Year, 1968 Cruise Book, Taylor Publishing Com-pany and the Naval Historical Center.

Above: SH2 West and McCarthy plying their trade. Photograph by B. D. Sullivan. Courtesy of the USS *Decatur* (DDG-31), The First Year, 1968 Cruise Book, Taylor Publishing Company and the Naval Historical Center.

Left: Lt. D. R. Pauling, navigator. Photograph by B. D. Sullivan. Courtesy of the USS *Decatur* (DDG-31), The First Year, 1968 Cruise Book, Taylor Publishing Company and the Naval Historical Center.

Right: Lt. Gneckow, weapons officer, USS *Decatur* (DDG-31), and assistants underway South from Boston Naval Shipyard, 1967. Photograph by and courtesy of Bruce Babbitt, then assistant supply officer.

Right: USS *Decatur* (DDG-31) passing through the Panama Canal, 1967. Photograph by and courtesy of Bruce Babbitt, then assistant supply officer.

Right: Lt. Gneckow, weapons officer, USS *Decatur* (DDG-31), and assistant taking a break between underway replenishments, 1967. Photograph by and courtesy of Bruce Babbitt, then Assistant Supply Officer.

Above: USS *Decatur* (DDG-31) in the Panama Canal at Sunset, 1967. Photograph by and courtesy of Bruce Babbitt, then assistant supply officer.

Right: USS *Decatur* (DDG-31) in home port of Long Beach, California, 1967. Photograph by and courtesy of Bruce Babbitt, then Assistant Supply Officer.

Above: Mustering the officers, USS *Decatur* (DDG-31), circa 1968. Photograph by and courtesy of Bruce Babbitt, then assistant supply officer.

Above: CWO2 Miller, electronics maintenance officer, USS *Decatur* (DDG-31), on the quarterdeck receiving visitors, 1967. Photograph by and courtesy of Bruce Babbitt, then assistant supply officer.

Right: Mustering the chiefs, USS *Decatur* (DDG-31), circa 1968. Photograph by and courtesy of Bruce Babbitt, then assistant supply officer.

Below: USS *Decatur* (DDG-31) pollywogs ready to cross the Equator, circa 1968. Photograph by and courtesy of Bruce Babbitt, then assistant supply officer.

Below: USS *Decatur* (DDG-31) shellbacks and one pollywog in action, while crossing the Equator, circa 1968. Photograph by and courtesy of Bruce Babbitt, then assistant supply officer.

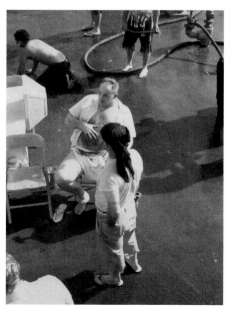

Above: An underway replenishment in the Western Pacific, as seen from the bow of the USS *Decatur* (DDG-31), circa 1968. Photograph by and courtesy of Bruce Babbitt, then assistant supply officer.

Above: USS Decatur (DDG-31) Royal Baby and other Shellbacks in action, while crossing the Equator, circa 1968. Photograph by and courtesy of Bruce Babbitt, then assistant supply officer.

Following completion of Post Shakedown Availability and her second, and this time successful, turn at refresher training *Decatur* began preparations for deployment. She took on her ordnance load out at NWS Seal Beach on July 3 and completed her Tender Availability alongside USS *Delta* (AR-9) from July 5 to 17, 1968.

Comdr. John B. Allen ready to relieve CDR Baggett, as commanding officer, USS *Decatur* (DDG-31), September 19, 1968. Photograph by and courtesy of Bruce Babbitt, then assistant supply officer.

Decatur got underway for her first deployment to WESTPAC on July 18, 1968. After a stop in Pearl Harbor and chop to COMSEVEN-THFLT on August 6, 1968, she held an upkeep period in Yokosuka, Japan, before her first Special Operations on Yankee Station, Gulf of Tonkin from August 23 to September 5, 1968. Following another upkeep in Subic Bay, P.R. *Decatur* returned to Yankee Station from September 12 to October 16. During this operation Comdr. John B. Allen relieved Comdr. Lee Baggett, Jr., as commanding officer. Decatur then visited Singapore and was back on Yankee

Station, where early in the morning of November 20 a Phantom II F-4 crashed on take-off from *Coral Sea* (CV-43). *Decatur* was detached for pilot rescue duty, but six hours of coordinated surface and air search resulted in the recovery of only slight debris at the scene. Following a brief R&R visit to Hong Kong in December, she visited Australia, New Zealand, and American Samoa before departing WESTPAC. Unfortunately, *Decatur* received some world-wide publicity while in Australia, when a locally sponsored hunting trip for twenty-five sailors attracted adverse mention in the press. Conservation authorities were upset that American sailors were hunting the national animal of Australia, but it was pointed out that they were there at the invitation of various Brisbane civic groups and in fact, Kangaroos were killed commercially in large numbers. The fuel stop in Pago Pago, American Samoa, was noteworthy because it typified the people-to-people program *Decatur* initiated through a basketball game, a baseball game, and a small party the crew threw for the local townfolk. After a brief stop in Pearl she arrived in Long Beach on February 26, 1969, following her first successful WESTPAC deployment.

Comdr. John B. Allen, USN, commanding officer, USS *Decatur* (DDG-31), September 19, 1968, to July 14, 1970. Photograph and following photographs by ETC Jerry Fugich. Courtesy of USS *Decatur* (DDG-31) Four Horizons WESTPAC Deployment 2, February 13 to August 29, 1970, Cruise Book, Tiffany Publishing Company, San Diego, and the Naval Historical Center.

After a period of upkeep and leave *Decatur* provided plane guard support to USS *Constellation* (CVA-64) from April 15 to 18, 1969, and then enjoyed an R&R visit to Acapulco, Mexico, from April 24 to 28. Decatur next participated in a Midshipman Cruise from June 8 to July 30, including visits to San Francisco for four days and Pearl Harbor for six days. She was also selected for the DESRON 13 Battle Efficiency, as well as departmental "E"'s in Operations, Engineering, and Missiles before undergoing a tender availability from July 30 to August 21. On August 4 Capt. T. R. Johnson relieved Capt. T. E. Groves as COMDESDIV 132 in a ceremony aboard the ship. Following various at-sea exercises and in-port upkeep periods from September to mid-December, she ended the year with a holiday leave period commencing December 8.

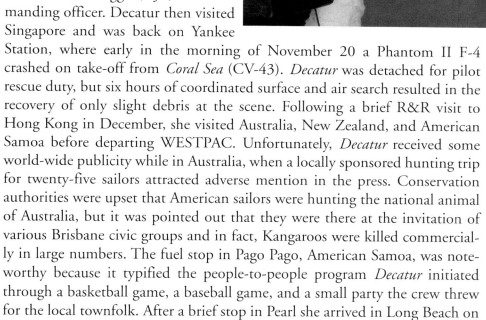

Above: CDR Baggett making his farewell remarks, September 19, 1968. Photograph by and courtesy of Bruce Babbitt, then assistant supply officer.

Right: Commander Baggett departing USS *Decatur* (DDG-31), September 19, 1968. Photograph by and courtesy of Bruce Babbitt, then assistant supply officer.

Left: Commander Baggett cutting his cake, September 19, 1968. Photograph by and courtesy of Bruce Babbitt, then assistant supply officer.

Above: Commander Allen, commanding officer, USS *Decatur* (DDG-31), with his boss on board in the Western Pacific, circa 1968. Photograph by and courtesy of Bruce Babbitt, then assistant supply officer.

Left: Lt. Mark Taylor, Missile System officer and relief, circa 1968. Photograph by and courtesy of Bruce Babbitt, then assistant supply officer.

Decatur spent the first of the year in preparation for her second deployment to WESTPAC and got underway for this deployment on 13 February 1970. After stops in Pearl and Midway, she CHOPPED to Seventh Fleet on 1 March, made a refueling stop in Guam, and arrived in Subic Bay, R.P.I., on March 8. Following a visit to Okinawa in April she performed Special Operations in the Gulf of Thailand in late May and early June and on Yankee Station in June and early July. She then made an R&R visit to Hong Kong, where Comdr. S. A. Swartztrauber relieved Commander Allen as commanding officer on July 14, 1970. After skirting Typhoon Ruby from July 15 to 17 followed by ten days in Subic, *Decatur* got underway on July 27 and visited Sydney, Australia, from August 1 to 5 and then Auckland, New Zealand from August 10 to 13. Upon returning to the West Coast and home port of Long Beach, she spent the rest of 1970 in local operations and in-port upkeep periods.

Following a regular shipyard overhaul in Long Beach Naval Shipyard from January to May 1971, *Decatur* got underway for local operations followed by refresher training out of San Diego in June and July. In August and September she performed local operations and began preparations for her third WESTPAC deployment. On September 10 1971 Comdr. T. J. Burke relieved the recently promoted Capt. S. A. Swartztrauber as commanding officer and on September 22 she got underway for a three-day training period.

On the night of September 22 *Decatur* was involved in a dramatic rescue, when while steaming through rough seas the starboard lookout heard a cry for help and man overboard procedures were initiated. After four musters were held and the entire crew accounted for, the search was about to be called off, when a paddle and lifejacket were spotted and the search resumed in earnest. Shortly afterward two people were sighted; a woman in a life jacket and a man clinging to a gas can. The survivors, identified as Mr. and Mrs. Ray Smith of Redondo Beach, California, were brought aboard and given medical aid by the ship's chief hospital corpsman. The Smith's were returned to Long Beach Naval Station that night. Their yacht had apparently struck a submerged object and flooded the battery compartment, so they were unable to radio for help. Forced to abandon ship in the dinghy when the yacht began breaking up, it soon swamped in the rough seas. Fortunately, *Decatur* happened along shortly thereafter.

Decatur departed Long Beach on her third WESTPAC deployment on October 1, 1971. Following stops in Pearl and Subic she was back on Yankee Station in November and December. After a short visit to Subic in between Yankee Station assignments and afterward, she deployed to the Indian Ocean for Special Operations with Task Force 74 from December 16, 1971 to January 11, 1972. Following an in-port Subic period she was back on Yankee Station from January 20 through February 1 before visiting Kaoshiung, Taiwan, and Hong Kong, B.C.C. After another stop in Subic in late February she was on her way home via Darwin, Fremantle, Perth, and Melbourne, Australia; Auckland, New Zealand; Pago Pago, American Samoa; and Pearl Harbor, Hawaii.

After completing this WESTPAC deployment in March 1972 *Decatur* returned to Long Beach on April 7 for a 30-day Post Deployment Stand Down. She spent further time in port through May before Engineering Sea Trials on June 15 followed by further in port time through June 20, while

Comdr. Sayre A. Swarzttrauber, USN, commanding officer, USS *Decatur* (DDG-31), July 14, 1970 to September 10, 1971. Photograph by ETC Fugich. Courtesy of *Decatur* Four Horizons WESTPAC Deployment 2 Cruise Book, Tiffany Publishing Company, San Diego, and the Naval Historical Center.

Lt. Comdr. Gordon L. Thorpe, USN, executive officer, USS *Decatur* (DDG-31). Photograph by ETC Fugich. Courtesy of *Decatur* Four Horizons WESTPAC Deployment 2 Cruise Book, Tiffany Publishing Company, San Diego, and the Naval Historical Center.

Comdr. Robert C. Hurd, USN, commanding officer, USS *Decatur* (DDG-31), April 20, 1973, to April 18, 1975. Photograph from the USS *Decatur* (DDG-31) WESTPAC Deployment, 1974–1975, Cruise Book. Courtesy of the Naval Historical Center.

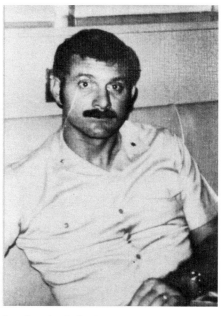

Lt. Comdr. J. D. Fontana, USN, executive officer, USS *Decatur* (DDG-31). Photograph from the USS *Decatur* (DDG-31) WEST-PAC Deployment, 1974–1975, Cruise Book. Courtesy of the Naval Historical Center.

embarking NROTC Midshipmen. From June 21 to August 3 she participated in Exercise PACMIDTRARON-72, including visits to Pearl, Seattle, and San Francisco before returning to Long Beach. She then spent August through December 1972 in port Long Beach and underway in local SOCAL operations before loadout at NWS Seal Beach and preparations for her upcoming WESTPAC deployment.

Decatur departed Long Beach for her fourth WESTPAC deployment on January 3, 1973, and after stops at Pearl and Guam arrived in Subic Bay on January 27. Following an upkeep period in Subic she deployed to the Gulf of Tonkin in February for operations in the Yankee Station Training Area, where she was on AAW Picket Station as Mutual Support Ship for USS *Fox* (DLG-33) and Plane Guard for USS *Enterprise* (CVN-65). *Decatur* then sailed for Kaohsiung, Taiwan, for tender availability from February 28 to March 9. On April 20, 1973, Commander Burke was relieved by Lt. Comdr. Robert C. Hurd as commanding officer.

The ship continued her WESTPAC deployment until July and then visited Subic and Yokosuka before starting home on July 19. She stopped at Midway Island and Pearl enroute and arrived in Long Beach on July 31. After an in-port period in Long Beach she then shifted her home port from Long Beach to San Diego on September 11, 1973. Following a TAV period from September to November she performed local operations finishing out 1973.

For the first half of 1974 *Decatur* was in and out of San Diego for upkeep and an RAV/TAV before departing for her fifth WESTPAC deployment on July 29, 1974. After stops in Hawaii, Midway, and Guam, she arrived in Okinawa on September 8 and participated in a PHIBTRAEX before continuing on to Subic, where she arrived on September 14. Following operations with HMS *Chicester* (F-59) and USS *Constellation* (CVA-64) *Decatur* visited Hong Kong for a little R&R. She then spent the rest of 1974 operating out of Subic with a brief RAV in Guam.

Decatur departed Subic for home on January 8, 1975, and arrived in San Diego on January 27. Following an in-port and upkeep period she commenced a regular overhaul in Long Beach Naval Shipyard on April 15. On April 18, 1975, Commander Hurd was relieved by Comdr. J. D. Korthe as commanding officer. She finished 1975 in the Long Beach Naval Shipyard.

The first three quarters of 1976 were spent on sea trials and underway qualifications and training before *Decatur* departed San Diego for her sixth WESTPAC deployment on September 25, 1976. After visits to Pearl and Sydney, Australia, she participated in an ASW exercise in the South China Sea before arriving in Subic on December 4. She then visited Hong Kong on December 30 to 31 to close out 1976.

Decatur completed her WESTPAC deployment with various training exercises in the South China Sea throughout early 1977. Comdr. G. C. Chappell relieved Commander Korthe as commanding officer on March 10, 1977. The ship then departed Subic for home on April 28, 1977. She arrived in San Diego on May 15 and spent the summer and fall in local southern California operations. She ended the year with a holiday and upkeep period in San Diego from December 14 to 31, 1977.

Following a Restricted Availability in January 1978 Decatur spent February and March in and out of San Diego for engineering drills and trials in the Southern California Operational Areas. In April she was off to Hawaii

Lt. Comdr. Thomas M. Mustin, USN, weapons officer, USS *Decatur* (DDG-31). Photograph by ETC Fugich. Courtesy of *Decatur* Four Horizons WESTPAC Deployment 2 Cruise Book, Tiffany Publishing Company, San Diego, and the Naval Historical Center.

Lt. Comdr. Jack L. Challender, operations officer, USS *Decatur* (DDG-31). Photograph by ETC Fugich. Courtesy of *Decatur* Four Horizons WESTPAC Deployment 2 Cruise Book, Tiffany Publishing Company, San Diego, and the Naval Historical Center.

Lt. Michael B. Tepovich, supply officer, USS *Decatur* (DDG-31). Photograph by ETC Fugich. Courtesy of *Decatur* Four Horizons WESTPAC Deployment 2 Cruise Book, Tiffany Publishing Company, San Diego, and the Naval Historical Center.

Lt. Kellie S. Byerly, engineering officer, USS *Decatur* (DDG-31). Photograph by ETC Fugich. Courtesy of *Decatur* Four Horizons WESTPAC Deployment 2 Cruise Book, Tiffany Publishing Company, San Diego, and the Naval Historical Center.

Lt. William B. Powers, weapons officer, USS *Decatur* (DDG-31). Photograph by ETC Fugich. Courtesy of *Decatur* Four Horizons WESTPAC Deployment 2 Cruise Book, Tiffany Publishing Company, San Diego, and the Naval Historical Center.

Right: Comdr. George C. Chappell, USN, commanding officer, USS *Decatur* (DDG-31), March 10, 1977, to June 19, 1979. Photograph and following photographs by W. D. Ellis. USS *Decatur* (DDG-31) WESTPAC, 1978–1979, Cruise Book. Courtesy of the Naval Historical Center.

to participate in RIMPAC 78 before returning to San Diego in May to begin a summer and fall series of Restricted and Tender Availabilities through October. Following Sea Trials and deployment preparation Decatur departed for her seventh WESTPAC deployment on November 10, 1978. After participating in various gun and missile qualifications and type training in the Hawaiian Area she CHOPPED to COMSEVENTHFLT on December 4. She then made brief fuel stops in Kwajalein and Guam before arriving in Subic for upkeep, training, and in-port Christmas Holiday season R&R. She ended 1978 underway in the South China Sea.

Decatur participated in Indian Ocean Contingency Operations in January and February 1979. She also paid a visit to Karachi, Pakistan, and was enroute to the Seychelles for a port call, when on February 13 she was ordered to return to the Arabian Sea and stand off the coast of Iran in support of the evacuation of American citizens. The night of February 21 she embarked eight American, one British, and twenty-five Thai citizens by small boat transfer from the *Margarett Root II*. Decatur then proceeded to Al Bahrain where all evacuees were disembarked on February 23. She departed Bahrain on February 24 and returned to Subic on March 11. She departed for home on March 19 and participated in Transit Exercise 6-79 in company with USS *Kincaid*, USS *Hoel*, USS *Bradley*, USS *Davidson*, and USS *Somers*. Following brief fuel stops in Guam and then Pearl, where she embarked male relatives of the crew as guests of the Navy, *Decatur* arrived in San Diego on April 8l. After leave and upkeep periods and partici-

USS *Decatur* (DDG-31) Tiger Cruise. Collage of photographs by W. D. Ellis and above photographers from the USS *Decatur* (DDG-31) WESTPAC, 1978–1979, Cruise Book. Courtesy of the Naval Historical Center.

pation in COMPTUEX in April and May, she began pre-overhaul preparations in June. On July 8 she sailed for a change of homeport to Bremerton, Washington, on July 16. On August 1 *Decatur* commenced a Regular Overhaul at Puget Sound Naval Shipyard for the remainder of the year during which Comdr. G. L. Dunn relieved Commander Chappell as commanding officer. The *Decatur* crew earned the Navy Expeditionary Medal and Humani-tarian Action Medal for services in the Indian Ocean during the months of January and February 1979.

Decatur continued her Regular Overhaul until August 26, 1980, during which her homeport was changed back to San Diego on June 15 in anticipation of its completion. She arrived in San Diego on August 31 and began a series of Ship's Qualification Tests and exercises that took

her into the Christmas Holiday season, where she was in port from December 18 to 31, 1980.

In January 1981 *Decatur* conducted Refresher Training and then participated in COMPTUEX 2-81 in February. Following a Restricted Availability and participation in READIEX 4-81 in the Eastern Pacific, she passed her Nuclear Weapons Acceptance Inspection on the second try on April 3. Main Feed Pump problems hampered her preparations for deployment, but she finally departed San Diego on April 25 for weapons loadout at Seal Beach and refueling at Long Beach before departing there on April 27 for her eighth WESTPAC deployment. She caught up with her Task Group in Pearl on 2 May. However, further Main Feed Pump problems caused her to delay departure until May 4 behind the Task Group once again. Following an independent transit of the Pacific with fuel stops in Kwajalein, Guam, and Sasebo, Japan, she finally joined the Task Group for the final days of SOJEX 81-3 on May 20. After a two-week upkeep period in Sasebo, she departed for Pusan, Korea, on June 12 for a four-day visit followed by a Joint Exercise with the Korean Navy. *Decatur* arrived in Subic on June 27 and Comdr. M. J. Mills relieved Commander Dunn as commanding officer on 3 July. After a short upkeep period she made a six-day visit to Hong Kong returning to Subic on August 5 for another eleven-day upkeep period.

Decatur departed Subic on August 17 for her trip "down under" with fuel stops enroute in Guam and Papua, New Guinea. She visited Brisbane, Australia, from August 30 to September 4 and Sydney from September 8 to 13 after which she participated in Sea Eagle 81-2 with our Australian allies from September 14 to 22 followed by Exercise Reconstruction in Sydney from September 23 to 25. Departing Sydney on September 26 she next visited Auckland, New Zealand, from September 29 through October 3. On October 4 *Decatur* sailed for home with stops along the way in Pago Pago, American Samoa, and Pearl arriving in San Diego on October 21. The rest of 1981 was spent accomplishing much needed repair work and preparing for INSURV inspection scheduled for January 1982.

On completion of a successful INSURV inspection *Decatur* began a Planned Restricted Availability on January 11, 1982, followed by preparations for an Operational Propulsion Plant Examination (OPPE) with a Mobile Training Team (MTT) Phase II on board from March 2 to 6. After conducting further MTT Phase II and other pre-deployment training through June she successfully passed the OPPE on July 12 to 14. She next joined FLEETEX 1-82 for two weeks and then commenced Refresher Training on August 2 followed by an upkeep period into September during which several SHIPALT's were installed. After final deployment preparations *Decatur* got underway from San Diego on October 30, 1982, with other DESRON Seven ships for her ninth WESTPAC deployment.

On November 8, 1982, the Office of the Secretary of Defense announced the planned decommissioning and retirement of *Decatur* in Fiscal Year 1983 along with the rest of her class. The ships to be decommissioned were programmed for transfer to the Navy's inactive fleet for use as mobilization assets or as sources of logistics support for active fleet ships.

Following a stop in Pearl the DESRON Seven ships arrived in Subic on Thanksgiving Day, November 25. *Decatur* departed Subic on November 29 to participate in Battle Week 83-1 along with more than twenty other ships

Capt. Gerald L. Dunn, commanding officer, USS *Decatur* (DDG-31), June 19, 1979, to July 3, 1981. Photograph courtesy of the USS *Decatur* (DDG-31) Pacific Cruise, Summer 1981, Cruise Book, Walsworth Publishing Company, San Diego, and the Naval Historical Center.

Capt. Dunne Change of Command with Captain Dunne being relieved by Comdr. Michael J. Mills, USN. Collage of Photographs on page 132 courtesy of the USS *Decatur* (DDG-31) Pacific Cruise, Summer 1981, Cruise Book, Walsworth Publishing company, San Diego, and the Naval Historical Center.

Comdr. Michael J. Mills, USN, commanding officer, USS *Decatur* (DDG-31), July 3, 1981, to May 28, 1983. Photograph courtesy USS *Decatur* (DDG-31) Pacific Cruise, Summer 1981, Cruise Book, Walsworth Publishing Company, San Diego, and the Naval Historical Center.

in the South China Sea, Yellow Sea, and Sea of Japan before visiting Hong Kong from December 22 to 25. Underway on December 26 to Thai waters on December 29, she visited Pattaya Beach, Thailand, in time to see the New Year in.

Departing Thailand on January 3, 1983, *Decatur* arrived back in Subic on January 7 to begin preparations for the Indian Ocean and Persian Gulf. She departed Subic on January 22 for a brief stop at Singapore for fuel and provisions on January 25 before transiting the Straits of Malacca the next day. On January 31 she arrived in Colombo, Sri Lanka for a four-day port visit. Getting underway again on February 4, she arrived in the Persian Gulf on February 12 and came under the operational control of COMIDEAST-FOR. Operating almost continuously at sea on the boundaries of the Iran-Iraq war zone, *Decatur* provided surveillance and intelligence support for JCS/USN/USAF mission roles. After completing her missions in the Persian Gulf on April 4 she received commendations for outstanding performances in surveillance operations. Following a stop in Colomba, Sri Lanka, for fuel and supplies, she participated in MEKAR 83-2, a joint USN-Royal Malaysian Navy exercise. *Decatur* then visited Singapore from April 14 to 17 before returning to Subic on April 21. On April 22 she got underway from Subic with DESRON Seven and arrived in Pearl on May 7, where she offloaded a majority of her weapons in preparation for decommissioning on June 30. She got underway from Pearl on May 8 and arrived in San Diego on May 14, where she began preparations for her decommissioning. On May 28, 1983, the executive officer, Comdr. R. G. Allee relieved Comdr. M. J. Mills as commanding officer in a formal Change of Command.

USS *Decatur* (DDG-31) was decommissioned on June 30, 1983. She was then transferred to the Naval Sea Systems Command Detachment, Naval Inactive Ship Maintenance Facility (NAVSEA Det NISMF) Bremerton, Washington, for custody and potential future use as a mobilization asset or as a source of logistics support for active fleet ships. (*Decatur*, DDG-31, Ship's History, pp. 1–20)

USS *Decatur* (DDG-31) underway off San Diego, June 24, 1976. Photograph by PH3 Burgess. Courtesy of the Naval Historical Center.

USS *Decatur* Insignia from Ship's Plaque. Photograph by John Ballou. Courtesy of the author.

Ex-*Decatur* Self Defense Test Ship Underway. Photograph by Naval Surface Warfare Center, Port Hueneme Division, circa 1994. Courtesy of Michael J. Wolfe, SDTS program manager, NSWC, Port Hueneme, California.

Ex-*Decatur* Self Defense Test Ship alongside pier at NSWC, Port Hueneme. Photograph by NSWC, Port Hueneme Division, circa 1994. Courtesy of Michael J. Wolfe, SDTS program manager, NSWC, Port Hueneme, California.

CHAPTER 11

DECATUR, THE SELF-DEFENSE TEST SHIP

On April 4, 1988, the Chief of Naval Operations authorized the Ex-*Decatur* to be demilitarized and stripped and then transferred to COMNAVSEASYSCOM (SEA 05R) for experimental purposes. NAVSEA DET NISMF Bremerton in was requested to coordinate the stripping to commence on July 18, 1988, and upon completion of all actions and when mutually agreeable transfer the ex-*Decatur* (DDG-31) to COMNAVSEASYSCOM (SEA 05R). (CNO to NAVSEA Letters) The ex-*Decatur* was towed to Puget Sound Naval Shipyard to begin conversion in 1992. The main propulsion steam plant was removed and replaced with diesel engines and remote controls installed to allow the ship to be operated remotely with no crew aboard. The original combat systems were stripped and replaced with the following anti-air warfare weapons and sensor systems:

Mk 23 Target Acquisition System (TAS) air search radar
Dual Director NATO Seasparrow Surface Missile System (NSSMS)
AN/SLQ-32A(V)3 Electronic Warfare System
Close In Weapons System (CIWS) Block I

She was then towed to her permanent home port in Port Hueneme, California, in April 1994. Here the final phase of her conversion was completed and sea trials were conducted. The ship has been supporting various test and evaluation operations since October 1994. (Wolfe, SDTS)

The ex-*Decatur* (DD-936/DDG-31) is being employed as a remotely controlled "drone-type" ship to upgrade current weapon systems and develop new ones. The ship tows a decoy barge about 200–300 feet aft and attacking aircraft or missiles fly directly at the ship until terminal engagement, when they then shift to the barge. (USNI Proceedings, August 1995, p.87)

In response to the new national defense strategy with emphasis on littoral warfare the Navy requires new and improved capabilities in several areas, especially ship self defense systems. New and

Ex-*Decatur* Self defense Test Ship in drydock, March 1992. Photograph by NSWC, Port Hueneme Division. Courtesy of Michael J. Wolfe, SDTS program manager, Port Hueneme, California.

upgraded self defense systems must be brought online and fully integrated and tested. Since rigorous testing of new or improved self defense systems has not been feasible in manned vessels because of the danger to the crew, the former *Decatur* (DDG-31) was converted to a Self Defense Test Ship or SDTS.

Designed primarily for unmanned operation on the Pacific Missile Test Range, the SDTS and its systems can be remotely piloted and operated. Therefore, constraints previously imposed for crew safety can be eliminated. The ship is controlled remotely by the Naval Air Warfare Center, Point Mugu, California, and the combat systems by the Naval Surface Warfare Center, Port Hueneme Division. When necessary to meet test objectives, a crew of up to sixty-four personnel can live aboard for up to 30 days with sufficient food and fuel. Since the sole mission of the SDTS is in support of Test and Evaluation missions, the user is in control of the ship's employment and is unencumbered by the daily routine of a fleet unit.

The SDTS was designed to support Test and Evaluation for approximately fifteen years operating out of Port Hueneme on an average of one month per quarter. In a typical operation a new combat system or element, such as a sensor or weapon system will respond to an air launched or surface launched threat to defend the ship. In order to protect the considerable investment in the ex-*Decatur*, a decoy barge will be towed approximately 200–300 feet behind the ship. Attacking missiles will fly directly at the ship until terminal engagement and then default to the decoy barge, which should not affect test objectives.

Although the ship's original watertight integrity offers protection from fire and flooding, HALON fire suppression systems and float-switch activated submersible pumps have been added to increase survivability in case of an accidental weapon strike. A Twin Wire Automatic Remote Sensing Evaluation System (TWARSES) has also been installed. TWARSES provides the capability to monitor fire, flooding, and smoke at forty-two remote locations throughout the ship from two shipboard locations, as well as remotely via a radio frequency modem. This system provides the ship's crew the exact location and nature of any damage before attempting to reboard.

The STDS offers the opportunity for realistic, integrated, synergistic testing that cannot be accomplished with a manned vessel. Multiple attacking weapons can be detected and engaged by multiple sensors and defensive systems. When pierside, the SDTS can act as a floating laboratory to address interoperability issues, verify computer programs, and resolve hardware related problems without the usual in-port scheduling problems of a manned vessel.

Below: Stern View of the Ex-*Decatur* Self Defense Test Ship, showing the stern drives from the diesel engines that replaced the old boiler fired main propulsion system. Photograph by NSWC, Port Hueneme Division. Courtesy of Larry Lee, Jr., Staten Island, New York.

All types and levels of test and evaluation can be supported by the SDTS, including contractor or advanced technology demonstrations and major or minor alteration testing, as well the Navy Technical Evaluations, Operational Evaluations, and Follow-On Test and Evaluation. Some of the systems being tested aboard the SDTS are the Rolling Airframe Missile (RAM) System, the Close-In Weapons System (CIWS), the High Order Language Computer (HOLC) Surface Mode, the SPARROW Missile Homing Improvement Program, the Evolved SEASPARROW Missile (ESSM) Program, and different configurations of the Ship Self Defense Systems (SSDS). Other potential users of the SDTS are the Electrothermal Chemical Gun, the Passive Countermeasures System, various foreign weapon systems, and new Navy sensors being developed.

The ex-Decatur SDTS is 418 feet in length with a 44-foot beam and 20-foot draft, and is propelled by two 1,200-Hp Caterpillar diesel engines and twin Ulstein stern-mounted outdrives. There is also a bow thruster installed, which makes the ship exceptionally maneuverable. Auxilliary power is provided by two 550 kW, 60-Hz diesel generators and three 400-Hz, 100 kva frequency converters. Since all of the original steam-powered equipment has been replaced with diesel or electrical equipment and the central refrigeration and air conditioning with packaged units, the ship requires 75 percent less engineering and maintenance personnel. (Port Hueneme Div. NSWC. SDTS.http://www.nswses.navy.mil/sdts.ht pp1-3 & Wolfe, SDTS)

Since becoming operational in October 1994, the SDTS has con-

Forward port side view of the Ex-*Decatur* Self Defense Test Ship at the pier at NSWC, Port Hueneme. Photograph by NSWC, Port Hueneme Division, circa 1994. Courtesy of Michael J. Wolfe, SDTS program manager, NSWC, Port Hueneme, California.

ducted numerous live-fire events on the Pacific Missile Test Range with a variety of threats, project users, and weapon and sensor systems. The SDTS has conducted test firing of a NATO Seasparrow missile, two different CIWS, and a combined test of CIWS and a tri-service infra-red system. The SDTS conducted operational testing of a Thermal Imaging Sensor System (TISS) against a wide variety of targets, including aircraft, high speed boats, Navy SEAL personnel, and floating mines. As a result, this system was approved for procurement and the test system was deinstalled from the SDTS and reinstalled on the USS *Ticonderoga* (CG-47). The SDTS has also conducted at sea noise measurements for a High Frequency Surface Wave Radar that is scheduled for test and evaluation on the SDTS in 1998. (Wolfe, SDTS)

On August 2, 1995, the SDTS conducted its first fully remote controlled operation on the Pacific Missile Test Range. The ship was evacuated using a support boat similar to the ones used to transport personnel to the offshore oil rigs, as well as a helicopter for the last few people off and first few back on the ship. These few are the engineers and technicians that turn on data recorders and arm or disarm the weapon systems. The ship was then navigated through the exercise scenario by the Point Magu Range Operations personnel, while the combat systems were operated by the San Nicholas Island

personnel. On April 3, 1996, the SDTS completed a live firing of CIWS against a VANDAL target, bringing the total of SDTS remote controlled firing operations to four. (Coasta Links, Port Hueneme, 9/15/95 & 5/10/96)

Ex-*Decatur* Self Defense Test Ship experimental radar. Photograph by NSWC, Port Hueneme Division, circa 1994. Courtesy of Michael J. Wolfe, SDTS program manager, Port Hueneme, California.

On May 18, 1996, Capt. Gered H. Beeby, USNR, was awarded the Legion of Merit by Capt. Scott Beachy, commanding officer, Port Hueneme Division, Naval Surface Warfare Center (PHD NSWC) on board the ex-USS *Decatur* SDTS. Captain Beeby received this high distinction for his exemplary leadership while serving as commanding officer of Naval Reserve PHD NSWC Headquarters Detachment 119 from October 1993 through September 1995. Captain Beeby was cited for integration of PHD NSWC's seven selected reserve units into a multi-functional team which supported conversion of ex-*Decatur* into the SDTS. The program was an excellent example of reserve utilization, as these detachments provided over 2,200 man-hours of contributory support to the SDTS conversion. The award was particularly unique in that Captain Beeby was believed to be the first Reserve Engineering Duty Officer to have received the Legion of Merit while serving in a Selected Reserve status. (News Briefs, Naval Reserve Association News, October 1996, p.23)

Christening of *Decatur* (DDG-73) by the ship's sponsor, Mrs. Joan E. Shalikashvili on November 9, 1996. Photograph by Bath Iron Works Corporation, A General Dynamics Company. Courtesy of the Aegis Program Executive Office, Naval Sea Systems Command.

CHAPTER 12

USS *DECATUR* (DDG-73)

USS *Decatur* (DDG-73) is the fifth U.S. Navy Ship to be honored with the Decatur name. In return she dignifies and pays tribute to the many dedicated sailors who have served in the previous ships of her namesake. All of these proud ships take their name from Commodore Stephen Decatur, Jr., U.S. Navy, of the Tripolitan War and War of 1812 fame. (*Decatur*, DDG-73, Christening Brochure, p. 2)

This fifth *Decatur* (DDG-73) was built by the Bath Iron Works of Bath, Maine, a General Dynamics Company, as an Arleigh Burke Class Guided Missile Destroyer. Her keel was laid on January 11, 1996, and she was christened by her sponsor, Mrs. Joan E. Shalikashvili, wife of the Chairman of the Joint Chiefs of Staff, General John M. Shalikashvili, United States Army, on Saturday, November 9, 1996, at Bath, Maine. However, *Decatur* was not launched until Sunday, November 10, 1996, because of the extremely high winds on Saturday. The prospective commanding officer of this newest *Decatur* is Comdr. Michael G. Knollmann from Cincinnati, Ohio, who is scheduled to become the commanding officer at the ship's commissioning in Portland, Oregon, on Saturday, August 29, 1998, just over 200 years from the day young Stephen Decatur was given his warrant as a midshipman from President John Adams, dated April 30, 1798.

Decatur is currently going through the final stages of construction at the Bath Iron Works and will be starting her sea trials in January 1998 in preparation for her delivery to the Navy in early 1998. The first two of these trials are a combined Alpha and Bravo Trial that will combine Engineering and Combat System Trials underway. The third or Charlie Trial will include the Navy Board of Inspection and Survey for acceptance of the ship by the Navy, which will take place approximately two months before actual delivery to the Navy. The Final Contract Trials are scheduled for approximately three months after ship delivery to complete the Combat System Ship Qualification Test. The ship will be armed, provisioned, and mission capable in major warfare areas for this trial.

The new crew for *Decatur* is being trained and phased in over four stages. The first increment reported to the Precommissioning Unit in Bath approximately twelve months prior to ship delivery. The second increment reported to Bath approximately eight months prior to delivery and the third approximately six months prior to delivery. The fourth and final increment will report approximately two months prior to delivery.

Cover of the launching brochure, "Launching the Aegis Guided Missile Destroyer *Decatur*, November 9, 1996." Courtesy of Bath Iron Works Corporation, A General Dynamics Company.

USS DECATUR

IN PURSUIT OF PEACE

DDG 73

Aerial view of *Decatur* (DDG-73) in "B" ways
at Bath Iron Works Corporation, 1996.
Photograph by and courtesy of Bath Iron Works
Corporation, A General Dynamics Company.

Inset: USS *Decatur* (DDG-73) insignia. "Patch"
Courtesy of Commander Michael G. Knollmann, USN,
prospective commanding officer, *Decatur* (DDG-73).

Unveiling artist Marty Reed Vinograd's portrait collage of "*Decatur* Meets the Macedonian" at *Decatur* House, December 1997, where the artwork will be on display until the ship is ready to receive it. Photograph by Nancy Birindelli. Courtesy of the author.

Portrait collage of "*Decatur* Meets the Macedonian" by Marty Reed Vinograd, 1997 being introduced by Chris Slusher, Curator of the Decatur House, December 1997. Photograph by Nancy Birindelli. Courtesy of the author.

The crew's training and certification has been scheduled over four phases with the first phase proceeding directly to the shipyard. The training during phase one included a review of planned and conducted training to support watch station qualifications, written or oral examinations of watchstands, and a review of Aegis directives that address safety, operations, and maintenance procedures. Phase two included a thorough audit of the ship's organization, administration, training plans, and programs with primary emphasis on safety in the areas of ship control, casualty control, and emergency procedures. Phase three and four are combined and will be completed during a two-week "Readiness For Sea" period following ship delivery. A Fast Cruise (at the dock) should also be conducted during this phase to emphasize evolutions and drills in preparation for sailaway from the shipbuilding site. This phase will also include a thorough audit of the ship's organization, administration, training plans, and programs with primary emphasis on safety in the areas of ship control, casualty control, and emergency procedures. (Precommissioning Handbook, PP. 4-1–4-21)

According to Comdr. John G. Morgan, first commanding officer of the USS *Arleigh Burke* (DDG-51), of the Aegis Program Executive Office, "There is more firepower per ton of ship here than on any other ship in the world," in describing these Arleigh Burke Class Guided Missile Destroyers. Their radar guided Tomahawk anti-ship missiles have a range of 250 km and their Tomahawk land attack-missiles a range of 2,500 km. Their vital areas are protected by two layers of steel and 70 tons of Kevlar armor, making them a "pocket-battleship"-style destroyer. Congress has authorized the construction of thirty-eight of these guided missile destroyers to date and they will probably be the most numerous ships in the U.S. Fleet after the year 2000. The contracts have been split between Bath Iron Works and Ingalls Shipbuilding of Pascagoula, Mississippi, a subsidiary of Litton Industries.

The design of these Arleigh Burke Class Guided Missile Destroyers has evolved from lessons learned from the cruiser *Belknap's* collision with the carrier *John F. Kennedy,* the Falklands war, and the Iraqi Exocet missile attack on the guided missile frigate *Stark.* Therefore, the entire ship is constructed from steel except for two aluminum funnels, so there is no longer an aluminum superstructure which can burn at extremely high temperatures. Fire control measures include larger foam tanks with quicker access and sprinkler systems in berthing and Combat Information Center areas. Anti-Nuclear, Biological, and Chemical warfare double air-locked hatches and anti-contaminant interior pressurization have also been incorporated into the design, as well as stealth features, such as angles and rounded corners to reduce radar signature.

These guided missile destroyers are 504.3 feet in length with a 67-foot beam and can accommodate a complement of 346. They are powered by four GE LM 2500 gas-turbines and two shafts of 100,000-shaft horsepower and are capable of 30+ knot speeds. With their two controllable pitch propellers they are capable of going from full speed to dead stop within a ship length. In

Aerial view of *Decatur* (DDG-73) in "B" ways at Bath Iron Works Corporation, 1996. Photograph by and courtesy of Bath Iron Works Corporation, A General Dynamics Company.

Decatur (DDG-73) collage presented to the Decatur House by Commander Michael G. Knollmann, USN, Prospective Commanding Officer, *Decatur* (DDG-73), November 1997. Photograph by Nancy Birindelli. Courtesy of the author.

addition to the Harpoon and Tomahawk missiles, they also carry Standard Surface-to-Air missiles in ninety Vertical Launch System cells. Other armament includes one 5-inch/54 caliber gun, two Phalanx Close-in Weapon Systems, and two triple torpedo tubes. They also have a landing platform and helicopter handling facilities on the fantail. These ships have definitely been designed "to go in harms way."

Right: *Decatur* (DDG-73) ready for christening, November 9, 1996. Photograph by and courtesy of the author.

Left: *Decatur* (DDG-73) ready for launching, November 10, 1996. Photograph by and courtesy of the author.

Comdr. and Mrs. Michael G. Knollmann, USN, Prospective Commanding Officer, and Lt. Comdr. and Mrs. Randall M. Hendrickson, USN, Prospective Executive Officer, *Decatur* (DDG-73) on the morning of the launching of *Decatur* (DDG-73), November 10, 1996. Photograph by and courtesy of the author.

Below: The author and artist, Marty Vinograd on the morning of the launching of *Decatur* (DDG-73). Photograph by Nancy Birindelli. Courtesy of the author.

Above: Artist Marty Vinograd with Nancy Birindelli on the morning of the launching of *Decatur* (DDG-73), November 10, 1996. Photograph by and courtesy of the author.

Right: Start of launching of *Decatur* (DDG-73) on the afternoon of November 10, 1996. Photograph by and courtesy of the author.

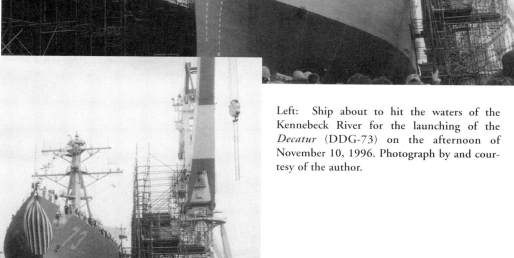

Left: Ship about to hit the waters of the Kennebeck River for the launching of the *Decatur* (DDG-73) on the afternoon of November 10, 1996. Photograph by and courtesy of the author.

STG1 Lunde, STG1 Butler, and SH3
Mann aboard *Decatur* (DDG-73) in transit
from Bath to Portland, Maine, on
November 14, 1997 for drydocking and
installation of the sonar dome. Photograph
by and courtesy of the author.

Lt. Kristen Fabry, supply officer, and Pat
Cornwell, administrative assistant, aboard
Decatur (DDG-73) on November 14, 1997.
Photograph by and courtesy of the author.

FC3 Clark, STG3 Beuge, and FC3 Day
aboard *Decatur* (DDG 31) on November
14, 1997.

EN3 Hembree, FA Siems, FN Connolly, and EN1 Simms aboard *Decatur* (DDG-73) on November 14, 1997. Photograph by and courtesy of the author.

CTRSN Luedke, OS2 Donaldson, and OS1 Worley aboard *Decatur* (DDG-73). Photograph by and courtesy of the author.

EM1 Mohler, GSM1 Massie, and EW1 Larson aboard *Decatur* (DDG-73). Photograph by and courtesy of the author.

Lieutenant Tim Shipman, STO and FCCS Moore aboard *Decatur* (DDG-73). Photograph by and courtesy of the author.

Larry Ross, Curator of the "Lindbergh Crate" and guest of the prospective commanding officer, IC2 Grev, and GSM3 Garrison aboard *Decatur* (DDG-73). Photograph by and courtesy of the author.

Pat Cornwell, administrative assistant, FC3 Sydorick, RMC Asbill, GSMC Pratt, FCC Smith, ETC Jervell aboard *Decatur* (DDG-73). Photograph by and courtesy of the author.

CTRSN Cable, FC3 Kleint, DC1 Orason, EN1 Simms, RMC Asbill, OS1 Worley, RM1 Ruis, and FCC Coyne aboard *Decatur* (DDG-73). Photograph by and courtesy of the author.

CTRSN Cable, CTRSN Luedke, and SK1 Joyce aboard *Decatur* (DDG-73). Photograph by and courtesy of the author.

SK1 Joyce, Lt. Kristen Fabry, supply officer, Pat Cornwell, administrative assistant, and SK2 Parayno aboard *Decatur* (DDG-73). Photograph by and courtesy of the author.

CTR1 Day, CTR1 Azzarello, and SK2 Parayno aboard *Decatur* (DDG-73). Photograph by and courtesy of the author.

Lieutenant Aiken, operations officer, aboard *Decatur* (DDG-73). Photograph by and courtesy of the author.

SN Rickaby, OSSA Stump, OSSA Thompson, OS1 Gulledge, OSSA Romero, CTR1 Day, CTRSN Cable aboard *Decatur* (DDG-73). Photograph by and courtesy of the author.

STGC Barker, Ensign Bohrer, DCA, DC1 Orason, and HT1 Conard aboard *Decatur* (DDG-73). Photograph by and courtesy of the author.

The author, EM1 Mohler, and GSM1 Massie aboard *Decatur* (DDG-73). Photograph by EW1 Larson. Courtesy of the author.

Ensign Skip Muller, ASWO, STG1 Butler, STG3 Benge, and STG1 Lunde aboard *Decatur* (DDG-73). Photograph by and courtesy of the author.

FC3 Clark, EW3 Dodge, CTRSN Luedke, FC3 Yoder, GMCS Scavo, GM3 Richardson, GMC O'Bannon, and Ensign Muller, ASWO, aboard *Decatur* (DDG-73). Photograph by and courtesy of the author

FC3 Sydorick, FC3 Clark, EW3 Dodge, CTRSN Luedke, FC3 Yoder, GMCS Scavo, GM3 Richardson, and GMC O'Bannon aboard *Decatur* (DDG-73). Photograph by and courtesy of the author.

HMC Ackerman, "Doc," and Ens. Skip Muller, ASWO, aboard *Decatur* (DDG-73). Photograph by and courtesy of the author.

Lieutenant Aiken, operations officer, his minister, and Larry Ross aboard *Decatur* (DDG-73). Photograph by and courtesy of the author.

Lt. Comdr. Randy Hendrickson, prospective executive officer, aboard *Decatur* (DDG-73).

OSSA Thompson, OSSA Stump, and OS1 Gulledge aboard *Decatur* (DDG-73). Photograph by and courtesy of the author.

OS1 Gulledge aboard *Decatur* (DDG-73).
Photograph by and courtesy of the author.

OS1 Hammer, CTRSN Luedke, SN
Rickaby, EW3 Dodge, EN3 Hembree, and
FC3 Tufts aboard *Decatur* (DDG-73).
Photograph by and courtesy of the author.

Lt. Kristen Fabry, supply officer, Pat
Cornwell, administrative assistant, Karl
Finnimore, Bath Iron works Aegis program
manager, aboard *Decatur* (DDG-73).
Photograph by and courtesy of the author.

SH3 Mann and Commander Knollmann aboard *Decatur* (DDG-73). Photograph by and courtesy of the author.

Mess caterer, Walter, in the ship's galley aboard *Decatur* (DDG-73). Photograph by and courtesy of the author.

Walter and associate, mess caterers, in the ship's galley aboard *Decatur* (DDG-73). Photograph by and courtesy of the author.

Ens. Shawn Bohrer, DCA, Ens. Skip Muller, ASWO, and Lt. (jg) John Carroll, disbursing officer, aboard *Decatur* (DDG-73). Photograph by and courtesy of the author.

QM1 Kenley, STGC Barker, STG1 Butler, and Commander Knollman aboard *Decatur* (DDG-73). Photograph by and courtesy of the author.

OS1 Parker, FN Chambers, FC3 Day, and OS2 Balla aboard *Decatur* (DDG-73). Photograph by and courtesy of the author.

ENC Jones and EN1 Simms aboard *Decatur* (DDG-73). Photograph by and courtesy of the author.

CTR1 Day, CTRSN Merrill, HMC Ackerman, and CTRSN Cable aboard *Decatur* (DDG-73). Photograph by and courtesy of the author.

SA Ferro aboard *Decatur* (DDG-73). Photograph by and courtesy of the author.

Right: OS2 Kershaw and OS1 Parker aboard *Decatur* (DDG-73). Photograph by and courtesy of the author.

Below: Line Drawing of *Decatur* (DDG-73) Profile. Courtesy of the Aegis Program Executive Office, Naval Sea Systems Command.

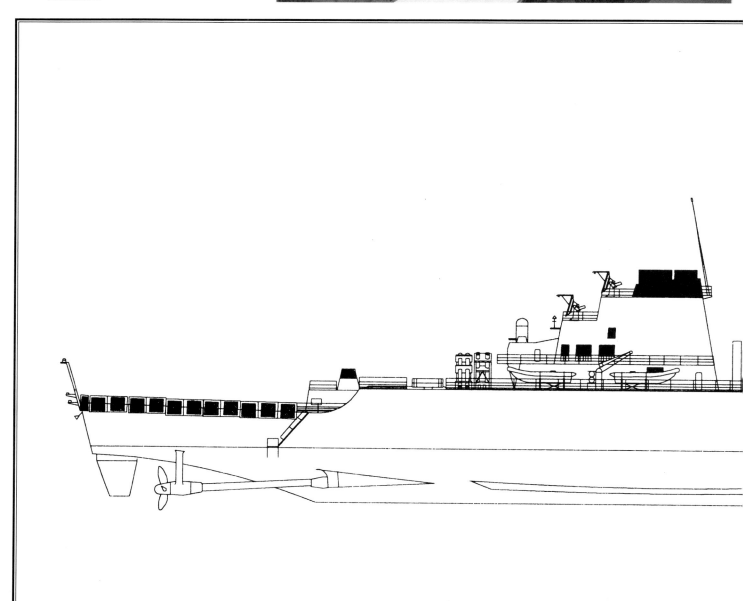

Commander Knollmann aboard *Decatur* (DDG-73) presenting the flag to Nick Nichols of Bath Iron Works for his retirement. Photograph by and courtesy of the author.

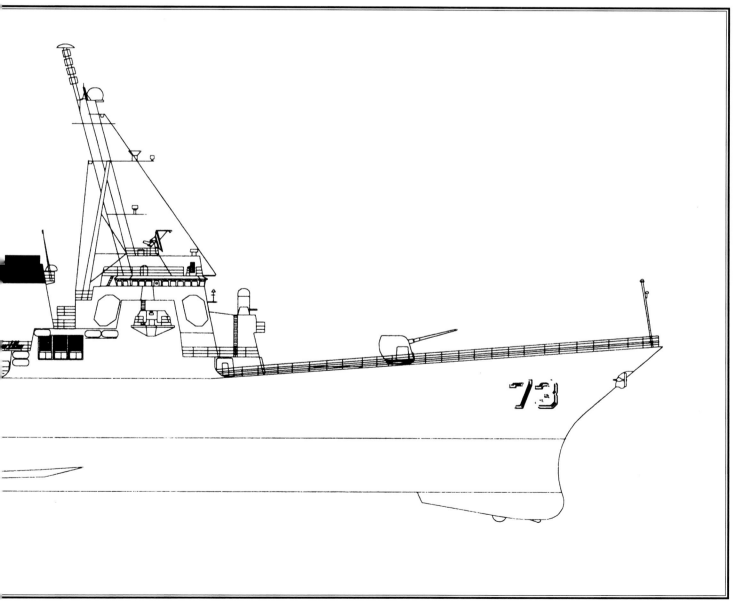

12.8 *Decatur* (DDG-73) in "B" ways at Bath Iron Works Corporation, 1996. Photograph by and courtesy of Bath Iron Works Corporation, a General Dynamics Company.

Right: Decatur High School, Decatur, Alabama. Photograph by Dixie Graphics. Courtesy of the Decatur Convention and Visitors Bureau.

Righ: City of Decatur, Alabama Seal. Photograph by Dixie Graphics. Courtesy of the Decatur Convention and Visitors Bureau.

Below: Sign for Bank Street, Old Decatur Historic District, Decatur, Alabama. Photograph by Dixie Graphics. Courtesy of the Decatur Convention and Visitors Bureau.

City Planner Rob Walker portraying Commodore Stephen Decatur, greets visitors to Decatur, Alabama. Photograph by Dixie Graphics. Courtesy of the Decatur Convention and Visitors Bureau.

City Planner Rob Walker portraying Commodore Stephen Decatur, welcomes Lt. Kristen Fabry, SC, USN, *Decatur* (DDG-73) Supply Officer, to Decatur, Alabama. Photograph by and courtesy of *The Decatur Daily*, July 21, 1997.

CHAPTER 13

DECATUR COUNTRY

The many Decatur schools, libraries, cities, towns, counties, and organizations that abound throughout the nation are too numerous to include in one easily readable chapter. Although this chapter is dedicated to all of those Decatur institutions in their entirety, only those Decatur cities, towns, and counties found by the author, as well as a few of the Decatur institutions could be selected to pictorially represent the whole cast. Accordingly, the complete list of Decatur institutions to the best of the author's knowledge has been included in Appendix B. Many of the Decatur cities and counties were founded in 1823 or soon after following an order of the U.S. Congress and President James Monroe in honor of the renowned U.S. naval officer Commodore Stephen Decatur.

DECATUR, ALABAMA

Decatur, Alabama was the first city to assume the name Decatur in early 1823 and along with her many sister cities and counties will be celebrating its 175th Birthday in 1998. In 1833 the Old State Bank opened in Decatur and served as a catalyst for the growth and development of Decatur from a settlement to a town. This impressive pre-Greek Revival building remains today as the city's oldest standing structure.

When the Civil War swept over the South, Decatur was engulfed in many skirmishes, because it was a key railroad junction. Both armies, Union and Confederate, occupied the town at one time or another. When the war ended in 1865, only four buildings were left standing in Decatur, including the Old State Bank.

Decatur's historic district dates back to an easier time in the Victorian era of 1870 through 1910. This charming district covers over 116 acres and is one of the most intact Victorian neighborhoods in Alabama. In modern times Decatur, Alabama, has continued its development with such attractions as the first American Wave Pool at Point Mallard, the Deep South's only Open-Air Ice Rink, Cook's Natural Science Museum, Wheeler National Wildlife Refuge, and the Alabama Jubilee, the state's original hot-air balloon festival. (Decatur, Alabama Convention & Visitors Bureau Internet web page)

Left: Houston McDonald House. One of the oldest buildings in downtown Decatur, Georgia, which was recently restored as "Gardentopia," a unique shop for gardeners. Photograph by Linda Harris. Courtesy of the Decatur Downtown Development Authority.

Below: Climax Depot has been restored and serves as the Climax City Hall and Community Center for Decatur County, Georgia. Photograph by Eddie Ledbetter, Register, Georgia. Courtesy of Frances Willis, Bainbridge, George.

Facing page top: City of Decatur, Georgia City Hall. Photograph by Bill Mahan. Courtesy of the Decatur Downtown Development Authority.

Facing page Bottom: Downtown Decatur, Georgia Masonic Temple building and By Hand South, a gift store with one-of-a-kind work by a variety of artists. Photograph by Linda Harris. Courtesy of the Decatur Downtown Development Authority.

DECATUR, ARKANSAS

After Arkansas became a state in 1836 people from the Eastern states migrated into the area on their way West. Some decided to settle in the area and eventually four townships came together in a corner near a spring, where they obtained their drinking water. They named the settlement "Corner Springs," Arkansas. These early settlers built a school, a water mill, and a general store.

In 1882 Corner Springs applied to the Postmaster General for a post office. There was some delay with map making regulations and they were told that the name of Corner Springs could not be used, since it had already been requested. However, one of the settlers had a relative by the name of Commodore Stephen Decatur, the naval hero of the Barbary and 1812 wars. He convinced them to apply for the post office as Decatur. So Decatur, Arkansas, got its start from there.

The Decatur Depot Library/Historic Museum and restored KCS Engine. From the Decatur, Arkansas, brochure.

Photograph of the "Welcome to Decatur, Arkansas" brochure.

Arthur Tillman published Decatur's first newspaper, the *Decatur Advance,* in August 1895 and told of beautiful Decatur, "where everything is right and everyone is happy." Through the early 1900s Decatur had numerous money crops from tobacco to strawberries to peaches to apples. However, after the largest apple year of 1919 things began to slow down around Decatur. Then the Decatur Development Corporation was established and started to develop a new sewer system, new deep water wells, a stock auction barn, and a new bank. By 1938 the poultry industry was moving into Arkansas and Lloyd Peterson began hatching baby chicks and Don Bredehoeft helped find farmers to raise them. Peterson then built a processing plant and Bredehoeft started a trucking business. By the 1950s the poultry business was booming in Decatur.

In 1950 a group of citizens gave the city enough money to buy ten acres of land and finance the Arkansas Game and Fish Commission to build a dam and create a lake. The lake was named "Crystal Lake" and was made available for everyone's enjoyment. Lloyd Peterson purchased land around the lake and built an air port. In 1954 Decatur won the "All American City" award in Kansas City from the National Municipal League.

Today Decatur has a high school and grade school, a city park, tennis courts, and a swimming pool. There is a low-income housing complex, a senior citizens complex, a modern post office, and a discount center to rival Walmart. Decatur claims the right to say, "We are helping feed the world." (Bredehoeft, Decatur, pp. 47–49)

DECATUR, GEORGIA

Through an act of the Georgia General Assembly on December 23, 1822, five commissioners were appointed to "fix on a public site for a Court House and jail for the new DeKalb County, and for that purpose to purchase one landlot (202-1/2 acres), and lay out a town, and dispose of lots . . . as they think most conducive to the interests of the county." The Commission selected landlot 246 in the 15th district and declared that the county town be named Decatur for Commodore Stephen Decatur, the naval hero of the Tripolitan War and War of 1812. The Commission stated that all business should be transacted in the town on and after the first Tuesday in September 1823. (Clarke, *The Story of Decatur,* p. 6) Decatur, Georgia, was incorporated on December 10, 1823, and as the seat of DeKalb County, is the second oldest municipality in the Atlanta metropolitan area.

In the 1830s early residents rejected a proposal by the Western & Atlantic Railroad to make Decatur a major stop on its new line. They did not want the noise, smoke, and confusion of a railroad town. Therefore, the railroad moved seven miles west to a small settlement called Terminus. In 1843 Terminus was renamed Marthasville and in 1845 became Atlanta.

Today Decatur, Georgia, adjoins Atlanta's city limits and is just six

The third DeKalb County Courthouse in Decatur, Georgia, was built in 1847 and survived the Civil War. It was demolished in 1898 to make room for a larger building. Photograph courtesy of DeKalb Historical Society, Decatur, Georgia.

COLOR SCENES FROM AROUND DECATUR COUNTRY

Top: Willis Park was originally the courthouse square. Photograph by Eddie Ledbetter, Register, Georgia. Courtesy of Frances Willis, Bainbridge, Georgia.

Right: Decatur County Courthouse, Bainbridge, Georgia. Photograph by Eddie Ledbetter, Register, Georgia. Courtesy of Frances Willis, Bainbridge, Georgia.

Above: Decatur County Courthouse, Greensburg, Indiana. Courtesy of the Greensburg Area Chamber of Commerce.

Statue of Stephen Decatur and bas relief of the "Burning of the frigate Philadelphia." The statue is in front of the Decatur, Illinois Civic Center. Photograph by Mary Talbott. Courtesy of the Macon County Historical Society, Decatur, Illinois.

miles east of the central business district. Decatur is home to some 17,200 residents and 8,000 households. The courthouse square has served historically as the community gathering place and continues today as the focus of festivals and special events, serving the heart of the community. The Old Courthouse on the Square stands on a rise where two Indian trails once crossed. It contains an interesting museum which covers DeKalb County history, as well as Civil War memorabilia. Visitors will also find helpful information at the Welcome Center located inside the front door of this beautiful old building.

The downtown district of Decatur is surrounded by beautiful, historic neighborhoods that reflect a variety of architectural styles. Decatur's tree-lined streets, nationally recognized public school system, and strong sense of community are its hallmark. This "City of Homes, Schools, and Places of Worship" continues to draw young families to the City of Decatur. Developers have been sensitive to Decatur's vision of maintaining its small town character, surrounding a vibrant retail center and a courthouse square that links the city's history. They have built highly successful new office buildings that swell the daytime population of Decatur to 28,000, which in turn nurtures the many fine restaurants and associated service establishments. (City of Decatur, Georgia What & Where Brochure)

DECATUR COUNTY, GEORGIA

Decatur County, Georgia, is in the southwest corner of Georgia adjacent to the Florida line. DeSoto and his band of explorers traversed the county as early as 1540. Following the War of 1812 Southwest Georgia was ceded to the United States by the Creek Indians in a treaty established by General Andrew Jackson. The Army built three forts in the county area. In 1818 two of them, Forts Scott and Hughes, were beseiged by the Seminole Indians, who refused to ratify the treaty with the general. General Jackson and troops from Georgia, Tennessee, and Kentucky came to their relief and continued into Florida, which then belonged to Spain. (*The Historical News,* p. 13)

During these Indian Wars, Camp Recovery was built when swamp fever (malaria) spread through the ranks at Fort Scott. The camp was established by the military surgeon on higher ground in order to get the soldiers away from the dampness of the swamp (without knowing it was the mosquitoes). (*Heritage Tours,* p. 16)

In 1823 Decatur County was established in honor of Commodore Stephen Decatur. The county seat was established at the site of Fort Hughes and named Bainbridge in 1824 in honor of that other distinguished naval hero of the War of 1812, Commodore William Bainbridge. This was a fitting

Left: Agnes Scott Hall, known as "Main," on the Agnes Scott College campus in Decatur. Photograph courtesy of DeKalb Historical Society, Decatur, Georgia.

choice, since the naval careers of the two were so inextricably entwined. As noted in Chapter 2, Decatur became the first lieutenant of the *Essex* in 1801, which was then under the command of Captain Bainbridge. (Anthony, pp. 69–70) After Bainbridge lost the *Philadelphia* on the rocks off Tripoli, it was Decatur who stealthily sailed into the harbor of Tripoli and torched the ship. During the War of 1812 Commodore Bainbridge redeemed the loss of the *Philadelphia* when in command of the USS *Constitution* (Old Ironsides), he defeated HMS *Java* on December 29, 1812. Congress later awarded Commodore Bainbridge a Gold Medal for this victory. (Martin, pp. 172–176 & 180)

The port at Bainbridge began activity as early as 1827 with steamships coming up the Apalachicola and Flint Rivers from the Gulf of Mexico. The height of this river trade occurred during the 1850s before the Civil War when Decatur County had two cotton factories and was trying to get a railroad established. Following the Civil War the river trade did not recover for forty years. (*The Historical News,* p. 13)

Eventually the railroad was established in Decatur County and became the Atlantic Coast Line (ACL) Railway. The town of Climax was laid out and named in 1833 with a train depot. The town acquired its unusual name because it was at the "climax of the grade" on the main line from the Chattahoochee River and Savannah. When the CSX Railroad, successor to the ACL, decided to demolish the depot, dedicated citizens relocated and restored it. The old Climax Depot now serves as the Climax City Hall and Community Center. (*Heritage Tours,* p. 17)

Camp Recovery, Decatur County, Georgia. Established in 1817 during the Indian Wars as a hospital camp to get the soldiers away from the dampness of the swamp so they could recover. Photograph by Eddie Ledbetter, Register, Georgia. Courtesy of Frances Willis, Bainbridge, Georgia.

DECATUR, ILLINOIS

Decatur, Illinois lies in the middle of the State of Illinois in Macon County approximately 30 some miles to the east of the State Capitol, Springfield, Illinois, the home of President Abraham Lincoln. By 1828 the population in the area that became Macon County had built up to the point that there was a clamor for organizing a new county. Three men, Benjamin R. Austin, Andrew W. Smith, and John Ward, were chosen to go to Vandalia, the state capital at the time, and present a petition for organization of a new county. As a result, the legislature passed an act establishing the county of Macon. John Fleming, Jesse Rhodes, and Easton Whitton were appointed as commissioners to locate a county seat. The legislature decreed that the county seat should be named Decatur, in honor of Stephen Decatur, the distinguished naval officer.

The James Ward home at Mt. Gilead was designated by the legislature as the temporary site for transacting business of the new county. The first elec-

Top: Newton County Courthouse, Decatur, Mississippi. Photograph by and courtesy of Mr. Bubby Johnston, East Central Community College, Decatur, Mississippi.

Above right: Decatur Park with Soldiers' Monuments, band stand, and WWI canon. Photograph by and courtesy of Ms. Eva Davis, Winchester, Ohio.

Left: Decatur, Mississippi, Plaque. Photograph by and courtesy of Mr. Bubby Johnston, East Central Community College, Decatur, Mississippi.

Wise County Courthouse, Decatur, Texas. The courthouse was built in 1895 of pink limestone from Burnet and is considered to be an architectural example of its type and era. Photograph courtesy of Ms. Susan Williams, Director, Chamber of Commerce, Decatur, Texas.

tion in Macon County, as directed by the legislature, took place in the Ward home on the second Monday in April 1829. Benjamin Wilson, Elisha Freeman, and James G. Miller were elected as members of the County Commissioners Court and William Warnick was elected as sheriff. On May 19, 1829, the first meeting of the County Commissioners took place at Ward's home and Daniel McCall was appointed county clerk and Benjamin R. Austin county treasurer.

Enterprise School, Decatur, Illinois. Photograph by Mary Talbott. Courtesy of the Macon County Historical Society, Decatur, Illinois.

Below: Peace Monument on Courthouse Square, Decatur, Indiana. Photograph by and courtesy of Gordon Gregg, Adams County Historical Society.

There was much public argument over the selection of the site for the county seat, as pioneer residents of Macon County were badly divided on where the seat of government should be. Three men were chosen from outside the county to make the selection, possibly for that reason. Once the rivalry over sites died down the site selection commissioners agreed to locate the county seat on the "fifteenth section of township 16 north, range 2 east, northeast quarter and east half of said quarter, the southeast corner of said above-named half quarter." On June 1, 1829, the County Commissioners Court ordered Benjamin R. Austin, county surveyor, to lay out the town of Decatur after the form of Shelbyville and make and return a complete plat of same by July 1, 1829.

The Commissioners then turned their attention to building a courthouse. The original courthouse was a log building of 18 by 24 feet and was erected on the southwest corner of the square, which is now a municipal park-

ing lot. The courthouse was a story and a half with the courtroom on the first floor and a room above. The building faced north with a door on that face and another on the south. It had a clapboard roof, an old fashioned fireplace, and puncheon floors. (Banten, *History of Macon County*, pp. 34–38)

The citizens of Decatur have erected a marvelous statue of Stephen Decatur backed by a Bas Relief depicting his exploits. This monument to the Commodore stands in front of the Decatur Civic Center.

As you enter the city, there is a handsome sign declaring "Welcome to DECATUR, the Pride of the Prairie."

Decatur, Indiana

Decatur, Indiana, is the county seat of Adams County, Indiana located twenty-one miles southeast of Fort Wayne and approximately six miles from the Ohio State Line. Decatur was first platted on June 23, 1836, as a small farming settlement and named for American naval hero Stephan Decatur. The City of Decatur was incorporated in 1853 and was connected to Fort Wayne by a road.

Decatur is a beautiful town with a pleasant mixture of modern and well kept older homes, tree-shaded streets and gardens, many churches, fine schools, and a friendly collection of area businesses and industries. The North Adams Community Schools district serves Decatur, as well as Northern Adams County. Decatur's local newspaper is the *Decatur Daily Democrat*. There are also local AM and FM radio stations, the Decatur Public Library, and Adams County Memorial Hospital.

The Adams County Court House is a landmark and the Court House Square is the site of the peace monument. It was the first World War I monument in the United States dedicated to peace. Court House Square is also the site of a memorial to Gene Stratton Porter, the county's best-known author and naturalist.

Decatur also blends the farm economy of the local rural area with thriving, diversified industries. Central Soya, a large soya bean processing plant, is located in Decatur and was the first such plant established in Indiana.

Above: Adams County Courthouse, Decatur, Indiana. Photograph by Affolder Photography, Decatur, Indiana, 1989. Courtesy of Gordon Gregg, Adams County, Indiana Historical Society.

There are many local attractions, such as the Adams County Museum, Peace Monument, and parks in Decatur. Nearby are attractions include Amishville, Heritage Village, the Covered Bridge, and Limberlost. (Decatur Chamber of Commerce Brochure & Historical Society Brief History of Adams County)

DECATUR, IOWA

Decatur, Iowa, is located in Decatur County, Iowa, and had a population of 7,458 as of the 1970 census. The beautiful parks and quiet neighborhoods of Decatur and Decatur County along with the friendly people offer a charm and courtesy that coupled with the luxury of modern convenience add to the ambiance of the area.

Decatur County was organized in 1850 and named in honor of Commodore Stephen Decatur. Leon, Iowa, was selected as the county seat and the original courthouse was built there in 1854. Decatur County has three active school districts and five public libraries, as well as being home to Graceland College, a private four year liberal arts college, and more than thirty churches.

County attractions include Liberty Hall Historic Center in Lamoni, which is the Memorial Home of Joseph Smith III, who was the son of the assassinated leader of the Restored Mormon Church. The Center is a beautifully restored eighteen-room Victorian farmhouse. The Decatur County Museum in Leon, the county seat is another historical site, as is the Trailside Historic Park that overlooks the Weldon River. It is also the site of a cemetary established by the Mormon pioneers who settled in Garden Grove. (Ruckman, Decatur County, Iowa Brochure)

Above: Liberty hall, the memorial home of Joseph Smith III, in Lamoni, Decatur County, Iowa. Courtesy of the Decatur County Inventory Map.

DECATUR CITY

Decatur City in Decatur County, Iowa, is a small community of 177 people. there is an elementary school which is part of the Central Decatur School District. Decatur City also has a Community Center that is home to the Decatur County Development Committee. (Decatur City Internet Web page)

Below: Mini-Sapa Festival the first weekend in October every year. Oberlin, Kansas. Photograph by Jeanie Louden Unger. Courtesy of the Decatur County Area Chamber of Commerce, Oberlin, Kansas.

DECATUR COUNTY, KANSAS

Decatur County, Kansas, was created by the act of the Kansas legislature of 1873. Decatur is in the northern tier of counties in the northwestern part of Kansas. There are ten counties between Decatur and the Missouri River and two before the Colorado border. Decatur County has an area of approximately 900 square miles and a population of over 4,100 people. The county was named after Commodore Stephen Decatur.

The first post office in Decatur County was established at Oberlin, which was then called Sappa. The first postmaster, J. A. Rodehaver, was appointed in April 1874. The first school in Decatur County was established near Oberlin during the fall and winter of 1875 and 1876.

Oberlin in Decatur County was the site of the last Indian raid in Kansas. It was attacked by the Cheyennes under the leadership of Chiefs Little Wolf and Dull Knife on September 30, 1878. Eighteen men were slain in Decatur County alone, as well as others in surrounding counties. A monument was erected in their honor at the Oberlin cemetery. One exception during the raid was Mr. H. D. Colvin and his brave wife, who managed to drive off the marauding band of over two hundred with an old Navy six-shooter and a shot gun.

Mr. J. C. Humphrey and Mr. James N. Counter issued *The Oberlin Herald* in June, 1879 and on November 1, 1879 a mass convention was held in Oberlin and selected Frank Kimball, John B. Hitchcock, and George W. Shoemaker as temporary County commissioners. On December 11, 1879 Governor St. John issued a proclamation organizing Decatur County and declaring Oberlin as the county seat. Oberlin was officially established as the county seat in an election on February 3, 1880. (Mathews, *Decatur,* pp. 1-5)

Most of Dull Knife's band were killed, while a few along with Dull Knife ended up on a reservation in Montana. Members of Little Wolf's band were returned to Dodge City, Kansas, and placed in the custody of "Bat" Masterson. They were put on trial for the murder of Decatur and Rawlins County settlers, but were found not guilty due to lack of evidence. (Farquhar, *Oberlin Herald,* p. 3H)

Above: Cheyenne Chiefs Little Wolf (on left) and Dull Knife. Photograph courtesy of the Decatur County Area Chamber of Commerce, Oberlin, Kansas.

Left: Decatur County Fair and Home-owned Carnival, Oberlin, Kansas. Photograph by Jeanie Louden Unger. Courtesy of the Decatur County Area Chamber of Commerce, Oberlin, Kansas.

Today the Decatur County Museum in Oberlin provides one of the finest collection of antiquities in the state of Kansas. The museum includes a number of historic buildings preserved from the ravishes of progress. They include a sod house, the old train depot, a one-room schoolhouse, an old jail built in 1886, a blacksmith shop, and an old "mom and pop" grocery store. (Farquhar, p. 3H)

BERLIN, MARYLAND

Although not named Decatur, Berlin, Maryland rightfully claims to be the birthplace of Commodore Stephen Decatur. Since Berlin is now where Sinepuxent, Maryland, and the two-room log house in which Stephen Decatur, Jr., was born used to be, its claim to that right and an appropriate place in Decatur Country is well deserved. Berlin is also the home of Stephen Decatur High School and Decatur Park with its monument to the Commodore.

Stephen Decatur High School NJROTC Unit 1995–1996, First Year. Photograph courtesy of Master Chief David Reynolds, USN (Ret), NJROTC Unit, Decatur High School, Berlin, Maryland.

Fittingly, there is a Naval Junior Reserve Officer Training Corps (NJROTC) at Stephen Decatur High School, in which many students participate very actively. In only its second year the NJROTC Program has expanded from 95 students in the 1995/1996 school year to 120 students in the 1996/1997 school year. That represents over a 26 percent growth in just one year and out of a total current school year enrollment of 1,020 the 120 student Corps represents almost 12 percent of the student body. That is not bad for just the second year of existence and indicates that many students are looking for that extra challenge that NJROTC provides. The activities offered by NJROTC include an Academic Team, a Rifle Team, a Drill Team, and a Color Guard that compete against other JROTC units throughout the United States. Rounding out these activities the unit has organized an annual Navy Ball, a Field Day and Picnic, and performed several fund raising events to finance these other extracurricular activities. (Reynolds, Blue Ribbon Report)

Mr. Dave Herman of Lockheed Martin presenting Principal Lou Taylor, Stephen Decatur High School, Berlin, Maryland, with a model of USS *Decatur* (DDG-73), as the prospective commanding officer, Comdr. Michael G. Knollmann looks on. Photograph by and courtesy of NASA Wallops Flight Facility.

Decatur, Michigan, Old Train Depot, circa 1900. Photograph courtesy of Ms. Toni Benson, Local History Librarian, Van Buren District Library, Decatur, Michigan.

DECATUR, MICHIGAN

Decatur, Michigan, is a small General Law Village of 1.1 square miles with a population of 1,760. It is located in the southern part of Van Buren County in southwestern Michigan just six miles off interstate 94. Over a dozen lakes are within five miles of Decatur. The village government consists of an elected six member council and mayor with a clerk, treasurer, and assessor also elected. Decatur has its own Fire and Police Departments, library and K-12 school system. *The Decatur Republican* is a weekly newspaper that has been published since 1867 and there are two area hospitals serving the needs of residents.

Following the Indians, who hunted the surrounding forests and fished the nearby lakes, the first settler arrived in 1829 and was soon followed by those from "York State" seeking the rich earth of "Little Prairie Rhonde." With the coming of the Michigan Central Railroad from Kalamazoo the village of Decatur was laid out and named after the township and Commodore Decatur. The village soon attracted many Irish workmen and was platted in 1848. The first village school house was also built in 1848. By resolution of the board of supervisors, the village of Decatur was incorporated on October 11, 1858, and later by legislative acts in 1861 and 1883.

When the swamp was cleared in the 1880s opening the muckland to cultivation, many Dutch immigrants were attracted. Many industries began thriving at that time attracting a growing number of inhabitants. Lumbering established sawmills and a stave factory. A tannery was established along with flour mills, grain and produce warehouses, as well as stockyards lining the railroad tracks. Immigrants from Central European countries began arriving on every evening train in the late 1920s to settle on the farmland East of Decatur. By the 1940s migrant farm workers came from the South every summer to assist with the harvests and many stayed on to become permanent citizens. Many retirement age people found a home in Decatur in the 1960s, as they left the crowded city life.

Decatur today offers many recreational and entertainment opportunities for residents and visitors alike. The many surrounding lakes offer water recreation throughout the year and the village owned Red Woolfe Park on Lake of the Woods provides a supervised beach, picnic tables, and grills throughout the summer. There are three excellent campgrounds nearby, as well as several of Michigan's finest wineries offering wine tasting tours.

DECATUR, MISSISSIPPI

Decatur, Mississippi, is the county seat of Newton County, Mississippi, a small town in east central Mississippi with a population of 1,248 as of the 1990 census. Newton County was organized in 1836, as part of the territory the U.S. purchased from the Choctaw Indians in 1830. The first settlers came from surrounding counties and were originally from Georgia and South Carolina. The town of Decatur was incorporated in 1906 and named in honor of Commodore Stephen Decatur.

The town of Decatur is governed by a part-time mayor and five-man board of aldermen. The mayor serves as chief executive officer and the aldermen are responsible for levying taxes, authorizing bond issues, and maintaining the town's infrastructure. Decatur has a volunteer fire department for fire protection and town water distribution and sewage systems. There are two medical clinics in Decatur and the school system is run by the county of Newton. Decatur is located twenty-five miles west of Meridian and sixty-five miles east of Jackson, Mississippi.

Decatur is home to the East Central Community College, which also serves the five surrounding counties. Decatur's main industry is the Peavey Research Center for Peavey Music Company that manufactures sound systems and instruments for entertainers worldwide. There is also a small chair factory in Decatur.

For recreation the Turkey Creek Water Park is just five miles southwest of Decatur. The park facilities offer camping, fishing, boating, swimming, and picnicking. Decatur also has a country club and golf course. (Decatur, Mississippi Welcome Brochure)

Decatur City Hall, Decatur, Michigan. Photograph by the *Decatur Republican Newspaper*, October 12, 1978. Courtesy of Ms. Toni Benson, Local History Librarian, Van Buren District Library, Decatur, Michigan.

DECATUR, NEBRASKA

Decatur, Nebraska, is a village in northeast Burt County at the eastern border of Nebraska. It is sited on the west bank of the Missouri River just below the bluffs, approximately sixty miles upriver from Omaha. Decatur was established in 1856 and is the second oldest settlement in Nebraska. Decatur currently has a population of 720.

Decatur had its beginning in September 1853, when the U.S. commissioner of Indian Affairs visited the Omaha Indians and negotiated the purchase of their lands. The first permanent settlement of Decatur was made in 1854. The town was named after Stephen Decatur, who claimed to be a nephew of Commodore Stephen Decatur. Decatur is rich in Indian legend, just as was discovered by Lewis and Clark during their 1804 expedition up the Missouri River to explore the Northwest Territories.

Bi-Centennial Parade, 1976, Decatur, Nebraska. Stagecoach built by William Deman, grandfather of Ms. Peggy Davis and Ms. Pam Nelson. Photograph by Ms. Pam Nelson. Courtesy of City Clerk, Ms. Peggy Davis, Decatur, Nebraska.

The first school term in Decatur began in the fall of 1861 at the town hall with Mrs. E. D. Canfield as the first teacher. Mrs. Samuels, mother of Frank and Jesse James, taught one term of school in Decatur in 1862. Over the years several different buildings were used to hold classes. The present school was built in 1936 and only holds classes for kindergarten through sixth grades. The seventh through twelfth grades were merged with the Lyons Public Schools in 1984.

The village of Decatur is governed by a chairman and four-member board of trustees. They are elected to four-year terms. Decatur also has a non-elected village clerk and village treasurer, two certified police officers, and a volunteer fire and rescue department.

Points of interest around Decatur include the famous "dryland bridge," which resulted from the Corps of Engineers temporarily diverting the Missouri River, the Decatur Marina, and Beck Memorial Park. Decatur also boasts of many interesting churches over 100 years old, the beautiful bluffs along the river, and an array of recreational activities. Every year over Father's Day weekend Decatur comes alive with its riverfront festivities in recognition of the importance of the Missouri River to the economy. (Nelson, *Burt County Plaindealer*, p. 14A)

Top: Beck Memorial Park, Decatur, Nebraska, on the Missouri River. Photograph by Ms. Pam Nelson. Courtesy of city Clerk, Ms. Peggy Davis, Decatur, Nebraska.

Bottom: Post Card, picturing an old ferry boat before the Bridge, Decatur, Nebraska. Courtesy of Ms. Pam Nelson and Ms. Peggy Davis, City Clerk, Decatur, Nebraska.

General stores in Decatur, Ohio. the building on the left is the J. P. Mann store built in 1882, now housing the Post Office. the building on the right was E. E. Black's store built in 1906. Photograph by and courtesy of Ms. Eva Davis, Winchester, Ohio.

DECATUR, OHIO

Decatur, Ohio is in Brown County, approximately fifty miles east south east of Cincinnati and is sited on the eastern part of Byrd Township. The village had originally been named St. Claireville in 1801, but was renamed Decatur in 1883. The change was required because Belmont County had a St. Clairville with a train stop. In those days the town with a train depot always retained its name. The name change to Decatur was approved by the state legislature approximately fifteen years later.

The town was originally laid out by town proprietors Basil Duke and John Coburn with lots measuring 66 by 188 feet. Outer lots of four to five acres were also platted and several of these were set aside for public use. (Davis letter)

The first house in Decatur was built about 1802 by Nathaniel Beasley. The first hotel was built by Thomas Moore in a log cabin built about 1804. Around 1830 Silas Thomas started another successful hotel in the village of Decatur. By 1883 Decatur contained two stores and blacksmith shops, a woolen factory, a carpenter and wagon-maker shop, a saddlery and harness-making shop, a paint shop, a butcher shop, a hotel, schoolhouse, and three churches. (Beers, p. 703)

Today Decatur has a beautiful park named Decatur Park with Soldiers' Monuments, a Band Stand, and WWI Commemorative Cannon. The tallest of the monuments was dedicated on September 12, 1908, in memory of those Civil War veterans from Byrd Township. A second monument was erected by the Lieutenant Byrd Chapter of the DAR in 1922 with an embedded bronze plate inscribed "In Honor of the Boys of Byrd Township who served in the World War of 1917–1919, for Liberty and Humanity." (Brown County Historical Society, pp. 93–94)

One of the general stores in Decatur, the J. P. Mann Store built in 1882, also houses the post office. The other store was E. E. Black's Store, which was built by James E. Branson in 1906. Decatur's communication system started with a manually operated switchboard and has progressed to today's computer-controlled switching system, something the "number please" girls never dreamed of having. (Davis Letter & Submission to Brown County Historical Society, pp. 70–71)

DECATUR COUNTY, TENNESSEE

Decatur County, Tennessee, is in west Tennessee, originally part of Perry County which was carved out of Hickman County in 1819 and was named in honor of Commodore Oliver Hazard Perry, the War of 1812 Naval hero of the Battle of Lake Erie. In time the inconvenience of having to cross a river to attend court led to the determination to form a new county in that part of Perry County lying west of the Tennessee River. In 1845 the Tennessee General Assembly passed an act creating the new county. The act stated that the new county was to be formed out of "that part of Perry County lying west of the river, to be known and distinguished by the name of Decatur County, in honor and to perpetuate the memory of Commodore Stephen Decatur, of the United States Navy, of whose services our nation should be proud and whose memory should be revered."

Decatur County Courthouse, Decaturville, Tennessee, county seat of Decatur County, Tennessee. The first log courthouse was built in 1848 and soon replaced by a frame building, which burned in 1869. A two-story brick courthouse was built in 1869, which burned in 1927, and was replaced by the current courthouse in 1928. Photograph from the *News Leader.* Courtesy of Edwin Townsend, Decatur County Historical Society.

Decatur County has a land area of 337 square miles and is bounded on the north by Benton County, on the west by Henderson County, on the south by Hardin County, and on the east by the Tennessee River. Fossils of shell-forming sea animals, fish, reef-building corals, and sponges of the Silurian period of the Paleozoic era have been found in the county by paleontologists.

Settlement of the area that became Decatur County appears to have begun in the 1790s. Jimmy Harris was the first settler of record. Coming up the Tennessee River, he landed at the mouth of a stream that was later named Cub Creek. His progeny named it in memory of the many bear cubs that "Uncle Jimmy" killed in that area. There were approximately 300 people living within the county area when it became Decatur County.

The old Washington Ferry connecting Highway 30 across the Tennessee River, which was replaced by a bridge in 1997. Photograph courtesy of Meigs County Tourism, Decatur, Tennessee.

DECATURVILLE, TENNESSEE

Decaturville, Tennessee, is the county seat of Decatur County, Tennessee, with a population of 9,457 as of the 1970 census. The first Decatur County Courthouse was a log structure built in 1848. It was soon replaced by a frame building which burned down in 1869 and was replaced by a two-story brick courthouse that same year for $9,000. That building also succumbed to a fire in 1927 and was replaced by the present courthouse in 1928.

DECATUR, TENNESSEE

Decatur, Tennessee, is the county seat of Meigs County with a population of 1,361 as of the 1990 census. decatur was established as the county seat when Meigs County was formed by the state legislature of 1835–1836. Named after Commodore Decatur, it is situated in the center of the approximately 30-mile-long and 10-mile-wide Meigs County, which lies between McMinn County and the Tennessee River.

This small rural county has seen almost everything that had affected the Uioted States in its history, but especially the Tennessee Valley Authority and the Great Cherokee Removal. The Cherokee "Trail of Tears" passed through Meigs County just south of Decatur.

Today the descendents of Decatur's early pioneers are developing the Cherokee Memorial Park on a bluff overlooking the river where many Cherokee families encamped on their arduous journey to Oklahoma. In the park will be the Cherokee Memorial Monument of granite representing the seven-pointed star of the Cherokee national seal. Its seven panels will be engraved with seventy names of heads of households that were recorded in the

1835 Cherokee census. A flame will burn in perpetuity from the top of the monument. (Meigs County Brochure and History)

DECATUR, TEXAS

Decatur, Texas, is a small town just twenty-five miles west of Denton in Wise County, North Texas, with a population of 4,869. Decatur was selected as a town site and the seat of Wise County in 1856. It was first known as Taylorsville. The famous Butterfield Overland Mail Route passed through town in the mid-1800s. Decatur was also the site of the trial and hanging of five Peace Party conspirators in 1862.

The Wise County courthouse in Decatur was built in 1895 of pink limestone from Burnet. The courthouse has been pronounced a perfect architectural example of its type and era. The Wise County Heritage Museum is also located in Decatur. The museum is housed in the administration building of old Decatur Baptist College, which was built in 1892. The museum exhibits include Indian artifacts, old post office fixtures from the Chico community, art, and mementos of the early history of the area. The museum also includes archives and a little theater.

Decatur is home to East Central Junior College, which was founded in 1914. Also nearby are lakes Bridgeport and Eagle Mountain. Decatur has become the trade center and shipping point for this agricultural and dairy region. (Decatur, Texas Internet Web page)

Top: Aerial view of Decatur, Texas. Photograph courtesy of Ms. Susan Williams, director, Chamber of Commerce, Decatur, Texas. Bottom: Decatur Elementary School, Decatur, Texas. The school is constructed of the same pink limestone as the county Courthouse. Photograph courtesy of Ms. Susan Williams, director, Chamber of Commerce, Decatur, Texas.

APPENDICES

APPENDIX A

Appendix A contains additional information on Chapters 1 — 12.

Chapter 2

1. Part of the Statement of Circumstances attending the destruction of the frigate *Philadelphia* with the officers and men employed on the occasion as laid before the president by the secretary of the Navy, November 13, 1804, from page 21 is continued below as follows:

The following is a list of the Officers, & the number of Men employed in the destruction of the Philadelphia.

Lieut. Stephen Decatur jr.
Jas. Lawrence Lieutenants.
Joseph Bainbridge
Jonathan Thorn
Louis Heerman Surgeon.
Ralph Izard Midshipmen.
John Rowe
Charles Morris
Alexr. Laws
John Davis
Ths. Macdonough
Thos. O. Anderson
Mr. Salvadore (Catalano)–Pilot
62 Men.
Lieut. Decatur has stated that all his Officers and men behaved with the greatest coolness and intrepiity, and Commodore Preble has informed me that Lieut. Stewart's conduct was judicious and meritorious.
Robt. Smith—
Secretary of the Navy."
(Note: Men who took part in the destruction of the Philadelphia.)
William Wiley, boatswain
James Robinson, seaman
William Hook, gunner
Mathew Yeates, seaman

George Crawford, quartermaster
William Ducket, seaman
George Brown, quartermaster
Andrew Espey, seaman
John Newman, quartermaster
William Tumbo, seaman
Paul Frazier, quartermaster
Thomas James, seaman
James Metcalf, boatswain's mate
Joseph Numond, seaman
Nicholas Brown, boatswain's mate
George Murray, seaman
Edward Kellen, master's mate
Robert McKnight,seaman
Samuel Endicott, quarter gunner
William Dixon, seaman
James Wilson, quarter gunner
Henry Davenport, seaman
John Ford, quarter gunner
Joseph Parker, seaman
Richard Doyles, quarter gunner
Dennis O'brian, ordinary seaman
Joseph Boyd, ship's steward
Jacob Kurgen, ordinary seaman
Edward Burk, seaman
John Burtson, ordinary seaman
Peter Munell, seaman
William Rodgers,ordinary seaman
Richard Ormond, seaman
Charles Robinson,ordinary seaman
Samuel Jackson, seaman
William Trippet,ordinary seaman
James Pasgrove, seaman
John Joseph, ordinary seaman
Joseph Goodwin, seaman
Michael Williams,ordinary seaman
John Boyles, seaman

Marines
Augustus C. Fleur, seaman
Solomon Wren, sergeant
1Charles Berryman, seaman
Duncan Mansfield, corporal
Daniel Frazier, seaman
Noble James, private
William Graham, seaman
John Quinn, private
Reuben James, seaman
Isaac Camfield, private
Robert Love, seaman
Reuben O'Brian, private
John Williams, seaman
William Pepper, private

Joseph Fairfield, seaman
John Wolsfrandorf, private
George Fudge, seaman
(Nav Docs, Knox, vol. 3, pp. 422–424)

Chapter 3

1. The list of killed and wounded on board the *United States* from Decatur's letter to Secretary of the Navy Hamilton of October 30, 1812 is as follows:

Thomas Brown New York Seaman—
Henry Sheperd—Philadelphia ditto—
William Murry Boston—Boy
Michael ODonnel New York private
marine—John Roberts— ditto—ditto—Killed -
*John Mercer Funk. Philadelphia Lieutenant.
*John Archibald—New York.
Carpenters crew
Christian Clark ditto Seaman
George Christopher ditto— ordinary seaman
George Mahai ditto—ditto
William James ditto—ditto
John Lalor ditto private marine—Wounded
- On board the *Macedonian* There were thirty six killed—& sixty eight wounded—Among the former were the Boatswain-one masters mate & the schoolmaster & of the latter were the first & third Lieutenants—one masters mate & two midshipmen—
*since dead
(Dudley, *The Naval War*, vol. 1, pp. 552–553)

Chapter 9

(1) Following is a list of the officers and crew of the USS *Decatur* (DD-936) during the

ship's Mediterranean cruise of 1959–1960, including the embarked Destroyer Squadron (DESRON) 8 staff. (USS *Decatur* (DD-936) Cruise Book, Mediterranean Cruise, 1959–1960, pp. last & inside back cover)

USS *Decatur*
Mediterranean Cruise
1959–60

Desron 8 Staff

Officers:
Capt. A. Coxe
Capt. C. Stephan
Lt. W. Delaney
Lt. J. Holmes
Lt. Comdr. G. Mahoney
Lt. (jg) G. Peloquin
Lt. (jg) G. Stallman

Enlisted:
RMC W. Goodwin
SM3 J. Farnan
YN3 J. Kovel
YN3 G. Magnuson
SD2 A. Mayes
RM3 E. W. Miller
TN A. Nalumen
YN1 E. Smith

Ship's Company

Ship's Officers
Comdr. S. Dombroff
Comdr. A. McLane
Lt. Comdr. R. Ewing
Lt. (jg) J. Chamberlain
Ens. J. Crandall
Lt. (jg) B. Davis
Lt. (jg) D. Elwell
Lt. (jg) D. Fitzgerald
Ens. R. Gramlich
LT W. Hamm, Jr.
Lt. (jg) P. Jacques
Ens. J. King
LT S. Lazarus
Lt. (jg) C. Nelson
LT A. Neustel
Lt. (jg) R. Rogers

Ens. C. Schoneman
Lt. (jg) R. Sweeney
LT P. Trimble
Ens. R. Waldman
Ens. R. Williams

1st Division
BMC X. Dietrich
SN R. Boushley
SN B. Bundy
SN W. Carter
SN E. Cowley
SN J. Donovan
SN S. Figura
SN R. Gaskell
SN R. Gendreau
SN E. Gopp
SA C. Graf
SN R. Harris
SN W. Herr
SN C. Hill
SN H. Jaderlund
SN E. Jenkins
SN D. Kerley
SN W. Macomber
SN C. Mallon
SN S. Manoski
BM3 T. McCary
SN T. McPhee
SN H. Merchant
SN J. Micheal
SN W. Middleton
BM3 D. Noble
SA H. Oestreich
SN J. Pomerleau
SA J. Pore
SN S. Rinebold
BM1 E. Roehrich
SN D. Service
SN E. Smith
SN R. St. John
SN L. Stukan
SN R. Urbanski
SN R. Vaden
BM2 C. Wallace
BM3 E. Whalen
SN T. Wiest
BM2 C. Wodarski

2nd Division
CM2 W. Adams
SN W. Bailey
GM3 J. Boyd
CM2 J. Cawley
FT3 J. Feehan
GM1 G. Ferguson
FT3 P. Fiebke
GM1 V. Gilliard
SN G. Harrigan
CM3 R. Harrison

SN G. Jordan
SN J. Keator
SN F. Marrone
FT3 G. Martin
SN E. Mayton
FT3 J. Merrill
CM3 A. Nolette
SN J. Parkinson
SN R. Paturalski
FT2 D. Peterlin
FT3 J. Pruiksma
GM3 G. Schreihofer
FT1 T. Schultz
GM3 J. Snyder
SN L. Spradlin
FT1 G. Stedman
SN S. Stella
SN H. Stevens
SN D. Sweeney
Gm1 R. Vaughan
SN B. Wade
CM2 C. Webb

OI Division
SN R. Caffery
RD3 P. Cahill
RD1 R. Campbell
ET3 C. Dellinger
SN L. Dingman
RD3 A. Dunnan
SN L. Eng
SN J. Gervais
SN V. Ghizzone
SN E. Klurman
RD2 C. Laney
ET2 C. Lauter
SN F. Longstreet
ET3 L. Rose
SN G. Specht
ET3 W. Tooke
SN L. White
M Division
BTC B. Ruzicka
FN C. Armiger
FN J. Armiger
FN J. Avery
FN E. Barr
FN J. Beaulieu
BT1 C. Bellflower
BT1 R. Benway
FN R. Bigbee
MM3 G. Black
MM1 G. Bowab
FN R. Briggs
FN J. Brouker
FN G. Burdick
FN M. Cope
MM3 M. Creager
FN E. Dieffenbach
BT3 F. Divonzo

FN R. Eppley
MM2 E. Farias
FN H. France
BT1 B. Fry
MM3 R. Crider
MM3 R. Guffey
FN O. Hammons
BT3 C. Harrison
BT2 H. Henson
MM3 D. Hill
FN G. Hoxmeier
MM3 M. Imel
FN L. Kautz
MM2 A. Kensil
FN G. Kimble
BT2 W. King
FN W. Leightley
FN L. Libetti
BT2 W. Loney
FN J. Maimone
FN D. Mathias
BT1 J. McElroy
Mm1 C. McChee
MM3 F. Menne
MM2 R. Michaud
FN R. Nivison
BT3 D. Norris
BT3 R. Pfanstiel
MM3 G. Pontius
FN M. Ruggerio
MM3 M. Runyan
FN N. Saltzman
FN F. Seeley
MM3 R. Senecal
FN H. Sexton
BT3 J. Sims
BT2 C. Sullivan
BT3 T. Ward

R Division
MMC R. Brown
EMC N. Hartling
MM1 E. Akens
FN B. Bill
MM2 J. Davis
FN M. Derato
SFP3 P. Dodge
IC3 D. Evans
FP1 H. Gooch
EM2 A. Hill
EN2 H. Huck
IC2 R. Judy
IC2 M. Kiese
FN C. Kirtland
FN R. Krauss
FN D. Luke
FP3 H. Martin
FN D. Miller
FP3 T. Montalbano
EM3 J. Moring

FN J. Onnestad
FN R. Rabideau
DC3 E. Reed
EM3 W. Stepp
FN C. Stratton

Supply Division
CSC H. Lowther
HMC C. Williamson
SN J. Baranauskas
CS2 B. Bethea
CS3 R. Bilyak
SN E. Brantley
TN F. Crowder
SN J. Erato
SH1 H. Gray
SN A. Gitsas
TN W. Hudson
SN S. Jablonski
CS3 T. Jaye
SD3 J. Johnson
SK3 P. Johnson
SN R. Lasek
SN R. Loomis
FN R. McCauley
SD3 G. Polite
SN C. Schafer
SN G. Schense
SD2 J. Smith
Sk1 M. Teles
SN W. Tyson
CS3 H. Vickers
DK3 J. Webster
SH2 R. Whitt
SD1 N. Williams
SH3 C. Ziegler
SK1 F. Zielinski

OC Division
RMC P. St. Pierre
QM3 D. Davidson
QM2 B. Decker
TE1 M. Demling
SN R. Gager
YN2 R. Gant
RM3 T. Gardner
SN D. Cavican
SN W. Gwinn
SN R. Hains
SM3 R. Hawk
RM3 H. King
PN3 P. Leahey
SN D. Leffler
SM1 L. Massie
SN R. McDonald
SN S. Milne
SN M. Newcomb
SN C. Peddycoart
SN D. Peters
SM3 R. Reilly

191

SN E. Robison
YN3 C. Scribner
QM3 C. Shepherd
QM3 M. Smith
SN E. Soucie
SN D. Watson

F Division
SN C. Cain
SO2 L. Carl
SN W. Conner
SO3 J. Crow
TM3 J. Davis
SO1 G. Herrington
TM2 S. Jenter
SN R. Kemper
SO3 J. Kreeb
SN R. Millett
SO3 D. Weatherby

Chapter 10

(1) Following is a list of the officers and crew of the USS *Decatur* (DDG-31) during the first year, 1967–1968. (USS *Decatur* (DDG-31) Cruise Book, *Decatur*–The First Year, pp. inside front & back covers)
DDG-31 Plank Owners
April 29, 1967

Comdr. Lee Baggett, Jr.,
    Commanding Officer
Lt. Comdr. Rodney B.
    McDaniel, Executive
    Officer

Navigation Department
Lt. David R. Pauling,
    Navigator
Administrative and Medical
    Divisions
Chief Petty Officers
Chief Signalman J. J. Mitchell
Chief Hospitalman E. L.
    Powers
Petty Officers First Class
T. E. McLamb
D. E. Rogers
B. E. Snow
Petty Officers Second Class
R. R. Fong
W. L. Hickey
P. R. LeFever
R. H. Ramey
Seamen
R. W. Carlson
J. F. Carver, Jr.
R. C. Cave

W. Terry
J. R. West
L. L. White

Engineering Department
Lt. Richard H. Rener,
    Engineering Officer
Lt. (jg) Stanley J. Snyder,
    Damage Control Assistant
Lt. (jg) Theodore F. Smolen,
    Main Propulsion Assistant
Chief Petty Officers
Chief Electrician W. R. Braden
Chief Boiler Tender R. E.
    Brenner
Master Chief Ship's
    Propulsionman J. B.
    Butler
Senior Chief Machinist Mate
    C. M. Dyer
Chief Boiler Tender C. E.
    Gratham
Chief Boiler Tender G. D.
    Jenkins
Chief Machinist Mate D. E.
    Ledoux
Chief Engineman C. Reed
Chief Machinist Mate L. W.
    Turner
Petty Officers First Class
L. F. Baier
W. Bilyeu
V. Craft
W. T. Dent
J. D. Farrell
K. P. Hawkins
G. M. Jones
W. F. Lavitich
F. E. Linebarger
D. G. Parker
D. C. Powell
W. J. Rhoden
R. P. Richardson
W. L. Rush
H. L. Shelton
F. M. Spilva
M. W. Stricker
A. O. Tolejkoski
K. E. Wulff
Petty Officers Second Class
J. P. Ahneman
C. D. Arkon
D. E. Crawford
R. O. Ellorin
L. J. Gregel
C. A. Haviland
N. W. Hill
W. D. Martin
J. Millar
C. E. Noe

M. B. Panaquiton
R. E. Paschall
A. N. Rogers
E. E. Staub
Petty Officers Third Class
H. T. Bowser
W. L. Cook
M. A. Desy
D. C. Ellington
R. D. Grandpre
R. Lampkin
G. M. Larson
D. L. Olsen
D. C. Shelter
T. L. Warzynski
W. B. Woodruff
S. F. Zentz
Firemen
D. E. Acklie
R. A. Allison
R. W. Berry
B. B. Blesi
R. D. Bower
R. G. Brown
L. G. Burnett
T. V. Cameron
R. E. Clark
L. L. Cooper
D. W. Crouch
R. S. Curry
W. J. Dennis
J. F. Fider
R. V. Goessling
M. M. Hiles
W. S. Hodge
L. W. Kirk
R. J. Kramer
A. Latham
B. R. Martinez
M. M. Miles
M. R. Montoya
G. L. Mooy
T. H. Myrick
N. T. Nagy
R. S. Nailor
J. A. Neufeld
R. M. Pasalski
M. J. Pounds
M. L Ramsdell
T. C. Rankin
R. E. Rush
K. P. Schmidt
R. N. Schurr
C. D. Sherry
J. E. Skoglund
J. H. Stewart
D. J. Stoffell
T. N. Terrell
W. D. Terrell

T. R. Vaughn
C. B. Warner

Supply Department
Lt. James B. Birindelli, Supply
    Officer
Ens. B. P. Babbitt, Assistant
    Supply Officer
Chief Petty Officers
Chief Commissaryman D. E.
    Bergbower
Chief Storekeeper J. M. Pilkus
Petty Officers First Class
M. T. Bleza
D. W. Goebel
H. J. Graham
G. Z. Majica
Petty Officers Second Class
F. C. Aspuri
R. L. Bendiske
F. C. Camacho
O. P. Cayagas
E. H. Lewis
J. A. Rastall
Petty Offices Third Class
A. T. Adams
J. W. Hunter
M. L. Langford
R. D. Ristow
J. O. Roberts
D. R. Schultz
E. G. West
H. B. West
H. Wilkerson
Seamen
R. J. Abrenilla
J. A. Badaraco
R. D. Bilbrey
J. L. Boehlke, Jr.
J. E. Butler
L. A. Clairmont
L. M. Crowe
D. R. Czikall
R. A. Diaz
R. L. Dominguez
J. A. Ferraro
J. A. Gonzales
E. V. Gossett
T. E. Harris
T. L. Howard
C. S. Nichols
D. L. Oliver
R. L Robinson
L. C. Rose
E. M. Sarmiento
E. L. Sears
J. D. Shields
D. E. Singleton
T. A. Sauza

D. M. Vail
B. M. Ward
J. J. Wilczek

Weapons Department
Lt. Gerald E. Gneckow,
  Weapons Officer
Lt. (jg) Jeffrey V. Wilson,
  First Lieutenant
Lt. (jg) Henry r. Morris, III,
  Missile Systems Officer
Lt. (jg) Thomas S. Moore,
  Undersea Warfare Officer
Lt. (jg) Marcus K. Taylor,
  Missile Officer
Lt. (jg) James Tyng
Petty Officers First Class
A. D. Jordan
B. J. McGarity
C. B. Morris
G. L. Smoker
G. S. A. Straw
J. W. Zagarac
Petty Officers Second Class
J. S. Augenbaugh
J. O. Bailey
A. T. Baltistpli
R. J. Burnz
R. A. Candel
R. L. Dias
B. W. Fryer
D. R. Gonzales
E. E. Kincaid
R. R. Lumley
M. J. Mandeville
R. E. Manual
G. Oden
H. W. Ogden
C. D. Petzold
J. J. Reamer
W. C. Rice
R. Rabbins
K. W. Smith
W. J. Smits
R. T. Willis
Petty Officers Third Class
E. R. Bauer
D. H. Delock
A. L. Graham
W. J. Gratza
H. M. Hamilton
J. L. Harless
L. D. Indvik
P. J. Justin
R. K. Kingsbury
N. T. Laney
J. W. Lawrence
A. J. Linardi
R. B. Lucas
N. D. Madore

G. L. Rosebraugh
E. G. Rosenthal
J. Schlitter
C. E. Schmitz
R. L. Wheeler
M. E. Whitmore
Seamen
M. W. Angel
A. D. Audi
J. C. Bahner
L. J. Bennett
G.L. Brook
C. C. Brown
K. P. Connelly
J. A. Copeland
W. E. Davis
M. J. DeSilva
J. V. Diaz
J. C. Falconer
T. L. Folk
P. G. Galle
J. H. Ganey
R. P. Groswirth
C. W. Hale, Jr.
K. W. Henderson
R. J. Kern
E. S. Kraft
G. A. Lake
C. D. Leffew
M. L. Lieberman
D. B. Matulich
J. E. McCarthy
R. D. McConchie
J. V. McNeely
R. G. Melcher
D. R. Miller
F. R. Mowrer
M. E. Parvu
D. T. Patterson
R. J. Peterman
L. D. Reed
D. K. Rice
R. L. Robinson
C. M. Robison
W. M. Scott
G. L. Smith
J. H. Stella
K. V. Stull
D. Z. Tully
J. Ulrich
W. H. Watson
D. A. Young

Operations Department
Lt. Martin S. Hellewell,
  Operations Officer
Lt. (jg) James S. Rugowski, CIC
  Officer
Lt. (jg) Jack O. Klass,
  Communications Officer

WO Phillip E. Miller, Electronic
  Material Officer
Chief Petty Officers
Chief Electronics Technician P.
  H. Godwin
Senior Chief Electronics
  Technician J. S. Parker
Chief Radarman V. A.
  Ringenberg
Chief Signalman N. E. Rollins
Petty Officers First Class
B. L. Bunn
C. W. Costilow
E. G. Jacobson
N. L. Ruthart
R. V. Spence
R. L. Whitlock
Petty Officers Second Class
V. P. Bell
W. R. Bellamy
B. L. Birkman
C. Cobb
L. A. Cubbage
V. V. Ellison
J. E. Hayslip
R. P. Inman
G. L. Knapp
J. H. Mishier
C. A. Ream
H. A. Rosbury
A. M. Serdline
R. E. Smith
A. I. Van Vleat
S. J. Wieczoski
Petty Officers Third Class
W. V. Ball
A. T. Barbiari, Jr.
W. F. Berst
E. E. Gearhart
G. F. Glynn
C. E. Ketchum
J. R. Marsh
J. E. Masic
W. D. Morrison
W. A. Myron
J. D. O'Brien
T. M. O'Hara
D. L. Robison
J. E. Rogers
L. L. Taft
E. F. West
K. C. Williams
M. L. Williams
R. L. Wilson
Seamen
W. N. Alexander
W. A. Barkowski
K. R. Baughn
B. F. Chaffinch
E. J. Chavez

R. D. Crouse
B. E. Downs
L. H. Gillilard
J. L. Holloway
J. A. Hoover
J. C. Kelly
D. M. Koehler
D. J. Larese
J. P. North
T. W. Ogden
L. G. Perry
J. H. Robinson
F. G. Swan
A. D. West
D. Whiteman

(2) Following is a list of the officers and crew of the USS *Decatur* (DDG-31) during the ship's second Western Pacific deployment from February 13 to August 29, 1970. (USS *Decatur* (DDG-31) Cruise Book, WESTPAC DEPLOY-MENT 2)

Comdr. John Bishop Allen
Commanding Officer, 19
  September 1968–14 July
  1970

Commander Sayre Archie
  Swarztrauber
Commanding Officer, 14 July
  1970–10 September 1971.

Lt. Comdr. Gordon L. Thorpe
Executive Officer

Department Heads
Lt. Comdr. Thomas M. Mustin,
  Weapons
Lt. Comdr. Jack L. Challender,
  Operations
Lt. Michael B. Tepovich, Supply
Lt. William B. Powers
Lt. Kellie S. Blerly

Division Officers
Ens. Robert K. Brands, First
  Lieutenant
Lt. (jg) Michael W. Hughey,
  Disbursing Officer
Lt. (jg) Franz J. Kurth,
  Communications Officer
Lt. (jg) George F. Leboutillier,
  Main Propulsion Assistant
Lt. (jg) Nelson R. Parda, Fire
  Control Officer

Lt. (jg) Gordon H. Pullin,
    Navigator
Lt. (jg) Richard A. Quinn,
    Electronic Material Officer
Lt. (jg) Paul A. Smith,
    Gunnery Assistant

Chief Petty Officers
MMCS J. Nelson
BTCS J. Whetstone
RDCS D. Wooten
MMC K. Bachler
DCC L. Bostdorf
SMC E. Carson, Jr.
BMC G. Crenshaw
SKC L. Dungo
ETC J. Fugich
STC S. Grimm
CSC M. Metts
YNC N. Parsons
GMGC K. Smith
RMC K. Stempion

First Class Petty Officers
MM1 R. Bacon
RM1 J. Been
GMM1 C. Collier
FTG1 T. Danzer
ST1 H. Dousharm
EM1 R. Ellorin
ET1 J. Fugich
MR1 K. Hawkins
MM1 D. Hibbard
BT1 I. Jackson
GMM1 R. Lang
PN1 J. Lynn
FTM1 W. Ramsey
MM1 R. Storey
RD1 A. VanVleet

Second Class Petty Officers
ETN2 M. Albert
RD2 W. Alexander
BT2 W. Brown
FTM2 R. Candel
RD2 C. Chain
MM2 L. Cooper
DC2 P. Dillard
MM2 J. Elder
MM2 G. Ellis
IC2 C. Faber
BT2 E. Gasque
GMG2 A. Hobbs
DK2 R. Hudson
FTG2 M. Kelley
PC2 E. Knight
RM2 D. La Plante
EM2 C. Lynch
SM2 D. Miller
MM2 R. Occhiline
194

FTM2 W. Pepin
MM2 P. Robinson
RD2 D. Scheo
FTM2 C. Schmitz
MM2 D. Shetler
BT2 J. Stewart
BT2 D. Stoffel
MM2 R. Trafton
MM2 C. Walker
RD2 A. West
SH2 H. West

Third Class petty Officers
STG3 M. Allen
ETR3 D. Asselin
DE3 A. Audi
STG3 B. Baker
FTM3 S. Bennett
CS3 K. Bilbrey
FTM3 J. Bond
FTM3 L. Burk
MM3 L. Burnett
EM3 D. Campbell
GMG3 G. Capra
FTM3 R. Collom
GMG3 M. Conatser
STG3 W. Craig
BT3 W. DeLaet
GMM3 L. Ely
MM3 S. Estep
RD3 S. Falcon
FTM3 P. Ferrara
MM3 R. Fleet
RD3 L. Fry
SK3 G. Glasco
MM3 J. Gonzalez
BM3 D. Griffin
SM3 R. Griffin
RM3 J. Harsh
SFM3 H. Hartmann
GMG3 R. Hayes
SK3 D. Hellman
MM3 J. Hurtado
GMM3 N. Jensen
RM3 E. Johnson
FTM3 P. Justin
FTM3 T. Korgie
SFPe R. Kramer
ETN3 J. Liebseck
STG3 R. Lowrey
SM3 G. Munn
FTG3 E. Nichtigal
Rm3 L. Norman
BM3 J. Otis
RD3 W. Perry
STG3 M. Peridas
RD3 J. Prise
BT3 M. Ramsdell
YN3 J. Rapp
RD3 C. Rich

MM3 P. Robinson
IC3 W. Saunoris
FTM3 D. Schaffbuch
FTM3 J. Schlitter
FTG3 R. Sechrist
EM3 T. Smay
FTG3 D. Smith
FTM3 T. Spiro
SFP3 W. Stewart
GMM3 D. Stille
RD3 R. Thomas
RD3 W. VanNess
ETN3 S. Waldenga
STG3 H. Walsh
ETR3 B. Wells
FTM3 D. White
IC3 T. Wilson
IC3 M. Young

Seamen
SN P. Andrews
EMFN R. Azcltine
FN S. Barchak
FA D. Barrett
RDSA L. Bell
SN D. Bettolucci
SN L. Brand
SN E. Collier
RMSA S. Collins
FN F. Craig
SN A. DeYoung
DCFN R. Dittemore
SMSN S. Dowdall
FN D. Duquette
FA R. Engelhorn
MMFN S. Estep
SN G. Falbo
FN M. Flores
SN R. Flynn
SN M. Fought
RDSN L. Fry
SN P. Garrett
MMFN W. Gehrke
SN D. Givens
FA J. Groat
PNSN I. Gutierrez
FTMSN M. Hamilton
SN E. Harness
SN D. Harris
SN J. Harsen
SN R. Heiple
BTFA C. Hembree
BTFN J. Hingey
FN H. Holstedt
GMMSN J. Houck
BTFN J. Irving
RDSN A. Jablonski
SA D. Jacobs
SN M. Jahnke
MMFN R. Jeffrey

SA R. Kelley
SN T. Kirkwood
SN D. Koczinski
SN T. Kolnik
SN P. Landry
ETNSN R. Lark
SN W. Lyons
RDSA D. McCullough
SN T. McGovern
SN G. McMahon
QMSN J. Miller
SN C. Monte
ETSN S. Morton
SN G. Newcomer
MMFN J. Newland
FA R. Norris
MMFN D. Offutt
MMFN J. Paglia
MMFN W. Paradiso
SA P. Parkinson
SN M. Patterson
SN D. Platzer
DCFN R. Provencal
SN J. Riggs
SN A. Risner
SA N. Schaffer
SN D. Schweiger
FA D. Scott
FN B. Smith
FN V. Spade
SA G. Splett
ICFN R. Steighner
FA E. Strader
SA D. Taylor
STGSN E. Taylor
SN S. Tessler
SN R. Thorbjornsen
BTFN D. Trammell
EMFN D. Utterback
FN M. Vanderleest
FN T. Vaughan
BTFA J. Walsman
Sn S. Wellman
SN D. Wilson
GMGSN R. Withrow
RMSN C. Wood
FA M. Zimmerman

(3) Following is a list of the officers and crew of the USS *Decatur* (DDG-31) during the ship's Western Pacific Deployment of 1974 to 1975. (USS *Decatur* (DDG-31) Cruise Book, WESTPAC Deployment, 1974-75)

Comdr. Robert C. Hurd,
    Commanding Officer

Lt. Comdr. J.D. Fontana,
    Executive Officer
Lt. Comdr. R. G. Katz,
    Engineer Officer
Lt. J. S. Fitzgerald, Operations
    Officer
Lt. D. R. Aurand, Weapons
    Officer
Lt. R. Loshbaugh, Supply
    Officer
Lt. M. B. Hanson, Supply
    Officer
Lt. (jg) S. D. Arnote, ASW
    Officer
Lt. (jg) R. Bolding, Disbursing
    Officer
Lt. (jg) E. D. Brady,
    Communications Officer
Lt. (jg) A. B. Coffer, Gunnary
    Officer
Lt. (jg) K. E. Craine, Navigator
Ens. H. Domis, Engineering
    Materials Officer
Ens. T. A. Grote, 1st
    Lieutenant
Lt. (jg) D. E. Hoffman, Fire
    Control Officer
Lt. (jg) R. C. Lloyd, CIC
Ens. C. D. Trestrail, DCA
Lt. (jg) G. Valade, EMO
Lt. E. Davis, MPA
Ens. R. Hartling, Navigator
WO1 M. Duyck

Weapons Department
BMC W. Pospisil
BM2 I. Jones
BM2 R. Starr
BM3 J. Lawhorne
SN H. Robinson
SN P. Bass
SN R. Best
SN C. Devera
SN R. Ellison
SN E. Evans
SN D. Kilgore
SN J. Lankford

1st Division
BM3 K. Verbic
SN B. McPhee
SN L. Rickard
SN J. Scott
SN R. Standriff
SN T. Stout
SN C. Turley

ASW Division
STCS R. Campbell
TM1 J. McDuffie

ST1 M. Proper
STG2 D. Jorns
STG2 G. Rose
STG2 J. Ruth
GMT3 M. Elwell
STG3 D. Graff
TM3 M. Houtz
STG3 K. Johnson
STG3 J. Tibbetts
STGSN J. Bonc
STGSN D. Draper
SN L. Hall
GMTSN W. Jones
SN G. Martinez
SN J. Pelz
SN T. Snider
GMT3 L. Yagi

SAM Division
STCS J. Cross
GMMC D. Pasola
FTM1 R. Gillock
FTM2 M. Barr
GMM2 G. McPherson
FTM2 R. Siebert
FTM2 L. Walton
FTM3 G. Bisig
FTM3 T. Johnson
FTM3 M. Rettig
GMM3 A. Roussel
FTM3 F. Whitney
FTMSN J. Augustine
SN J. Browning
SN L. Dominguez
FTMSN R. Eddings
SN G. Mabey
SN M. Safranek

F Division
FTGC J. Jay
GMG2 B. Wegmueller
GMG3 J. Butler
FTG3 T. Westlake
GMG3 N. Woods
SN J. Bowden
SN G. Currier
SN F. Leniek
SN M. ormsbee

Operations Department
EWC L. Pollard
EW1 R. Harris
ETN2 T. Augustine
ETR2 B. Byrum
EW2 M. Goldammer
ETN2 A. Ritchie
ETR3 R. Arsenault
ETRSN R. Dunlap
ETNSN S. Gorsuch
ETRSN D. Mauro

ETNSN D. Yant

OC Division
RM1 M. Pearsall
RM1 W. Vetzel
RM2 J. Bigelow
RM2 R. Biswell
RM2 E. Skillings
RM2 J. Helmig
SM3 C. Bridges
RM3 R. Dandridge
RM3 D. Johnson
RM3 J. McCord
SM3 G. Smith
RMSN T. Cogan
SMSN I. Decker
RMSN J. Morken
SMSN C. Owens
RMSN P. Talbert

OI Division
OSC B. Jones
OS1 R. Crow
OS1 R. Peterson
OS3 A. Tate
OSSN R. Aguirre
OSSN E. Geathers
OSSN J. Hesse
OSSN R. Wooldrige
SN T. Gosh

Supply Department
SKC I. Balmaseda
CSC C. Raybourn
SH1 R. Corgin
SK1 T. Gladney
SK1 J. Holtwick
SD1 D. Legaspi
CS1 J. Wieland
DK2 R. Delacruz
SK2 J. Kosel
SK2 N. Millan
CS3 T. Aguilar
SH3 P. Paelmo
SH3 H. Petterson
SH3 R. Unruh
SN E. Andal
SDSN R. Arimbuyutam
CSSN M. Blackwell
DKSN M. Carrasco
SN W. Christian
SN J. Cogswell
CSSN R. Fleischacker
SN M. Hall
SN L. Heiert
SN B. James
SCCN D. Kelly
SN D. Lloyd
MSSN P. Mucci
CSSN K. Patterson

SN M. Perez
SKSN J. Plenty
SKSN K. Schaefer
CSSN D. Suhler

Engineering Department

M Division
MMC B. O'Brien
MM2 W. Craig
MM2 J. Gonzales
MM2 J. Mundy
MM2 M. Olin
MM2 J. Warnock
MM3 K. Gotcher
MM3 M. Hamley
MM3 G. Moore
MM3 B. Phillips
FN A. Barker
FN J. Beasley
FN J. Goodrich
FN L. Heinzer
FN T. Hiltner
FN M. Klawitter
FN R. Martin
FN M. Manupella
FN J. Meek
FN G. Ozuna
FN J. Roberts
FN E. Saldivar
FN I. Sales
FN G. Schmidt
FN D. Tolrud
FN D. Webb
FN D. Adams

B Division
BTC C. Jones
BT1 P. Wing
BT2 R. Saienni
BT3 M. Whitlock
BT3 L. Sealey
BT3 J. Rigsby
FN P. Arnold
FN D. Bjorge
FN C. Borza
FN W. Brockway
FN P. Gallagher
FN R. Gilbert
FN J. Girdler
FN J. Hass
FN C. Lynch
FN D. McCauley
FN J. Mc Dougle
FN R. Mitchell
FN C. Scripture
FN B. Waterhout
FN G. Yribe

R Division
EMCS A. Smith

EMC R. Johnson
HTC E. Speakman
MMC M. Woods
HT1 H. James
EM1 K. Morris
IC2 R. Riner
MM2 F. Olsen
EM2 L. Pruiett
HT3 J. Barger
IC3 M. Grabowski
EM3 L. Larson
MM3 J. Nance
IC3 K. Cutting
IC3 J. Thompson
FN F. Alo
FN P. Aniva
FN D. Baker
FN L. Broussard
FN E. Evagelista
FN D. Haney
FN W. Lake
FN D. Lamela
FN R. Langley
FN S. Lewis
FN R. Loiselle
FN J. Ortega
FN L. Puckett
FN T. Shields
FN W. Solonika
FN E. Weisner

N and X Divisions
PNC J. Bruno
HMCS P. Gerard
YN1 R. Richardson
QM1 A. Von Werder
PN2 W. Dove
YN2 W. Gonzales
QM2 W. McMillan
PC2 G. Zamore
HM3 F. Burke
PN3 M. Francis
PN3 R. Gordon
JO3 D. Hager
SN K. Hare
SN M. Schweizer
SNSN D. Wilaon

(4) Following is a list of the officers and crew of the USS *Decatur* (DDG-31) during the ship's Western Pacific Cruise of 1978–1979. (USS *Decatur* (DDG-31) Cruise Book, WESTPAC, 1978–1979, pp. 10–42)

Comdr. George C. Chappell, Commanding Officer

Lt.Comdr. B. W. Young, Executive Officer

Operations Department
Lt. Jordan
Lt. Lane

On Division
QWC Conductor
QM3 Harmon
QMSN Gallahan
QMSR Olszewski
FA Bellipanni

OE Division
Lt. (jg) Edwards
Ens. Denton
ET1 Wade
ETR2 Boyle
ETN2 Frank
ETR3 Fansel
ETR3 Gootz
ETR3 Scott
SN Clutter
ETC Coutts
ETNSN Lackner
ETNSN Liccese

OI Division
Lt. (jg) Bloss
Ens. Rose
OD1 Ryker
OS1 Wasacz
OS2 Boyd
OS2 Brandt
EW2 Doane
EW2 Ellis
OS2 Foote
OS2 Francis
OS2 Tante
OS2 Thurman
OS2 Williams
OS3 Fiut
OR3 Foote
OS3 Gasaway
EW3 Hamner
EW3 Heup
OS3 Lincoln
OS3 Reed
OS3 Robinet
OS3 Shown
OD3 Sparks
OS3 Stone
OSSN Capaldo
OSSN Greeze
EWC Greger
OSC Parks
OSSA Smith

OC Division
Lt. (jg) Van Dyke
SM1 Murphy
RM1 Scott
RM2 Etienne
SM2 Houston
RM2 Speights
RM3 Coleman
RM3 Kallio
RM3 Kerns
RM3 Kilponen
RM3 Moreno
SM3 Thompson
RM3 Tobin
RMSN Carnes
RMSN Chatman
SMSN Hauff
SMSN Henderson
RMSR Mc Quay
RCC Shewmake

Engineering Department
Lt. Comdr. Giannotti
EM1 Almotie
IC1 Harness
EM2 Wright
IC3 Cassler
EM3 Collins
EM3 Cruz
EM3 Finley
IC3 Knott
EM3 Lemons
IC3 Palkovich
EM3 Perez
EM3 Voight
CWO4 Castillio
ICFN Gaska
EMSN Kressig
EMC McCammon
ICFN Woodley

R Division
MM1 Albano
HT2 Baney
HT2 Johnson
MR2 Powell
HT2 Stewart
MM3 Carl
EN3 Deguzman
MM3 Gallagher
MMC Bryant
HTFR Buckalew
FR Feldapausch
FN Gifford
ENFA Golding
HTFN Hirst
FN Lackey
HTFA May
HTC MC Govern
ENFN Sokoloski

HTFA Worstman

M Division
ENS Wahler
MM1 McCrary
MM1 Rupe
MM2 Magsaan
MM2 Roa
MM2 Viehmann
YN3 Cisar
MM3 Dye
MM3 Swanson
MM3 Wilheim
FA Alger
MMFN Base
MMFR Crabill
MMFN Johnson
MMFN Kiesow
MMC Lyle
MMFN Saari
MMFN Schoelsel
FA Sessions
MMFA Shuck
MMRN Tuel
MMFN Vincell

B Division
ENS Gilmore
BT1 Epps
BT2 Adasa
BT2 Cayas
BT2 McKaughan
BT2 Nielson
BT2 Ruba
BT3 Azzapardi
BT3 Barreras
BT3 Berlinger
BT3 Burkhart
BT3 Hogrebe
BT3 Kutcher
BT3 Mikaele
BTFN Dawley
BTFN Dingus
BTFN Feliciano
MMFN Helson
MMFN House
BTFN Kessler
BTFN Laposky
BTFN Longmire
FR Pugh
BTC Ren
BTFN Reynolds
FR Rose
BTFN Zerbie
BTFA Seising
FA Tryjillo
BTC Ware
MMCS Weisser

Weapons Department
Lt. Hagstrom
Lt. (jg) Delaney

ASW Division
STG1 Norris
STG2 Capaccio
GMT2 Miller
STG2 Oney
GMT2 Schwietz
TM2 Starke
STG3 Barnes
TM3 Benjiman
GMT3 Brandenburg
STG3 Cammack
STG3 Dubque
GMT3 Felczak
STG3 Henderson
STG3 Horn
TM3 Hull
STG3 Nottage
STG3 Owen
STG3 Peterson
STG3 Winter
GMTSN Allen
STGSN Colon
GMTSN Elam
STGSN Smith
STGSN Vargas
GMTSN Wunder
STGC Severn

Fox Division
Lt. (jg) Mallory
FTG1 McKinney
FTG1 Plasket
GMG2 Buchanan
GMg2 Cates
FTG2 Geiger
GMG2 McPherson
GMG3 Fletter
GMG3 Malone
FTG3 Mullen
FTG3 Neaves
FTG3 Nelson
FTG3 Wright
GMGSN Dreyfus
FTGC Jackson
GMGC Stark

Sam Division
Lt. (jg) McLoughlin
FTM1 Catterton
GMM1 Ely
FTM1 Gregg
FTM1 Groth
FTM1 LaPlante
FTM2 Dollar
FTM2 Gallipo
GMM2 Grantham

FTM2 Harless
FTM2 Kendall
FTM2 Klein
GMM2 Knievel
GMM2 Meyers
FTM2 Norris
FTM2 Povisen
FTM2 Sturgill
FTM3 Amaya
FTM3 Betancourt
FTM3 Denault
GMM3 Everett
FTM3 Lutrell
FTM3 Martin
FTMSN Clauson
FTMSN Ellingson
FTMC Holden
GMMSN Nelson

First Division
BM1 Lancaster
BM2 Hollowman
BM2 Sznajder
BM3 L. Coppinger
BM3 Jones
BM3 Wilson
SN Bitner
SN Carrol
SN Carter
SN Cato
SN Chamberlin
SR Clark
SN R. Coppinger
SA Harris
SA Hicks
SA Jacobsen
SN Kendrick
BMSN Kluver
SN Kuykendall
SR Lyle
SN McCutcheon
BMSN McKinley
BMC Moran
BMSN Mortimer
SR Olawumi
SN Rodriguez
SA Sarino
BMSN Saxton
SA Tittle
SN Wood

Supply Department
Lt .Bianco
Ens. Church
SH1 Gonzalvo
SK1 Johnson
SK1 Mayenschein
SH1 Rawls
BM1 Santos
MS1 Trajano

MS2 Cortez
SK2 Kazar
MS2 Santos
MS3 Aguon
MS3 Anderson
SH3 Bennett
SK3 Domantay
SK3 Gibbons
MS3 Hafften
SH3 Hall
SK3 Hernandez
SMS3 Morrow
MS3 Peralta
MS3 Richardson
MS3 Smith
MS3 Wolf
DKSN Douglas
SHSA Galich
SKSN Gonzalez
MSSR Hickey
SKSN Lanski
MSSN Miranda
SKSR Moore
MSC Papa
SHSR Story
SN Tyson
SHSA Vest

X Division
YN1 Abueg
NC1 Grodzicki
YN2 Bryant
YN3 Bolich
PN3 Crabtree
HM3 Wilson
YN3 Wright
HMC Hernandez
MAC Jenkins
PNC Wilde
SKCS Wilson

(5) Following is a list of the officers and crew of the USS *Decatur* (DDG-31) during the Pacific Cruise, Summer 1981. (USS *Decatur* (DDG-31) Cruise Book, Pacific Cruise, Summer 1981, pp. 7–49)

Capt. Gerald L. Dunn, Commanding Officer
19 June 1979–3 July 1981

Comdr. Michael J. Mills, Commanding Officer
July 3, 1981–May 28, 1983

Executive Division
Comdr. David F. Walsh, Executive Officer

CMA R. Sullivan
NC1 S. Alguire, Command Career Counselor
HM1 D. Banag
YN1 C. Cristobal
PN1 J. Nevling
YN2 J. Gustafson
HM2 T. Hughes
YN2 M. Staten
YN3 H. Davis
PC3 P. Hunkins
PC3 M. Nash
YNSNT. Eiesland
PNSN D. Gregory
PNC E. Trujillo
HN B. Warden

Navigation Division
Lt. Roger A. Gilmore, Navigator
QM1 S. Cook
QM3 M. Palo
QMSN P. Iten
QMSN H. Tolson, III
SN S. Mapes

Engineering Department
Lt. Comdr. Fred Orchard, Chief Engineer
Lt. Alfred Nugent, Damage constol Assistant
Lt. (jg) Tom Williams, Main Propulsion Assistant
Ens. Jim Dillingham, Electrical Officer
Ens. Jim Clemson, M Divison Officer
Ens. Steve Green, B Division Officer
MMCM J. Shepherd
YN3 D. Florez

B Division
BT1 J. Bender
BT1 I. Hayes
BT2 M. Benton
BT2 G. Dawley
BT2 K. McKaughan
BT2 R. Oden
BT2 J. Rath
BT2 P. Reid
BT3 E. Adrianzen
BT3 D. Burnett
BT3 S. Chapmna
BT3 T. Gonzales
BT3 R. Herring
BT3 T. Holike
BT3 E. Howington
BT3 N. Jerkovic
BT3 R. Kesslar

BT3 J. Kounse
BT3 J. Rebel
BTFR T. Bedway
BTFN D. Bentti
BTFN C. Circolo
BTFR R. Crane
BTFR J. Cull
BTFA T. Diggs
BTC S. Epps
BTFA E. Grieshaber
BTFR M. Howse
BTFA A. Jackson
BTFR T. Jackson
BTFA P. Johnson
BTFA T. Lashier
BTFA E. Lauch
BTFN G. Lyons
BTFN E. Mack
BTFR K. McIntyre
BTFR G. Nichols
BTC R. Ren
BTFN W. Sawyer
BTFA v. Trujillo
BTFA C. Vanornum
BTFA J. Winchester

M Division
MMCS R. Lyle
MM1 T. Graff
MM1 L. Rupe
MM2 J. Allen
MM2 R. Hermatz
MM2 M. Howard
MM2 J. Jeffers
MM2 J. Kiesow
MM2 D. Meyer
MM2 T. Schoelzel
MM2 B. Tuel
MM2 L. Wilheim
MM2 D. Wolz
MM3 D. Baker
MM3 H. Decatur
MM3 F. Irkinas
MM3 P. Stegner
MMFA D. Aubuchon
MMFA C. Boone
MMFN M. Brunnmeire
FA J. Corey
MMFA G. Daniel
MMFN C. Eash
MMFA C. Engwell
MMFA R. Gold
MMFN K. Kupka
FN R. McCrite
MMFN D. Newson
MMFR J. Reeves
FN B. Reichard
MMFN I. Williams

E Division
EM2 B. Dale
EM2 R. Perez
EM3 J. Blackketter
EM3 L. Davis
EM3 C. Niedzielski
EM3 F. Tala
FN A Gayda
EMS S. McCammon
EMFN T. Noegel
FN C. Tate

IC Division
IC1 D. Schulz
IC2 R. Butler
ICFN M. Buckley
ICFA S. Ross
ICFA J. Webb

R Division
HT1 W. Rachel
HT2 S. Gremillion
HT2 K. Kirst
HT2 A. Savage
HT2 C. Seider
HT2 F. Walthers
HTC J. Rogers
HT3 J. Bates
HT3 R. Coleman
HT3 E. Tscherteu
HT3 C. Williams
HTFN D. Carron
HTFN B. French
HTFN J. Martinez
HTFN R. Wyant

A Division
MMC B. Bryant
MM1 R. Rametes
EN1 D. Wigley
EN2 K. cole
MR2 T. Gifford
MM2 J. Jeffers
MR2 C. Searl
MM3 S. Gamble
EN3 D. Horn
MMFR R. Moriarty
MM3 Thanh Pham
FN R. Portugal
ENFN D. Schoene
MM3 l. Starr

Weapons Department
Lt. Kevin Barry, Weapons
    Officer
Lt. (jg) Don Urquidez, Missle
    Officer
Lt. (jg) Jonathan James, ASW
    Officer
Lt. (jg) Mark Kershner,
    Gunnery Officer
Ens. Alan Knuth, Gunnery
    Assistant
Ens. Dave Beilharz, First
    Lientenant

BM Division
BM1 M. Collins
BM1 R. Haugen
BM2 K. Mushrow
BM2 W. White
BM3 D. Clark
BM3 S. Rodgers
BMC T. Vigil
First Division
SN J. Buffano
SN R. Cato
SA M. Catron
SA S. Cochrane
SN T. Cridebring
SN C. Gaines
SN G. Gilleland
SN J. Goodrich
SA D. Green
SA J. Hardin
SN S. Harris
SA K. Healey
SN C. Hiatt
SA L. Kamrowski
SN M. Keeling
SR T. Keslar
SA K. Lomas
SN R. Mason
SA P. Nush
SN R. Owens
SN W. Robison
SR J. Sheldon
SA S. Valen

F Division
FTG1 J. Federuik
GMG1 J. Kovach
GMG1 W. Noell
GMG2 J. Baskerville
GMG2 A. Peront
FTG3 B. Carlin
FTG3 C. Harper
GMG3 S. Pridemore
GMG3 B. Stropp
FTGSN F. Gainley
GMGSN D. Joachim
FTGC Plamondon
FTGSN K. Slocum
GMGSN B. Tharpe
GMGSN T. Vigil

SAM Division
R. Alverez
R. Amaya

B. Arnold
R. Boone
J. Dowler
F. Dunn
R. Everett
L. Gregg
J. Head
M. Howser
F. Johnson
R. Kendall
A. Meyers
A. Mickey, Jr.
R. Mills
M. Povlsen
M. Ramos
R. Reeves
B. Schruender
R. Tatum

Operations Department
Lt. Greg Ostrowski, Operations
    Officer
Lt. Lin Wong, Asst OPD/EMO
Ens. Carlos Rivera,
    Communications Officer
Ens. Tom Greene, CIC Officer

OI Division
EM1 M. Faulkner
OS1 E. Redding
SO1 J. Ryker
OS2 C. Capaldo
EW2 S. Dershem
OS2 D. Freeze
OS2 E. Gasaway
OS3 M. Fields
OS3 M. Krogman
OS2 R. Sparks
OS2 N. Wheeler, Jr.
OS3 P. Scardina
E3 R. Simmons
OS3 M. Urtz
OSSR C. Adair
OSSN T. Deering
OSSA M. Lovell
OSSA K. Magill
OSSA R. Petersen
OSSN S. Putas
OSSN P. Riley
EWSN M. Smith
EWC T. Steinbert
OSSN K. Wiest

OC Division
SM1 R. Murphy
RM2 S. Baldwin
SM2 T. Huston
RM3 G. Finn
SM3 R. Henderson
RM3 B. Quail

RM3 W. Whitaker
RMSN B. Dunton
RMSN R. Koehler
SMSN W. Mize
RMC I. O'Neal
RMSN C. Reeves
SMSN A. Sheehan
RMSN R. White

OE Division
ET1 L. Livermore
ET1 C. Swanson
ET2 T. Boyle
ET2 R. Fansel
ET2 R. High
ET2 T. Kelleher
ET2 C. Montgomery
ET2 M. Tiede
ET3 V. Anderson
ET3 K. Benham
ET3 R. McCutcheon
ETC T. Huffine

Supply Department
Lt. Wayne Boren, Supply
    Officer
Lt. (jg) Kurt Hyttel,
    Disbursing Officer

DK Division
DK1 V. Tomas
DKSN N. Harper

MS Division
MS1 F. connolly
MS1 C. Mercado
MS2 R. Diaz
MS2 R. Greenwood
MS2 P. Reyes
MS3 B. Burns
MS3 R. Cox
MS3 R. Davis
MS3 D. Street
MSC J. Elpedes
MSSN D. Merchant
MSSN V. Walker
SA K. Wallace
SK Division
SK1 D. Perkins
SK2 E. Kernodle
SK2 O. Tamayo
SK3 A. Howard
SKSN W. Holden
SKCS J. Lyttle
SKSA T. Talley
SH Division
SH1 B. Even
SH3 S. Carroll
SH3 C. Olvera
SHSN D. Bimslager

SHC R. Gonzalvo
SHSN R. Kendrick
SN R. Kupsch
SN S. Lojewski

Chapter 12

(6) Following is a list of the
Officers and Chief Petty
Officers of the *Decatur*
(DDG-73)
Precommissioning Unit as
of January 20, 1998:

Comdr. Mike Knollmann,
    USN, Commanding
    Officer
Lt. Comdr. Randy
    Hendrickson, USN,
    Executive Officer

Navigation/Administration
    Division
Lt. (jg) Steve Corlon, USN
PNC Cynthia Trotter, USN
Command Master Chief
EMCM(SW) P. Quayle, USN
HMC(SW) Mike Ackerman,
    USN
DSC(SW) Tomothy Brown,
    USN

Weapons Department
Lt. Chris Zaller, USN
GMCS Charles Scavo,USN

Undersea Warfare (USW)
    Division
Ens. Skip Muller, USN
STGC(SW) David Barker,USN
Ordnance Division
Ens. Jill Cesari, USN
GMC(SW) Steve O'Bannon,
    USN

Weapons Control Division
Ens. Molly McCabe, USN
FCC(SW) Britt Smith, USN

Combat Systems Department
Lt. Tom Olsy, USN
FCCS(SW) Robert Moore,
    USN

Electronics Material Officer
ETC(SW) Bill McKeithen,
    USN

Systems Test & Integration
    Division
Lt. (jg) Tim Shipman
FCC(SW) Lee Humphrey,
    USN

AEGIS Weapons System
    Division
Lt. Phil Certariano, USN
FCC(SW) Mike Coyne, USN

Engineering Department
LT Tom McGrath, USN
GSCS(SW) Carlos Timirez,
    USN

Propulsion Division
Lt. Dan Meyer, USN
GSEC(SW) Chris Knem, USN
GSMC(SW) Lee Pratt, USN

Damage Control Repair
    Division
Ens. Shawn Bohrer, USN
DCC(SW) Lee Shahagon, USN
Auxilliaries Division
Ens. Colleen Carlton, USN
ENC(SW) Oscar Jones, USN

Electrical Division
Ens. Kurt Fischi, USN
EMC(SW) Eric Williams, USN
Operations Department
Lt. Jim Aiken, USN
CTRC(SW) David Renwick,
    USN

Combat Information (CIC)
    Division
Lt. (jg) Shane Corres, USN
OSC(SW) John Crewdson,
    USN

Electronic Warfare Division
Lt. (jg) Jim Caroland, USN
EWC(SW) Scott Bonsem, USN

Communications &
    Information Systems
    Division
Ens. Kathy Sandaz, USN
RMC(AW) Toni Asbill

First (Deck) Division
Ens. Jay Mihal, USN
BMC(SW) Earl Breon, USN

Supply Department
Lt. Kristen Fabry, SC, USN
MSCS(AW) Evelyn Banks, USN

Supply Services Division
Lt. (jg) John Carroll, SC, USN
SKC(SW) Leonardo Sy, USN

Training Department
Lt. Joe Garry, USN
FCCS(SW) Tom Ward, USN

APPENDIX B

Appendix B contains the composite list of Decatur Country, including all Decatur cities, towns, counties, schools, libraries, and other municipal and civic organizations, as best identified by the author to date.

DECATUR COUNTRY

DECATUR, ALABAMA

Decatur Chamber of Commerce
515 6th Avenue
Decatur, Alabama

Decatur Convention & Visitors Bureau
719 6th avenue SE
Decatur, Alabama

Decatur Daily (Newspaper)
201 1st Avenue SE
Decatur, Alabama 35601-2333

Decatur Heritage Christian Academy
13412 Riverview Avenue SE
Decatur, Alabama 35601-3241

Decatur High School
1011 Prospect Drive SE
Decatur, Alabama

DECATUR, ARKANSAS

Decatur City Hall
310 Maple Avenue
Decatur, Arkansas 72722

Decatur High School

Decatur Elementary School

Decatur Public Library

DECATUR, GEORGIA

Bainbridge-Decatur Chamber of
Commerce
P.O. Box 736
Decatur, Georgia 31717

Decatur Downtown Development
Authority of the City of Decatur
P.O. Box 220
Decatur, Georgia 30031

Decatur DeKalb News Era
739 DeKalb Industrial Way
Decatur, Georgia 3033-5703

Decatur Public Library
215 Sycamore St.
Decatur, GA 30030-3413

Decatur County Law Library
Courthouse
Bainbridge, Georgia 31717

DECATUR, ILLINOIS

Decatur Area Convention and Visitors
Bureau
202 E. North Street
Decatur, Illinois 62523

Metro Decatur Chamber of Commerce
100 Merchant Street
Decatur, Illinois 62523

Macon County Historical Society
5580 North Fork Road
Decatur, Illinois 62521

Decatur Tribune
265 S. Part Street
Decatur, Illinois 62523-1307

Decatur Public Library
247 E. North Street
Decatur, Illinois 62523

Stephen Decatur High School
Educational Park
Decatur, Illinois 62526

Decatur Herald and Review Library
601 East William St.
Decatur, Illinois 62523-1142

Decatur School–Practical Nursing
300 E. Eldorado St.
Decatur, Illinois 62523-1037

Decatur Memorial Hospital
2300 N. Edward St.
Decatur, Illinois 62526-4163

"The Stephen Decatur Collection"
Millikin University
Stanley Library
1184 W. Main St.
Decatur, Illinois 62522

Decatur Christian Elementary School
3475 N. Maple Ave.
Decatur, Illinois 62526-1458

Decatur Christian School
3770 N. Water St.
Decatur, Illinois 62526-1952

Decatur Classical School
7030 N. Sacramento Avenue
Chicago, Illinois 60645-2848

DECATUR, INDIANA

Decatur Chamber of Commerce
125 E. Monroe Street
Decatur, Indiana

Adams County Historical Society
P.O. Box 262
Decatur, Indiana 46733

Decatur Public Library
128 S. 3rd Street
Decatur, Indiana 46733-1676

Decatur Daily Democrat
141 S. 2nd Street
Decatur, Indiana 46733-1664

Stephen Decatur Elementary School
3935 W. Mooresville Rd.
Indianapolis, IN 46221-2359

DECATUR, IOWA

Decatur County Development
4th & National
Decatur City, Iowa 50067

Central Decatur Community Schools

DECATUR COUNTY, KANSAS

Decatur County Area Chamber of
Commerce and Visitors Bureau
132 S. Penn
Oberlin, Kansas 67749-2243

Decatur Community Junior-Senior High
School
605 E. Commercial Street
Oberlin, Kansas 67749-2104

BERLIN, MARYLAND

Stephen Decatur High School
9913 Seahawk Road
Berlin, Maryland

Decatur Community Center
Clinton, Maryland

Decatur Middle School
Clinton, Maryland

Stephen Decatur Highway
Maryland

DECATUR, MICHIGAN

Decatur City Hall
114 N. Phelps Street
Decatur, Michigan 49045-1009

Van Buren District Library
200 N. Phelps Street
Decatur, Michigan 49045

Decatur, Mississippi
Decatur Public Library
Decatur, MS 39327-0040

DECATUR, NEBRASKA

Village of Decatur, Nebraska
Chairperson of the Village Board
Jack Dunning
P.O. Box 156
Decatur, Nebraska 68020
Village Clerk: Peggy Davis
Sigonella, Sicily

Stephen Decatur Junior/Senior High
School
U.S. Naval Air Station
Sigonella, Sicily
FPO NY 09523

DECATUR, TEXAS

Decatur Chamber of Commerce
203 East Main
P.O. Box 474
Decatur, Texas 76234

Decatur Middle School and High School

Decatur Public Library
1700 S/FM/51
Decatur, TX 76234-36313

DECATUR COUNTY, TENNESSEE

Decatur County Historical Society
P.O. Box 700
Decaturville, Tennessee 38329-0700
& P.O. Box 608
Parsons, Tennessee 38363

Decatur County Chamber of Commerce
201 Tennessee North
Parsons, Tennessee 38363

The News Ledger
46 Tennessee Avenue South
Parsons, Tennessee 38363

Meigs Decatur Public Library
104 Main Street and Highway 30
Decatur, TN 37322

Decaturville Elementary School
Decaturville, Tennessee 38329

Decatur County Library
Decaturville, Tennessee 38329-0488

WASHINGTON, D.C.

Decatur House Museum
748 Jackson Place NW
Washington, D.C.

Decatur Carriage House
1610 H Street NW
Washington, D.C.

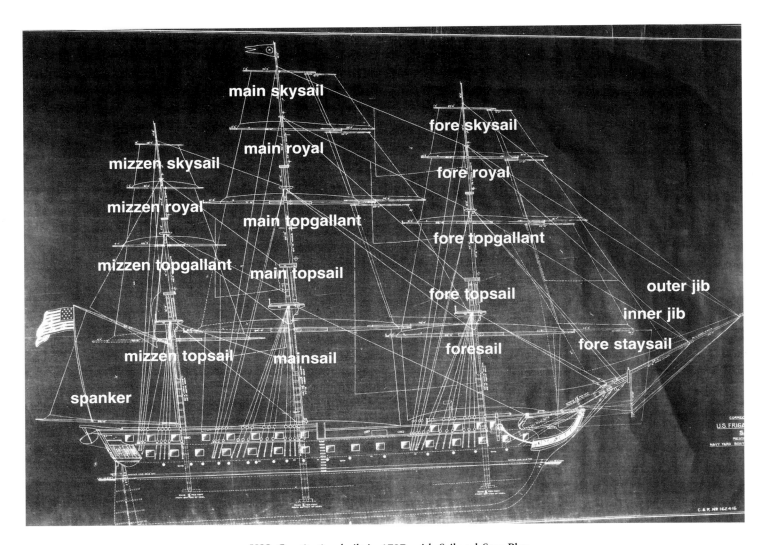

USS *Constitution,* built in 1797, with Sail and Spar Plan drawn about 1929 for the ship's restoration. Photograph courtesy of the National Archives.

GLOSSARY

a-back: setting the sails against the mast, so that sails are blown by the wind in front to give a ship sternway.

abaft: back of a ship

abaft the beam: back of the center or middle of a ship.

amidship(s): the middle of a ship midway between the bow and the stern.

approbation: formally or authoritatively approving something as proper or commendable.

bar: any long narrow bank in a body of water forming a shallow place.

bark: a three-masted ship with the foremast and mainmast square-rigged and the mizzenmast fore and aft rigged.

beam: the breadth of a ship at its widest point.

before-the-wind: sailing directly with the wind.

birth deck [berth deck]: that deck containing the sailors' hammocks for berthing.

boarding-pike: a long handled pike for boarding or repelling boarders.

boatswain (or bos'n): the warrant officer or petty officer in charge of the deck crew and other aspects of the deck, such as sails, rigging, anchors, and boats.

bombard: a bomb ketch, usually mounting a naval mortar for bombarding stationary targets.

bow: the front part or prow of a ship.

bowsprit: a spar projecting forward and usually slanted upward from the bow of a ship.

brig: abbreviation for a Brigantine; a two-masted square-rigged ship. (also a place of confinement aboard ship)

broadside: the simultaneous firing of all the guns on one side of a warship.

cable: a heavy rope or hawser composed of three plain-laid ropes of three strands each measuring from 10 to 26 inches in circumference and 100 to 140 fathoms in length.

cannister: grape-shot from a cannon, consisting of iron bits, nails, and other fragments to scatter the shot and wound or maim.

caps: stout blocks of wood joining the bottom of one mast to the top of another; as where the main topmast joins the mainmast.

carronade: a short chambered piece of ordnance used in naval engagements at close quarters.

cartridge: a charge for a firearm or cannon in a case or shell of metal, paper, pasteboard, or cloth.

cat-o'-nine-tails: an instrument consisting of nine pieces of cord each with three knots, attached to a thick rope handle that was used for flogging.

cimetar (same as simitar): a convex edged sword, extremely curved and a popular weapon with the Barbary pirates.

close hauled: setting the sails for sailing as close to the wind as possible.

cockade: a rosette or knot of ribbon or leather or the like worn on the hat as a party badge.

cockpit: an compartment below the waterline of a warship, where the wounded may be received and treated during an engagement.

Commodore: a naval rank next below Rear Admiral and next above Captain; the Commander of a squadron or division of a fleet.

commission: to put a ship within the direct command of a designated officer after the ship has been fitted out for sea service.

convoy: a protecting force accompanying property in the course of transportation, as a ship or fleet at sea.

coppered: covered with copper to protect against marine growth and organisms.

corsairs: those who, without commission or authority from any state, sail the high seas in an armed vessel taking booty; a pirate; a freebooter. Also, a corsair's vessel.

cutlass: a short, heavy, sword slightly curved for cutting and used mostly in hand-to-hand naval warfare.

decommission: to retire a ship from active service permanently or temporarily.

dundebuss: a 17th Century shotgun.

equipage: the outfit, including all essentials to make a ship ready for sea.

fantail: the part of the main deck at the stern of a ship.

fathom: a six foot measure of length used principally in marine measurements of depth.

fell-in: the joining up of two ships whose outcome is to be determined.

foremast: the mast that is foremost on a vessel.

foretopmast: the next mast above the foremast.

foresail: the lowest sail bent to the foreyard on a square-rigged vessel.

foreyard: the lower yard on the foremast.

frigate: a war ship in use from 1650 to 1840, smaller than a ship of the line carrying 24 to 50 guns.

gaff: a spar for extending the upper edge of a stayless fore and aft sail.

galley: a strongly built two-masted vessel, formerly partly square-rigged forward and often mounting guns or mortars for naval service; also, that part of a ship where meals are prepared.

grounding: running a ship aground on the shore, a reef, rocks, or a sandbar.

gun boats: formerly, a small vessel with one gun propelled by sails and sweeps.

gun ports: an opening in the side of a ship through which cannon may be fired.

haillard (halyard): a rope or line for hoisting a sail, a yard, or a flag.

hove: to heave or to linger about or lie at anchor.

howet (or howitzer): a short light cannon for projecting shells at a low elevation.

hull down: a distant vessel with the hull hidden by the horizon.

in ordinary: laid up or out of commission.

Inst.: a date within the current month.

jib boom: a spar forming a continuation of the bowsprit to support the forward corner of the jib sail.

ketch: a strongly built two-masted vessel, formerly partly square-rigged forward and often mounting guns or mortars for naval service.

larboard: the left hand side of a vessel when facing the bow or forward. Later changed to port to avoid confusion with starboard (the right side).

league: a marine league is approximately equal to 1/20th of a degree or three geographical miles.

lee: the side or direction opposite to that from which the wind comes from.

Lieutenant: an officer authorized to fill the place or discharge the duties of a superior in his absence, or to act for him under his direction.

Lieutenant Commandant: a lieutenant in command of a ship.

lighter: a barge or similar vessel used in loading and unloading ships.

luffed: to bring the head of a vessel near to the wind as to cause the sails to luff or lose their driving power.

mainmast: the principal mast of a vessel, which is the second mast from the bow except on ketches and yawls.

mainsail: the lowest sail set from the main yard on a square-rigged vessel or the large sail set from the mainmast on a fore and aft rigged vessel.

main yard: the lower yard on the mainmast.

mainstay: the stay or line leading from the mainmast forward to stay or support the mast in that direction.

maintopmast: the next mast above the mainmast.

man-of-war: an armed vessel of a navy or marine military.

master: the officer formerly responsible, under the captain, for the navigation of the ship in both the British and American Navies.

main top galt.: top gallant mast, yard and sails about the maintopmast.

Master Commandant: the equivalency of a Commander in today's Navy.

midshipman: a naval rank that is literally an officer to be in training.

messmates: a number of persons who habitually take their meals together.

mizzen-mast: the mast next aft of the mainmast.

moiety: one half.

Navy Enlisted Ratings

1. The below Enlisted Ratings are followed by the individua'ls Rate to designate pay grade as follows:

Rate	Definition	Pay Grade
CM	Master Chief Petty Officer	E-9
CS	Senior Chief Petty Officer	E-8
C	Chief Petty Officer	E-7
PO1	First Class Petty Officer	E-6
PO2	Second Class Petty Officer	E-5
PO3	Third Class Petty Officer	E-4
SN or FN	Seaman or Fireman	E-3
SA or SA	Seaman or Fireman Apprentice	E-2
SR	Seaman Recruit	E-1

2. Ratings as seen aboard the Decatur ships and followed by (SW) for Surface Warfare or (AW) for are as follows:

General Seamanship:
BM–Boatswain's Mate
SM–Signalman

Ships Operations:
OS–Operations Specialist
QM–Quartermaster

Marine Engineering:
BT–Boiler Technician
EM–Electrician's Mate
EN–Engineman
GS–Gas Turbine System Technician (used at Pay grade E-9 only)
GSE–Gas Turbine System Technician (Electrical)
GSM–Gas Turbine System Technician (Mechanical)
IC–Interior Communications Electrician
MM–Machinist's Mate

Ship's Maintenance:
HT–Hull Maintenance Technician
IM–Instrumentman
MR–Machinery Repairman
OM–Opticalman
DC–Damage Controlman

Weapons Control:
ET–Electronics Technician

FC–Fire Controlman
FT–Fire Control Technician

Ordnance Systems:
GM–Gunner's Mate (used at pay grade E-7 and above)   GMG–Gunner's Mate (Guns)
GMM–Gunner's Mate (Missiles)
MT–Missile Technician
TM–Torpedoman's Mate

Sensor Operations:
EW–Electronics Warfare Technician
OT–Ocean Systems Technician (used at pay grade E-9 only)   OTA–Ocean Systems Technician (Analyst)
OTM–Ocean Systems Technician (Maintainer)
ST–Sonar Technician
STG Sonar Technician (Surface)

Data Systems:
DP–Data Processing Technician
DS–Data Systems Technician

Health Care:
HM–Hospital Corpsman

Administration:
LN–Legalman
NC–Navy Counselor
PN–Personellman
PC–Postal Clerk
YN–Yeoman
RP–Religious Program Specialist

Logistics:
DK–Disbursing Clerk
MS–Mess Management Specialist
SH–Ship's Serviceman
SK–Storekeeper

Master-at-Arms:
MA–Master-at-Arms
Cryptology:
CT–Cryptologic Technician
CTA–Cryptologic Technician (Administrative)
CTI–Cryptologic Technician (Interpretive)
CTM–Cryptologic Technician (Maintenance)
CTO–Cryptologic Technician (Communications)
CTR–Cryptologic Technician (Collection)
CTT–Cryptologic Technician (Technical)

Communications:
RM–Radioman

Intelligence:

IS–Intelligence Specialist
(Johnston, *All Hands,* pp. 42-43)

ordnance: weapons and their associated hardware and appliances.

overboard: over the side of or out of a ship and into the water.

overhaul: to overtake or catch up with, when in pursuit.

pantaloons: men's garments closely fitting from the waist down below the calves and there fastened with buttons or ribbons.

poop deck: a short deck built over the after part of the spar deck of a vessel; generally the stern of a vessel.

port: the left hand side of a vessel when facing the bow or forward.

port tack: sailing or tacking with the wind blowing on the port side.

post captain: a full grade captain in command of a post (or rated) ship (ie; no less than 20 guns) entitled to a Master, who was responsible for the navigation of the ship.

privateer: a vessel owned and officered by private persons, but carrying on maritime war under a Commission from a belligerent state, commonly known as letters of marque.

quarter: the after part of a vessel's side from the beam to the stern.

quarterdeck: that part of a warship's spar deck between the poop deck and the mainmast, reserved for the use of officers. In today's Navy it is usually manned by the Officer of the Deck only when in port.

quarters: a sailor's proper or assigned station, position, or place.

recommission: to put a ship back into active service under the command of a designated officer.

rigging: the entire cordage system of a ship, divided into standing rigging (set) and running rigging (movable).

schooner: a fore and aft rigged ship, having two to three or more masts.

shoal: a shallow place within a body of water, such as a sand bar.

shoal draft: draft of a vessel able to encounter and survive shoal waters.

sloop-of-war: a vessel of war rigged either as a ship, a brig, or a schooner, mounting between 18 and 32 guns.

spar deck: the upper deck of a vessel that extends from bow to stern, including the quarterdeck and forecastle (or foc'sle).

speak or spoken: to hail a passing ship and speak with same via megaphone or plain voice.

squadron: an assemblance of two or more war vessels detailed for independent service under one command.

starboard: the right hand side of a vessel when facing the bow or forward.

starboard tack: sailing or tacking with the wind blowing on the starboard side.

steerage: the portion of the berth deck just forward of the wardroom in a warship; usually the quarters for midshipmen or junior officers.

stern: the rear or after end of a ship or boat.

stood off: to stand away from.

sweeps: long oars to propel a ship.

swell: a succession of large waves or the long continuous body of a wave.

tack: changing the direction of a vessel by bringing the wind round by the head or bow to the other side (the opposite of wearing); or sailing on a course just off the wind (ie; a port or starboard tack).

tompion: a wooden disk fitting into the bore of a muzzle-loading gun to keep out seawater, rain, and debris.

top galt. (top gallant): the mast, yard, sail, or rigging immediately above the top-mast and topsail.

topmast: the next mast above the lower mast (foremast, mainmast, or mizzen-mast).

tops: the uppermost masts, sails, and yards.

ultimo: a date from the proceeding month.

wardroom: the compartment aboard a warship used by the commissioned officers for eating and lounging.

warrant officer: an officer ranking above an enlisted person but below a commissioned officer and holding offic on a warrant rather than a commission.

wear: to turn or change the direction of a vessel by swinging its bow away from the wind and bringing the wind round by the stern to the other side (opposite of tacking).

weather guage: a position to windward; the advantage of receiving the wind first; figuratively, the advantage or upper hand.

wore: past tense of wear.

xebec: a small three masted vessel with both square and lateen sails in various arrangements that was often used by the Algerine pirates.

yard: a long slender spar, nearly cylindrical but tapering from the middle toward the ends, suspended crosswise and ath-wrtships on a mast and used to support sails (square, when the yard is parallel to the deck and lateen, when it hangs obliquely).

yardarm: either end of a yard.

yataghan: a Turkish sword, smitar, or knife with a double curved-blade running to a point without a guard.

yaw: to move about from side to side unsteadily or irregularly.

BIBLIOGRAPHY

PRIMARY SOURCES

Chief of Naval Operations Memorandum 3900, Ser 982F3/7U356398 of 9 Oct. 1987. Department of the Navy, Washington, 1987.

Chief of Naval Operations Letter 4780, Ser 03/8U578932 of 18 Feb. 88 w/end. Department of the Navy, Washington, 1988.

Chief of Naval Operations Letter 4780, Ser 325E/8U578984 of 4 April 1988. Department of the Navy, Washington, 1988.

Davis, Eva Mae. Ms. letter to Ben Birindelli, Winchester, Ohio, March 4, 1998. Falls Church, Va., author's files.

Decatur Action Reports, various. College Park, Maryland: National Archives, Textual Reference Branch: WWII.

Decatur Action Reports, various. Washington: Naval Historical Center, Operational Archives Branch: Post WWII.

Decatur Deck Logs, various. Washington: Naval Historical Center, Ships History Branch, Ships' Deck Log Section: Post 1961.

Decatur. Navy Board of Inquiry. Cavite, P.I., September 10, 1915. Washington: National Archives, Record Group 45, Navy Subject File, 1910–1927, OS, USS *Decatur*.

Decatur Photographs, various. Washington: Naval Historical Center, Curator Branch, Photographic Section.

Decatur Ship's Annual Command Histories, various. Washington: Naval Historical Center, Ships History Branch.

Decatur War Diaries, various. College Park, Maryland: National Archives, Textual Reference Branch: WWII.

Decatur War Diaries, various. Washington: Naval Historical Center, Operational Archives Branch: Post WWII.

Latrobe, B. H., Mrs. Letter to Mrs. Juliana Miller, Washington, D.C., December 12, 1812. Washington: Decatur House Museum Archives.

Manual of the Judge Advocate General, Basic Final Investigative Report concerning the collision of the USS *Decatur* (DD-936) and the USS *Lake Champlain* (CVS-39) which occurred on May 6, 1964. Alexandria, Va.: Office of the Judge Advocate General.

Manual of the Judge Advocate General, Basic Final Investigative Report concerning circumstances connected with the damage incurred by the USS *Decatur* (DDG-31) to the sonar dome on January 15, 1968 in San Diego Harbor in the vicinity of Buoy 20. Alexandria, VA: Office of the Judge Advocate General.

Reynolds, David, MCPO, USN (Ret), ed. "Naval Junior Reserve Officer Training Corps (NJROTC) at Stephen Decatur High School, Berlin, Maryland." *Blue Ribbon Report*. Berlin: NJROTC Unit, 1997.

Tingle, Melvin R. Letter to Ben Birindelli, Decatur, Mississippi, January 27, 1998. Falls Church, Va., author's files.

Wilson, Jeffrey V. First hand report on the USS *Decatur* (DDG-31), San Diego mooring buoy snagging of January 1968. Oxnard, Cal., December 22, 1997. Falls Church, Va., author's files.

SECONDARY SOURCES

Addy, Pat and Rodney Bounds. Welcome to Decatur, Newton County, Mississippi. Map Brochure. Decatur: Newton County Tax Assessor and Circuit Court Clerk.

Alden, John D., Comdr., USN. *Flush Decks and Four Pipes*. U.S. Naval Institute, Annapolis, 1965.

Anthony, Irvin. *Decatur*. Charles Scribner's Sons, New York-London, 1931.

Babbitt, Bruce P., ed. *Decatur* (DDG-31) Cruise Book. *The First Year*, 1968.

Banten, O. T., ed. *History of Macon County*. Decatur, Illinois: Macon County Historical Society, Decatur, Illinois, 1976.

Barnes, James. *Naval Actions of The War of 1812*. Harper & Brothers Publishers, 1896.

Beers, W. H. ed. *The History of Brown County, Ohio*. Chicago: W. H. Beers & Co., 1883.

Bredehoeft, Nellie. "Decatur." *Benton County Revisited*. Dallas: Curtis Media Corporation, 1991.

Brown County Historical Society, ed. *Brown County, Ohio History and Families, 1818–1993*. Georgetown, Ohio: Brown County Historical Society, 1993.

Bullock, Helen Duprey and Terry B. Morton. *Decatur House*. Washington: National Trust For Historic Preservation, 1967.

Christian, W. Asbury, D. D. *Richmond, Her Past and Present*. Virginia State Library Edition, Richmond, 1912. Reprinted, The Reprint Company, Spartanburg, S.C., 1973.

City of Decatur, Georgia What & Where, A Guide to Good Eating, Interesting Places and Great Services, 1997. Decatur, Georgia: Decatur Downtown Development Authority, 1997.

Clarke, Caroline McKinney. *The Story of Decatur, 1823-1899*. Atlanta: Higgins-McArthur/Longino & Porter, 1973.

Cochran, Hamilton. *Noted American Duels and Hostile Encounters*. Chilton Company, Phildelphia, PA. and Ambassador Books, Ltd., Toronto, Canada, 1963.

Cranwell, John P., and William B.Crane. Men of Marque: *A History of Private Armed Vessels out of Baltimore During the War of 1812*. New York: Norton, 1940.

Decatur, Alabama Convention & Visitors Bureau. *Decatur, Alabama* Internet Web Page.

Decatur (DD-936) Cruise Book. *Mediterranean Cruise, 1959-1960*. Fall River, Mass.: R. E. Smith Co., Inc.

Decatur (DDG-31) Cruise Book. *WESTPAC Deployment, 1974–1975*.

Decatur, Indiana Chamber of Commerce & Historical Society. "Brochure & Brief History of Adams County." Decatur, Ind.

Decatur City, Iowa Internet Web page. http://www.netins.net/itcweb/community/leon/leon.htm

Decatur County, Tennessee Internet Web page. http://www.usit.net/tngenweb/decatur.htm#HISTORY

Decatur, Newton County, Mississippi Welcome Brochure and Maps.

Decatur, Texas Internet Web page. http://www.fnbtexas.com/decatur.htm

deKay, James Tertius. *Chronicles of the Frigate Macedonian, 1809-1922*. New York-London: 1995.

Dudley, William S., and Michael J. Crawford, eds. *The Naval War Of 1812, A Documentary History*. Washington: Naval Historical Center: GPO, 1985—. Vol. 1, 1812; Vol. 2, 1813.

Dudley, William S. and William M. P. Dunne. *Stephen Decatur, A Most Bold and Daring Man*, Video. Washington: Decatur House, 1995.

Dunne, William M. P. *A Most Bold and Daring Man, Commodore Stephen Decatur, Jr*. Video from the National Trust for Historic Preservation Decatur House. New York: Triune Pictures, L.P., 1995.

Dye, Ira. *The Fatal Cruise of the Argus, Two Captains in the War of 1812*. Annapolis, Maryland: Naval Institute Press, 1994.

Dye, Ira, Captain, USN(Ret). "Toasting Decatur's Gallant Exploit." *Naval History*, U.S. Naval Institute, August 1995.

"Early History of Bainbridge & Decatur County." *The Historical News*, special Thanksgiving edition, November 1997, vol. 17, no. 99-GA. Hiram, Geo.: The Southern Historical News, Inc. Reprinted from *The Tri-State Vista*, July 1988 issue.

Ellis, William D., ed. *Decatur* (DDG-31) Cruise Book. *Western Pacific, November 10, 1978–April 8, 1979*.

Farquhar, Brodie. "Decatur Museum is filled with historical treasures." *The Oberlin Herald*. Oberlin, Kansas: April 30, 1997.

Forrester, C. S. *The Age of Fighting Sail, The Story of The Naval War of 1812*. Doubleday & Company, Inc., Garden City, N.Y., 1956.

Funk, Isaac K., D.D., L.L.D., ed-in-chief. *Funk & Wagnalls New Standard Dictionary of the English Language*. New York & London: Funk & Wagnalls Company, 1913.

Goodrich, Marcus. *Delilah*. Farrar & Rinehart, 1941. Republished with an introduction by Gilliland, C. Herbert, Jr., U.S. Naval Institute Press, Annapolis, Maryland, 1985.

Hagan, Kenneth J. *This People's Navy, The Making of American Seapower*. The Free Press Division of Macmillan, Inc., New York, 1991.

Heritage Tour Bainbridge, Georgia. Bainbridge: Bainbridge-Decatur County Chamber of Commerce.

Johnson, Warren B., Captain, SC, USN (Ret). "Shall We Let It Crumble?" *Shipmate*. U.S. Naval Academy Alumni Association, Annapolis, Maryland, May 1996.

Johnston, Marie G., ed. *All Hands 1997 Owner's and Operator's Manual*. Washington: Naval Media Center, 1997.

Keister, Kim. "Influence and Ambition." *Historic Preservation, March/April 1995, Vol. 47, number 2*. Washington: National Trust for Historic Preservation, Reprinted for Decatur House, 1995.

King, Dean with John B. Hattendorf and J. Worth Estes. *A Sea of Words, A Lexicon and Companion for Patrick O'Brian's Seafaring Tales*, Second Edition. Henry Holt and Company, New York, 1997.

Knight, Robert. "Stephen Decatur: American naval hero." Berlin, Maryland News, April 3, 1985.

Knox, Dudley W., Commodore, USN. *A History of the United States Navy*. G. P. Putnam's Sons, New York, 1936, Revised 1948.

Knox, Dudley W., Captain, USN(Ret). *Naval Documents related to the United States Wars with the Barbary Powers*. Washington: GPO, 1941. Vol. 1, 1785 through 1801, vol. 3, September 1803 through March 1804, vol. 4, April 1804 to September 6, 1804.

Lee, Lawrence W., Jr. *Decatur (DD-936/DDG-31)*. New York: unpublished, 1995.

Leech, Samuel. *Thirty Years From Home, or A Voice From The Main Deck*. Boston: Charles Tappan, Publisher, 1844.

Lewis, Charles Lee. *The Romantic Decatur*. Philadelphia: University of Pennsylvania Press; London: Oxford University Press, 1937.

Lloyd, Christopher and Jack L. S. Coulter. *Medicine and the Navy, 1200-1900, vol. 3, 1714-1815*. Edinburgh: E. and S. Livingstone Ltd., 1961.

Mackenzie, Alexander Slidell, USN. *Life of Stephan Decatur, A Commodore in the Navy of the United States*. Boston: Charles C. Little and James Brown, 1846.

Maclay, Edgar Stanton, A.M. *A History of American Privateers*. New York and London: D. Appleton and Company, 1924.

Mahan, Alfred T. *Sea Power in its Relations to The War of 1812*. Boston: Little, Brown, 1905. 2 vols. (Reprinted 1968 by Greenwood; 1970 by Haskell).

Marryat, Frederick, Captain, R.N. With an introduction and notes by Evan L. Davies. *Mr. Midshipman Easy*. London: Saunders and Otley, 1836; London: J. M. Dent & Boston: Little, Brown, 1896 edition; reprinted Annapolis, Maryland: U.S. Naval Institute, 1990.

Martin, Tyrone, Commander, USN (Ret). "A Loved and Respected Machine." *Naval History*, U. S. Naval Institute, August, 1997.

Martin, Tyrone G. *A Most Fortunate Ship, A Narrative History of Old Ironsides*, Revised Edition. Naval Institute Press, Annapolis, Maryland, 1997.

Mathews, John. Decatur County Kansas History. Oberlin, Kansas: January 19, 1998.

McKee, Christopher. *A Gentlemanly and Honorable Profession, The Creation of the U.S. Naval Officer Corps, 1794–1815*. U.S Naval Institute Press, Annapolis, Maryland, 1991.

Meigs County, Tennessee, brochure. Decatur, Tenn.: Meigs County Tourism.

Meigs County, Tennessee, History.

Mooney, James L., ed. *Dictionary of American Naval Fighting Ships*, vol. 2. Washington: Naval Historical Center, Ship's History Branch: GPO, 1963, Reprint 1977.

Naval History. Annapolis, Maryland: U. S. Naval Institute, August, 1995.

Nelson, Pam. Decatur–"Nebraska's Second Oldest Settlement". *Burt County Plaindealer*. Decatur, Neb.: May, 1982.

"News Briefs: Award of Legion of Merit Medal for CAPT Gered Beeby, USNR." *Naval Reserve Association News*. Alexandria, Va.: October, 1996.

Niedzielski, Craig T., ed. *Decatur* (DDG-31) Cruise Book. *Pacific Cruise, Summer 1981*. San Diego: Walsworth Publishing Co., 1981.

O'Brian, Patrick. *Post Captain*. New York, London: W. W. Norton & Company, 1972.

O'Brian, Patrick. *The Letter of Marque*. New York, London: W. W. Norton & Company, 1988.

Parda, N. R., ed. *Decatur* (DDG-31) Cruise Book. *Four Horizons, WESTPAC Deployment 2, February 13–August 29, 1970*. San Diego and Norfolk: Tiffany Publishing Co., 1970.

Precommissioning Handbook for Aegis CG 47 Class Cruisers and DDG 51 Class Destroyers (Draft), March 1992. Washington: Aegis Program Executive Office, Naval Sea Systems Command, 1992.

Port Hueneme Division Naval Surface Warfare Center. *Self Defense Test Ship*. http://www.nswses.navy.mil/sdts.html.

Potter, E. B. *Nimitz*. Annapolis, Maryland: Naval Institute Press, 1976.

Richmond, The Pride of Virginia, An Historical City, Illustrated. Philadelphia: Progress Publishing Company, 1900.

Richmond Times Newspaper. Richmond: September 27, 1900.

Roosevelt, Theodore. *The Naval War of 1812: Or, the History of the United States Navy During the Last War With Great Britain: To Which is Appended an Account of the Battle of New Orleans*. Presedential ed. New York and London: Putnam, 1882. (Republished 1970).

Ruckman, Lisa. The Good Life, Decatur County, Iowa. Leon Iowa: Decatur County Tourism Council.

Sabine, Lorenzo. *Notes on Duels And Duelling, Alphabetically Arranged with a Preliminary Historical Essay*. Boston: Crosby, Nichols, and Company, 1855.

Smith, Charles Henry, LL.D. *Stephan Decatur and the Suppression of Piracy in the Mediterranean*. New Haven, 1901.

Smith, Edgar Newbold. *American Naval Broadsides, A Collection of Early Naval Prints (1745-1815)*. New York: Phiadelphia Maritime Museum and Clarkson N. Potter, Inc./Publisher, 1974.

Spears, John R. *The History of Our Navy From Its Origin to the End of the War With Spain, 1775-1898*. New York: Charles Scribner's Sons, 1899.

Truxton-Decatur Naval Museum. *Commodores Thomas Truxton and Stephan Decatur and the Navy of Their Time, An Exhibition*. Washington: 1950.

United States. Congress. Senate. Committee on Labor and Public Welfare. Subcommittee on Veterans' Affairs. *Medal of Honor Recipients*. Washington: 1968.

Village of Decatur, Van Buren County, Michigan. Decatur: Decatur Chamber of Commerce.

Virginia, Rebirth of the Old Dominion. vol. 5. Chicago and New York: The Lewis Publishing Co., 1929.

Wolfe, Michael J. *Self Defense Test Ship: Affordable Live Fire Testing At Sea*. Seattle: ITEA 1996 Symposium, October 14-18, 1996.

Wolfe, Michael J. "Test ship conducts first remote control operation." *Coasta Link Newsletter*. Port Hueneme: Naval Surface Warfare Center, Port Hueneme Division, September 15, 1995.

Wolfe, Michael J. "Self Defense Test Ship survives three attacks." *Coasta Link Newsletter*. Port Hueneme: Naval Surface Warfare Center, Port Hueneme Division, May 10, 1996.

Wood, Virginia Steele. *Live Oaking, Southern Timber for Tall Ships*. Annapolis, Maryland: Naval Institute Press, 1981.

211

214

About the Author

Ben Birindelli is a retired Naval Reserve Captain, but still attached to the Reserve Unit at the Naval Historical Center, Washington Navy Yard, as a volunteer. There he is working on a project to document the histories of 558 Landing Ship Medium (LSM) ships for the Dictionary of American Naval Fighting Ships. During his active duty with the Navy, Ben was the Prospective Supply Officer of the rebuilt Decatur following her collision with the USS *Lake Champlain* (CVS-39) and while undergoing her conversion to a guided missile destroyer. Ben then became the Supply Officer following the recommissioning of the USS *Decatur* (DDG-31) for the start of her second life. Thus, the seeds for the *200 Year Legacy of Stephen Decatur* were sown. Although this is his first book to be published, one covering those LSMs is in process. He has also authored several technical papers for two technical societies. Ben resides with his wife, Nancy, in Falls Church, Virginia.

About the Artist

Marty Reed Vinograd has attracted international attention for her unique collage works. She creates with fabric, fur, flax, silk, leather, beads, wood, and any other materials that will help her bring the work of art to life. The innumerable "pieces" applied to the surface create an extraordinary reality, and the clever use of these materials gives the viewer a strong second impact. But the artist also deliberates the relationship between the material and the personality of her subject. "Quilts, clothes, dresses, fabrics, hold onto a personality. Old dresses have an essence of who was once in them." says Vinograd. "It grabs a primitive 'rag, bone and hank of hair' idea that is tribal," relates the artist. As Frank Getlein, the dean of Washington, D.C. art critics said of these distinctive works, "Vinograd likes to start with a fabric or a garment, even actually used and liked by her subject. That's Voodoo, of course, for capturing the soul. It works." Vinograd has created portraits of such "larger-than-life" figures as John Lennon, Winston Churchill, Lillian Gish, Louise Nevelson, Jesse Jackson, Alexander Solzhenitsyn, and William Faulkner among others.

The Florida-born Vinograd, now residing in Oxford, Mississippi, has enjoyed noteworthy success with her art. Recent exhibitions include two consecutive summer solo shows in France, as well as solo shows at the University of Mississippi Museum, the Midtown Gallery in Washington, D.C., The Heritage International Bank, Waterford in Weston, Connecticut, and The Massillon Museum in Massillon, Ohio. She has also shown her work at the Wolfe/Hoggen Gallery in Santa Fe, New Mexico, NOVA Community College in Fairfax, Virginia, and her 1984 series of political portraits was seen on the CBS Morning News and was the subject of a feature article in *Washington Woman Magazine*. Vinograd has prepared many commissions which include all the Prime Ministers of Israel for an Israeli bank and Civil War Generals Lee and Jackson for the George C. Marshall Museum. Her art work is represented in the permanent collections of the Heritage International Bank, The University of Mississippi Museum, The United States Aegis Missile Cruiser *Chancellorsville* and numerous private collections.

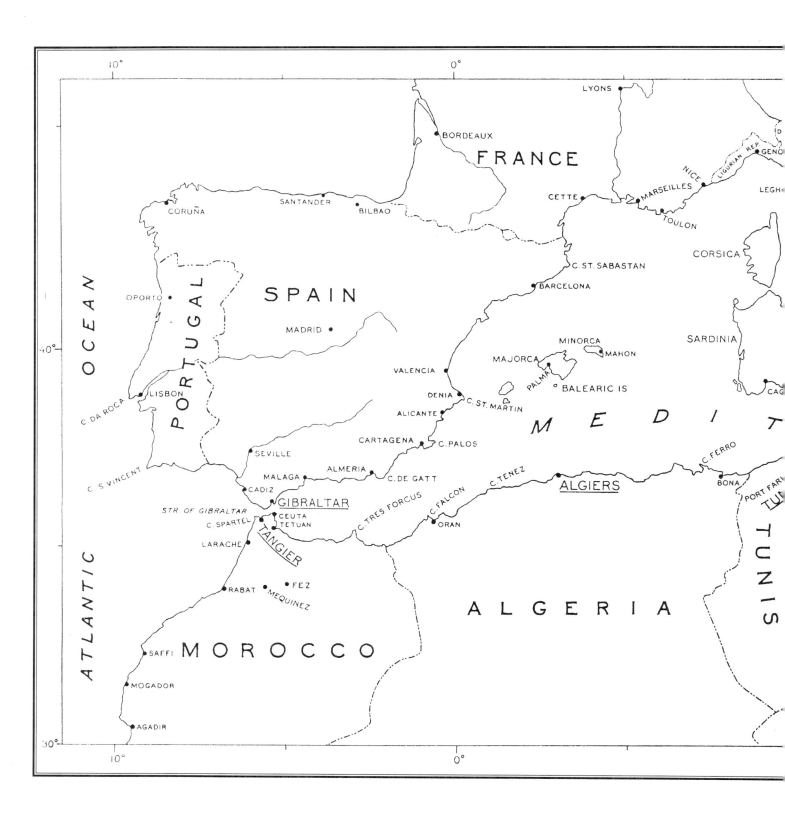